Dancing Longer
Dancing Stronger

D0964986

Dancing Longer
Dancing Stronger

A Dancer's Guide to Improving Technique
and Preventing Injury

Andrea Watkins
University of Massachusetts, Amherst

Priscilla M. Clarkson
University of Massachusetts, Amherst

Photography by Vicki Johnson
Illustrations by David A. Gabriel

A Dance Horizons Book
Princeton Book Company, Publishers
Princeton, NJ

© 1990 Princeton Book Company, Publishers

A Dance Horizons Book
Princeton Book Company, Publishers
POB 57
Pennington, NJ 08534

Editorial Coordinator: Roxanne Barrett
Cover Design by Main Street Design
Interior Design by Meg Davis
Typeset by Peirce Graphic Services, Inc.

ISBN 0-916622-98-3

Cover Photograph by Vicki Johnson

Library of Congress Cataloging-in-Publication Data

Watkins, Andrea.
    Dancing longer dancing stronger : a dancer's guide to improving technique and
preventing injury / Andrea Watkins, Priscilla M. Clarkson ; photography by Vicki
Johnson ; illustrations by David A. Gabriel.
        p.   cm.
    Includes bibliographical references and index.
    ISBN (invalid) 0-916622-96-3 : $24.95
    1. Dancing.   2. Physical fitness.   3. Dancing—Physiological
aspects.   4. Dancing—Accidents and injuries.   5. Dancing—Safety
measures.   I. Clarkson, Priscilla M., 1947–   .   II. Title.
GV1588.W387   1990
792.8—dc20   89-64300
                                                                              CIP

Contents

PART III. The Foot, Ankle, and Lower Leg

PART IV. The Knee, Upper Leg, and Hip

PART V. The Trunk and Neck

PART VI. The Shoulder and Arm

PART VII. Putting it All Together

Acknowledgments

Many people have contributed to the completion of this project. We are particularly indebted to the following individuals: Vicki Johnson for her photographic work and unfailing commitment to excellence; David Gabriel for his care and expertise in preparing the anatomical illustrations; Ken and Kathryn Fredgren, directors of the Arlington Center for Dance and the Center Dance Company, for their generous donation of studio space; Karen Menter and Steve Brown for their work as models throughout the major part of the book; Amy Cox and Scott Henderson for their work as models primarily in Chapter 23; Margaret Ann Fredgren for her work as a model primarily in Chapter 19; Sally Gardner for her assistance in developing the illustrative concepts; and to the dance faculty at the University of Massachusetts, Amherst, for encouragement and cooperation. We are also grateful to Susan Anthony, Karen Blank, Melanie Calitri, Gail Collins, Robert James, and Margaret Skrinar whose questions, concerns, and ideas helped to motivate our work. Finally, we would like to thank Lorna Watkins for her constant encouragement and Ronald Pipkin for his kind and generous support as well as computer expertise. Without their understanding and assistance, this book would not have been possible.

Preface

Many dancers have had the frustrating experience of repeatedly being told to correct a weakness in their technique such as an unstable balance, bent knees, or bent arms. Conversely, a majority of dance teachers have had the frustrating experience of repeating the same correction to the same student numerous times without seeing any improvement. In many of these situations the problem is not the student's desire to change, nor the teacher's ability to identify and communicate the change that is needed. The problem is that the student lacks the necessary physical strength and/or flexibility to bring about the desired change.

Unfortunately, another problem common to many dancers is that of overuse or traumatic injury. In the majority of cases, these are caused by faulty technique. Poor technique can be the result of bad instruction, poor coordination, or a lack of strength and flexibility. If the latter is true, then a conditioning program to correct these deficiencies can help correct technique and thereby prevent injury.

Why is it that taking dance class does not always condition the body to meet the demands of the technique? The answer essentially is time. In a one-and-one-half or two-hour dance class there is not enough time to strengthen and stretch every muscle in the body and still have time to *dance*. The time spent in class must primarily be used to perfect the patterns of coordination that produce dance movement, as well as refine the aristry of performance and communication.

This book is designed to help ballet, modern, aerobic, and jazz dancers improve their dance technique and prevent injury. By presenting both general principles of injury prevention as well as specific exercises for increasing strength and flexibility, this book provides information that dancers of all ages and skill levels can use to improve their performance. Beginning dancers will find the book particularly helpful in reinforcing the explanations and corrections made in technique class. It will also help them better understand the correct way to work, and why working correctly is so important. More experienced dancers will also find the book helpful in answering some of their questions regarding technique and injury.

The dance conditioning exercises presented in this book are designed for use in a variety of exercise environments. The exercises do not use extensive or expensive equipment, nor do they require a large space. They can be performed at home or in the dance studio. They are designed for students of all skill levels, and should be used to *compliment* the work performed in technique class.

This book can be used by dancers studying in private dance studios as well as dancers studying in colleges and universities. If used as a college text, it would be appropriate reading for both non-major and dance-major technique courses.

Dance majors could also use this book as an introduction to Dance Anatomy or Dance Kinesiology courses. In many cases, dance majors are overwhelmed by the body of scientific knowledge to be learned when they take these courses. An introduction to some of the concepts and vocabulary would help to prepare them. Furthermore, the practical application of the material presented in this book may inspire an interest in dance science. In situations where dance majors do not have access to specific courses in dance science, this book could help them apply their general anatomical studies to the field of dance.

Dancers have long recognized that there are many factors that contribute to improved technique and injury prevention. Some of these include taking class, aerobic exercise, proper nutrition, adequate rest, and a healthy mental outlook. In addition, a carefully planned dance conditioning program can enhance technique and help to minimize or prevent injury.

This book includes general information about conditioning as well as presenting specific information concerning anatomical structure, common problems in dance technique, common dance injuries, and exercises to help improve technique and prevent injury. When dancers become familiar with this material, they will be better prepared to explore and enjoy the unique world of dance.

Note

The exercises suggested in this book are meant to be used by noninjured dancers as a complement to their regular schedule of dance technique classes. The exercises are not designed for the general public, nor are they meant to be used by injured dancers in self-prescribed treatment and injury rehabilitation programs. Dancers who are injured should see a physician. In addition, dancers are urged to carefully follow the exercise instructions, and listen to their bodies. If an exercise hurts, it should not be continued. Previous injuries or other preexisting factors may make an exercise inappropriate. Dancers should always check with their physician before starting this or any other exercise program.

PART

I

Before You Begin

Strength and flexibility training outside of dance class is a concept new to many dancers. Consequently, the majority of dancers do not realize what a conditioning program can do to improve their ballet, modern, aerobic, or jazz dance technique. Although some dancers may realize they need additional strength and flexibility, they may not know how to begin such a program. In this part we present the basic principles of conditioning. Once these are understood, dancers can begin a program of training for strength and flexibility.

1

How to Use This Book

Evaluation

The first step to beginning a conditioning program for strength and flexibility is to determine your personal strengths and weaknesses or, if you are a teacher, the strengths and weakness of your students. To do this you need to assess the areas of technique that are difficult to perform correctly or difficult to perform with the desired range of motion. Next, you must determine the muscle groups which need to be strengthened or stretched.

It may take careful thought to discover the fundamental cause of a technical problem and thereby assertain which muscle groups need conditioning. The body is an amazingly complex instrument. Sometimes the more obvious problem may in fact be just the tip of an iceberg. Unless the underlying problems are identified and corrected, efforts to improve will not be completely successful. For example, a dancer who has difficulty straightening her knees when *en pointe* may at first think the problem is weakness in the muscles that straighten the knee. A closer examination, however, might reveal alignment problems elsewhere in the body that cause the knees to bend in an effort to compensate. Unless these fundamental problems are corrected, the dancer will not be successful in solving her knee problem, no matter how much conditioning work she performs for her knee muscles.

If you are a dancer and are uncertain how to evaluate your strengths and weaknesses, you should discuss your needs with your teacher. The information in this book will also help you evaluate your problems and define your conditioning requirements.

How to Find the Information You Need

This book is organized into seven parts. Part I discusses the physiological principles involved when strength and/or flexibility is increased, and it explains how a dance conditioning program can improve dance technique and help prevent injury. Understanding this information will help you design your own conditioning program as well as evaluate other programs.

Part II explains the correct way to use the dance conditioning exercises presented throughout this book. It is most important that you carefully read Part II before attempting to perform any of the exercises. Part II contains vital information that is not repeated in the individual exercise instructions.

Parts III through VI deal with the dancer's instrument, the body. These parts present specific problems in dance technique and the recommended exercises to help solve those problems. Much of this information will help you in the personal evaluation discussed previously. In addition, specific dance injuries are presented and possible preventative measures are suggested. These parts also present a brief anatomical description of the bones, joints, and muscles.

Part VII discusses various dance conditioning programs. Several programs are outlined that integrate the exercises presented in this book. In addition, basic information is presented concerning strength conditioning with exercise machines.

We hope you will read the book from cover to cover. However, if you have an immediate problem you want to correct, you may want to turn to a specific section. For example, if your feet wobble from side-to-side when you try to balance, you can turn to Part III that discusses problems related to the foot and ankle. Begin by reading the anatomy of the foot and ankle in Chapter 10. Then look at Question 8 in Chapter 11 so you will understand exactly what your problem is and why specific exercises may help. Finally, read Part II, then follow the instructions for the exercises specifically recommended to help correct wobbling feet. These exercises are found in Chapter 12.

If you should read the sections of the book out of sequence, you may find unfamiliar terminology. Should this happen, we recommend that you use the index. For the most part, a term or concept will be defined and explained the first time it is used, and will not be explained again thereafter.

A Dance Conditioning Program for Strength and Flexibility

The best way to improve technique and help prevent injury is to follow a complete dance conditioning plan. Chapter 22 outlines several appropriate programs. It also includes information that will help you should you decide to organize your own program. Dancers who do regular conditioning work will develop bodies that are balanced in strength and flexibility. They will be better prepared for class, rehearsal, and performance.

2

The Purpose of Strength and Flexibility Conditioning

For a muscle to become stronger, it must be worked for increasingly longer periods of time, worked more frequently, or worked with increased intensity. For a muscle to become more flexible, it must be stretched for specific lengths of time. In a dance class of one-and-one-half or two hours, there is not enough time to continually increase the strength and flexibility of each muscle group in the body. The majority of class time needs to be spent developing the patterns of coordination required for specific dance movements, as well as working on artistic performance.

In the process of taking class, some increase in strength and flexibility does occur. There is a limit, however, to the degree of strength and flexibility that can be reached. For some dancers, the technique acquired during class seems to be sufficient. Many others, however, cannot build the strength and flexibility necessary to meet all of the technical challenges of dance merely in class. If you find yourself on a plateau and are unable to improve your technique, part of the problem may be that you lack the necessary strength or flexibility. If so, you will find your technique improving if you follow a conditioning program in addition to your dance classes.

Not only is it difficult to increase strength and flexibility continually just by taking class, most dance techniques do not develop equal strength and flexibility in all muscle groups. Such muscular imbalances can result in injury. In ballet, for example, *pointe* work develops strength in the calf muscles at the back of the lower leg. Ballet exercises may not, however, provide equal opportunity for these muscles to stretch out. As a result, the calf muscles often become tight and the ankle becomes vulnerable to certain painful conditions, such as tendonitis. The problem is not unique to ballet; muscular imbalances may develop in any dance style or idiom.

A good dance conditioning program will complement the work in technique class. Such a program can help prevent injury by balancing the strength and flexibility of each muscle group. As strength and

7

flexibility improve, technical skill will also improve. Conditioning can help professional dancers lengthen their performing careers, as well as improve the quality of those careers, and can do the same for nonprofessional dancers. It can help them dance longer and stronger.

Many choreographic works require dancers to dance continuously for a relatively long time, when compared with the short exercises performed in class. A dancer may not be fully prepared for these works by classroom activities alone. In fact, dancers often lack aerobic training. It is therefore recommended that dancers incorporate aerobic activity into a total training program.

Aerobic conditioning involves low-to-moderate intensity exercises that are performed continuously for ten minutes or more. Brisk walking, bicycling, swimming, and of course, low-impact aerobic dance fit into this category.

Recognizing the Benefits

While the concept of conditioning the body for dance may be new to many dancers, conditioning has long been part of Olympic and professional athletic programs. Participants at the elite levels of gymnastics and figure skating, two sports closely related to dance, have known for many years that conditioning the body needs to be performed separately. Consequently, gymnasts and skaters follow weight and aerobic training programs in addition to practicing their gymnastic and skating skills.

Because the value of a conditioning program for strength and flexibility has been well documented in athletics, a dance conditioning program is recommended by physical therapists who work with dancers, as well as by others who are involved in exercise science and dance medicine research. These professionals know many injuries can be prevented when conditioning is combined with careful work in technique class.

Many dancers, however, do not understand how important a conditioning program for strength and flexibility can be to their success. If you are one of these dancers, now is the time to learn. If you are a teacher, you should learn about conditioning the body so that you can help your students achieve greater success with less chance of injury. Dancers who condition their bodies outside of class come to class with an instrument that is ready to *dance*. These dancers will be less vulnerable to injury and better prepared to meet the challenges of technique and performance.

The Past and the Present

Many dancers wonder why they should begin a conditioning program when they read about famous dancers who were successful performers without undertaking extra conditioning work. It is difficult to say whether past dancers were involved in personal conditioning programs. If we assume that they did not work outside of class to correct muscular imbalance and improve technique, we would have to say that these dancers were "natural" performers. Their bodies adapted easily to the technical demands of dance. It is possible to argue that these dancers would have been even greater technicians had they participated in a conditioning program.

Furthermore, we will never know how many potentially stunning dancers never had the chance to perform. Technique classes may not have offered sufficient exercise to fully develop the height of their jump or *développé,* for example. Consequently, they may have been passed over in favor of another dancer with better *ballon* or extension. Perhaps injury cut short or completely prevented one of these unknown performing careers. A dance conditioning program could have helped these dancers.

It is also important to recognize that dance technique has continually increased in difficulty. What was technically demanding fifty years ago is now common dance vocabulary. In many instances it was easier for dancers of past generations to acquire the necessary technique by class participation alone.

Just as the level of difficulty in dance technique has increased with time, so have the physical demands of a performing career. Today's dancers often perform more frequently. Furthermore, members of today's *corps* are asked to dance difficult choreography rather than stand posed in group formations. Today's dancers are also asked to perform in a wider range of movement styles. Because dancers in earlier times did not have to meet these demands, their regular technique class was often sufficient preparation for a successful performing career.

3

Conditioning for Strength

Three principles serve as the foundation for strength training programs. They are: overload, specificity, and reversibility. *Overload* refers to increased exercise demands. *Specificity* indicates the similarity of a conditioning exercise to the dance idiom that an individual is performing. *Reversibility* describes the loss of strength when you stop training. The strength conditioning exercises in this book are based on these principles.

The Overload Principle

The overload principle states that strength cannot be increased unless the muscles are stressed beyond their normal work load. They need to be worked to the point of fatigue. To achieve this overload, you can increase the frequency, duration, or intensity of your exercise program. Here, *frequency* means how often an exercise is performed; *duration,* how long an exercise lasts; and *intensity,* the difficulty of an exercise.

There are many factors that help to determine the intensity or difficulty of an exercise. In this book, intensity will be primarily determined by the amount of weight a muscle must lift or move. The overload principle also suggests that the frequency, duration, or intensity must be progressively increased for consistant gains in strength.

Overload and Flexibility
Some dancers are concerned that flexibility will decrease if they begin a program that uses weights to increase strength. This will not happen if flexibility exercises are also performed. All of the strength conditioning exercises in this book have flexibility exercises included as part of the conditioning program.

Overload and Muscle Size
Many dancers and teachers are worried that working with weights will build big muscles. In fact, one of the most common misconceptions

about strength training is that it will *always* result in large bulky muscles, even in women. This is not true. *Hypertrophy,* an increase in muscle mass, is influenced by several factors. One is the presence or absence of certain hormones, another is the type of exercise program that is followed.

Before puberty, growth hormone increases the size of the muscles, in both men and women, as the body grows. After puberty, the male hormone, testosterone, continues to increase muscle size. If men perform certain types of strength training exercises, the presence of testosterone makes it possible for them to increase the size of their muscles even further. Because the female body produces very little testosterone, women who engage in strength training do not develop the same muscle mass as men.

Muscular hypertrophy is also affected by the type of strength-training program that is followed. Exercise programs that use maximal resistance result in greater hypertrophy. *Maximal resistance* is afforded by a weight so heavy that it can be lifted only a few times before fatigue occurs.

When the weight to be lifted is light enough that the exercise can be performed a moderate number of times, very little hypertrophy will result. The small degree of hypertrophy that does occur is considered *muscle tone.* A strength training program that involves moderate resistance and moderate repetitions will not cause muscular hypertrophy, but it will result in modest, functional increases in strength. It can also help delay muscular fatigue. The exercises provided in this book are moderate resistance, moderate repetition exercises and will not produce excessive muscular hypertrophy.

Muscular Size and Strength

Two main factors determine strength. The first is the size of the muscle and the second is the ability of the nervous system to control the muscle. Inside each muscle are numerous muscle fibers. When these fibers receive a signal from the nervous system, they shorten or contract. If a task requires very little strength, then relatively few muscle fibers will be directed to contract. As more strength is required, more muscle fibers are called into action. When you consider that a skeletal muscle may contain as many as three hundred thousand fibers, you can understand the complexity of the controlling process. Through strength training, the nervous system "learns" to better coordinate the contraction of muscle fibers. This increases the strength of muscles without increasing their size.

Exercises in the Gym

Although we recommend the exercises in this book, many fine exercise programs can be found in gyms. Those dancers who have access to a gym and would like to use it will find information about weight machines in Chapter 23. Exercise machines allow you to add more resistance than simple conditioning exercises. Consequently, greater gains in strength and more muscular hypertrophy are possible. These weight machines can be particularly helpful to male dancers who would like to build strength for partnering, increase upper-body muscle mass for aesthetic reasons, or develop leg strength for powerful jumps.

The Specificity Principle

The *principle of specificity* states that the exercises you choose for your strength conditioning program should be as similar as possible to the dance movements you perform in class and on stage. It has been suggested that dancers could adhere to both the specificity and overload principles by wearing ankle weights to class. In this way they would be able to add resistance while performing specific dance movements. This resistance could be increased by wearing heavier weights.

There is some question as to whether wearing ankle weights is wise. For some warm-up exercises, light ankle weights may be all right. There is always the possibility, however, that extra weight at the ankle could hurt a knee or ankle that is not yet strong enough to support the additional weight. Another problem is that ankle weights distort the timing of your movement. To produce movement, the muscle fibers inside each muscle act in a complex coordination of contractions and relaxations. The timing of these contractions and relaxations is altered by ankle weights. Ankle weights also distort the centrifugal force your muscles have to control when you turn.

For these reasons, we believe a dance conditioning program is a better way to build muscle strength than wearing ankle weights during dance class. A dance conditioning program will allow you to condition your body with exercises that incorporate the principles of overload and specificity without the problems associated with ankle weights.

The Reversibility Principle

Reversibility refers to the fact that a loss of strength occurs rapidly when a person stops exercising. In fact, two weeks after training ends, a marked decrease in strength can occur; as much as a 35 percent loss in strength can occur after one month. To maintain gains in strength, one must continue a strength conditioning program. Generally speaking, a muscle needs to be conditioned at least two times a week in order to maintain its level of strength.

4

Conditioning for Flexibility

Flexibility is increased by stretching the muscle, especially the connective tissue within the muscle. Each muscle fiber is surrounded by a layer of connective tissue. In addition, bundles of muscle fibers and their sheaths of connective tissue are grouped together in another layer of connective tissue. Finally, the whole muscle is surrounded by a layer of connective tissue. This connective tissue maintains the structural integrity of the muscle and is one of the primary determinants of the muscle's elastic property. When the muscle is stretched, the connective tissue stretches and the flexibility of the muscle is increased. Temperature is an important factor in increasing the length of connective tissue. When the body is warm, the connective tissue is more amenable to elongation.

The Relationship Between Strength and Flexibility

Movement occurs when muscles pull on the bony structure of the body. Muscles always *pull*. They *never push*. Muscles also work in pairs. When one member of the pair contracts and pulls, the other member of the pair will relax and stretch. The more the one muscle contracts, the more the other is stretched. In any pair of muscles, the contracting muscle is called the *agonist* and the relaxing muscle is called the *antagonist*.

The same muscle can be the agonist in one movement and the antagonist in the opposite movement. For example, when you point your foot and extend your ankle, the *gastrocnemius* muscle (located in the back of the calf) contracts. The *gastrocnemius* is the agonist. The *tibialis anterior* muscle (located in the front of the lower leg), acts as the antagonist and relaxes. When you flex the ankle, the muscles switch roles. The *tibialis anterior* becomes the agonist and contracts to flex the ankle. The *gastrocnemius* becomes the antagonist and relaxes.

Because the same muscles act in both agonist and antagonist roles, they must be both strong and flexible. They must be strong enough to act as agonists to produce movement, and they must be flexible enough to stretch when they are in the antagonist position. If the muscle pairs are not balanced in strength and flexibility, technique can suffer and injury can result. For example, a muscle that is not flexible can be torn when it acts as the antagonist; furthermore, its lack of flexibility can prevent the agonist from fully contracting. This limits both motion and strength.

A flexible body without strength is a useless dance instrument. A strong body without flexibility is a very limited dance instrument. That is why a well-rounded dance conditioning program develops both strength and flexibility. Such a program prepares the muscles to act as either agonists or antagonists.

5

Basic Information

There are several concepts you will need to understand before reading the chapters that follow. These include six anatomical terms, as well as information about muscular action and proper alignment of the body. The six anatomical terms will be used primarily in Parts III through VI. These parts introduce the bones and muscles of the body, and we will assume you have an understanding of this basic vocabulary. Figure 5.1 shows the general location of the bones in the dancer's body. As you read Parts III through VI, you may find it helpful to reexamine this illustration. The information concerning muscle action and alignment is central to many of the comments and explanations made throughout the book. You will need to understand this material before you can evaluate dance techniques and conditioning exercises.

Anatomical Terms

Throughout the text, the following descriptive, anatomical terms are used:

Anterior: The front side of the body or part of the body.
Posterior: The back side of the body or part of the body.
Medial: Part of the body closest to the midline of the body.
Lateral: Part of the body furthest from the midline of the body.
Ligament: Tissue that attaches bones to other bones.
Tendon: Tissue that attaches muscles to bones.

Types of Muscular Action

There are three types of muscular action: concentric, eccentric, and isometric. In a *concentric muscle action,* the muscle shortens as it exerts force, while in an *eccentric muscle action* the muscle lengthens as it exerts force. In an *isometric muscle action* the muscle neither shortens nor lengthens as force is exerted.

A forward kick, or *grand battement* to the front, can be used to illustrate both concentric and eccentric muscular actions. When you lift your leg to the front, the hip flexor muscles are responsible for the

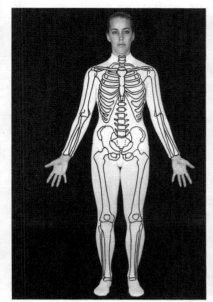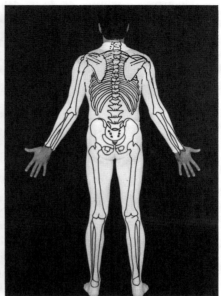

Figure 5.1 The skeleton

action. These muscles, located at the front of the hip, shorten as they exert force to pull the leg upward. This is an example of concentric muscle action.

Once the leg has been lifted, there are three ways to lower the leg. If the leg is to be lowered slowly, then muscles must exert enough force to counter gravity and control the descent of the leg. The muscles that perform that action are the hip flexors. After performing a concentric muscle action to lift the leg, the hip flexors perform an eccentric muscle action to slowly lower the leg. They lengthen as they exert force.

The second way to lower the leg is to completely relax the hip flexor muscles and let gravity pull the leg back down. If the leg is to lower very quickly, however, gravity will not be able to move the leg fast enough. The third way to lower the leg uses the hip extensor muscles. These muscles, located at the back of the hip, will shorten as they exert force to rapidly pull the leg downward. They will perform a concentric muscle action.

When a muscle performs an isometric muscle action it exerts force without any change in length. Holding the leg in *arabesque* is an example of an isometric muscle action of the hip extensors. Holding the arms in second position requires the arm abductors to perform an isometric muscle action. It should be noted that lifting the leg into arabesque or arms into second position requires a concentric muscle action. However, an isometric muscle action is performed once the limbs reach the position and are held in place.

Proper Alignment

Correct alignment is one of the best ways to prevent injury and improve performance because it allows the body to move in harmony with its structural architecture. This means there is less wear and tear on the muscles, bones, joints, ligaments, and cartilage. When you are correctly aligned, your muscles can work efficiently. You can dance better for longer periods with less chance of injury.

The body is correctly aligned when its weight is transferred through the center of each joint. The weight of the head should be transferred through the center of the first vertebra. The collective weight of the head and first vertebra should be transferred through the center of the second vertebra. This process continues down the spine, until the collective weight of the head, arms, and torso is transferred through the center of the hip to the center of the knee, and from there to the center of the ankle and foot.

A plumb line is often used to measure alignment. When a correctly placed body is viewed from the side, a plumb line will pass through the ear lobe, through the center of the shoulder, the center of the hip, just slightly in front of the center of the knee joint, and slightly in front of the outside ankle bone. The arms should hang easily, with the hand resting near the center of the hip. Figure 5.2 illustrates proper alignment of the body. In this example, the dancer's hand has been moved slightly forward so the center of the hip can be seen.

When alignment is incorrect, the weight of the body is not transferred through the centers of the joints. Depending on the alignment problem, the weight may be displaced toward the front, back, or sides of a joint. This puts a strain on the bones, cartilage, and ligaments. If the misalignment continues, the unnatural wear and tear can result in chronic pain. Continued further, it can cause a structural breakdown and injury.

Muscles are also adversely affected by improper alignment. They can become overstretched, or they can shorten and become very tight. In either case they are less able to meet the requirements of dance movement and are susceptible to injury. Dancers who habitually stand with an overarched back, for example, will generally find that their abdominal muscles are weak and their back muscles are tight. This is

Figure 5.2 Proper alignment.

because the hyperextended posture stretches the abdominals and allows them to "hang" in a relaxed state. Conversely, the back muscles adapt to the overarched position by tightening and shortening.

Another reason that correct alignment is so important is that the body is a *closed system.* This means that all its parts are connected. If one part is out of alignment, the alignment of the entire structure is adversely affected. For example, a head that is too far forward will cause alignment problems through the entire body and down to the feet. Badly aligned feet will cause stress in hips and knees as well as in the upper body.

Unfortunately, it is easy for a dancer to sacrifice correct alignment in order to solve a movement problem temporarily. Consequently, we see dancers forcing turnout from the knee and ankle, twisting the hip in *arabesque* to get the leg higher, and thrusting the ribs forward in order to improve their "presentation." These solutions are temporary because they are muscularly inefficient. Eventually they can lead to injury.

Bad alignment can be corrected. This is usually accomplished by combining a conditioning program to correct muscular imbalances with a reeducation program to establish correct habits. In Parts III through VI, we have provided information about specific alignment problems and conditioning exercises that can help correct the muscular imbalances associated with them.

PART

II

How to Perform the Exercises

This part of the book provides the basic information you will need before you begin the exercises. You will need to know how many repetitions to do, how fast to do them, what rhythm to use, how to stretch properly, and how to increase the training intensity for continued improvement. The information in this part applies to all the exercises throughout the book.

The majority of the exercises we recommend were chosen from those used by physical therapists for rehabilitation from injury. In many instances, it was necessary to choose among several effective exercises. The following criteria were used: (1) exercises had to be simple enough to be taught by written description; (2) exercises had to be performable without the assistance of a partner; and (3) any equipment required had to be easily obtained.

6

Exercise Equipment

What Equipment Is Needed

Although the exercises do not require elaborate equipment, several small items are necessary. These items are:

1. A small pillow or bath towel folded to make a small pillow.
2. A clock with a second hand.
3. A pair of cotton tube socks.
4. A bath towel and hand towel.
5. Elastic resistance in *one* of the following forms:
   a. A box of large rubber bands, approximately $1/8$ inch wide and 7 inches long. These can usually be purchased in stationery stores.
   b. Commercially prepared exercise rubber bands. Some sporting goods stores sell rubber bands especially made for resistance exercise. These rubber bands are cut in different widths and sold in sets. Each set usually contains three bands, the widest band providing more resistance than the narrowest band.
   c. Surgical tubing, $1/4$ inch $\times$ $1/16$ inch. Rolls of surgical tubing may be purchased from a hospital supply store. You will need at least 18 feet.
   d. *Thera-band* (brand name). This product, which resembles a six-inch wide piece of rubber fabric, comes in five color-coded resistances. It can be purchased from a hospital supply store, and is sold in rolls of varying lengths. We recommend most dancers purchase an 18 foot roll of the blue, or heavy resistance, *Thera-band*.
6. A pair of ankle weights. These are usually sold in sporting equipment stores, and come in sets identified by the total weight for the pair. A 5 pound set, for example, means each weight is 2.5 pounds. Ankle weights can be used around your ankles or your wrists, as well as being held for hand weights. When joined together they can be used around your waist. Throughout the book the weights will be identified as "ankle weights," "wrist weights," "hand weights," or "waist weights" to indicate the way in which they are to be used in a

25

particular exercise. We recommend that a 5 pound and 10 pound set of ankle weights be purchased at first. These weights, which can be used in combination, will be sufficient for most dancers. As you work with these and increase your strength, you will be able to decide if you need to purchase additional weights.

Pennypak is another type of ankle weight. This product is designed so you can control the weight you are using by adding or subtracting pennies. The pockets hold either loose or rolled pennies, and a "pennies to pounds" conversion chart is included. *Pennypaks* are sold as single packs and come in four sizes. Sizing designates circumference and weight capacity. If you use this product, we suggest you begin by purchasing two of the medium-size packs.

7. Optional equipment:
   a. Some dancers may be more comfortable exercising on a padded surface rather than on a hard floor. They may want to use padding such as a rug, blanket, or the foam rubber pad used by campers.
   b. Chain of elastic resistance. The strength conditioning exercise for the arm adductors (exercise 21.D) requires a 40-inch length of elastic resistance. If you are using rubber bands to provide resistance, you will need to make a chain from the rubber bands. Directions for making this chain of elastic resistance are given in the material that follows.
   c. Barbell. Dancers building strength for partnering will need to work with increasingly heavier weights. Most women can provide this resistance by working with a barbell. Men can begin working this way, but will need to work on an exercise machine for maximum benefit. We will describe how to make a homemade barbell in the material that follows. Exercising with weight machines is discussed in Chapter 23.

How to Prepare the Exercise Equipment

Preparing the Elastic Resistance

If you are using rubber bands, put four or five together in one circle. Check for any possible cracks, then stretch the circle to be sure you have a good strong resistance. If not, add more rubber bands. Next, pull one tube sock through the circle of rubber bands and tie the ends to form a fabric loop. Finally, use *several lengths of very strong twine* to attach the rubber band circle to the leg of a heavy piece of furniture (Figure 6.1a). It is most important to check the rubber bands, the knot on the tube sock, and the twine before each use.

Figure 6.1 Elastic resistance.

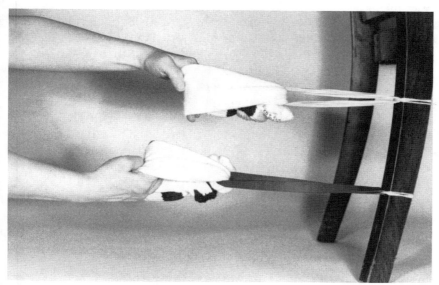

Stationery store rubber bands (a) are held by the upper hand. **Commercially prepared exercise rubber bands (b)** are held by the lower hand.

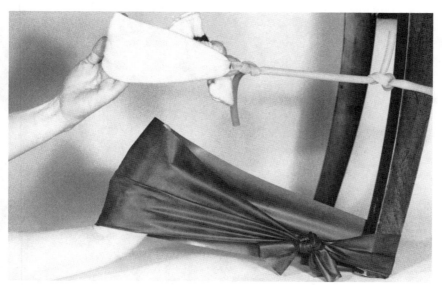

Surgical tubing (c) is held by the upper hand. **Thera-band (d)** is held by the lower hand.

If you are using commercially prepared rubber exercise bands, check for any cracks, then choose the band that provides a strong resistance when you stretch it. Next, pull one tube sock through the rubber band and tie the ends of the sock to form a fabric loop. Finally, use *several lengths of very strong twine* to attach the rubber band circle to the leg of a heavy piece of furniture (Figure 6.1b). It is most important to check the rubber bands, the knot on the tube sock, and the twine before each use.

If you are using surgical tubing, cut a 40-inch length. Next, take one tube sock and tie the ends together to form a fabric loop. Then tie one end of the surgical tubing to the fabric loop. Use enough tubing to tie several knots and still have one or two inches left over. Pull several times to secure each knot. Finally, tie the other end of the surgical tubing to the leg of a heavy piece of furniture (Figure 6.1c). Once again, use enough tubing to tie several knots and still have one or two inches left over. Pull several times to secure each knot. It is most important to check the knot on the tube sock and the knots in the surgical tubing before each use.

If you are using *Thera-band* cut a 40-inch length. Wrap the *Thera-band* around the leg of a heavy piece of furniture and tie a knot (Figure 6.1d). Be sure the knot is pulled tight, and check it before each use.

Constructing a Chain of Elastic Resistance
Group four or five rubber bands together in a circle. Twist the circle in half to form a smaller circle. Pull a tube sock through the smaller circle

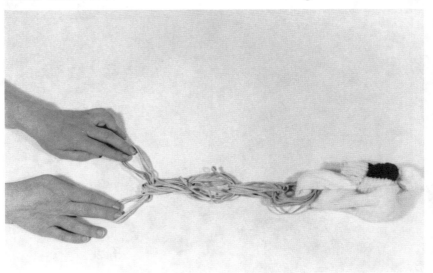

Figure 6.2 Chain of elastic resistance.

and tie the ends together to form a fabric loop. Next, make 14 more groups of rubber bands containing four to five rubber bands each. Do not twist these in half. Loop the circles through one another to form a 40-inch chain (Figure 6.2).

Preparing the Ankle Weights

As you begin to build strength you will need to increase weight resistance. If you use the *Pennypak* style of ankle weight, you can do this by adding pennies. If you use the other style of ankle weight, you can wrap more than one weight around the same body part. The second weight can be placed above or on top of the first weight. If necessary, a tube sock can be used to help hold the second weight in place (Figure 6.3).

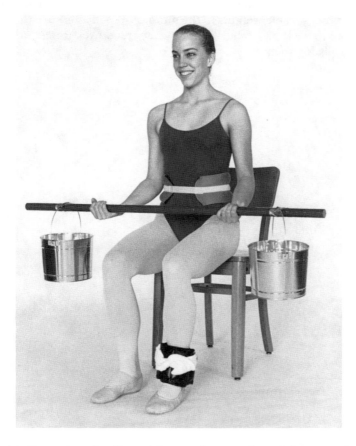

Figure 6.3 Examples of ankle weights used as a waist weight; strapping two ankle weights around one ankle; and a homemade barbell.

For certain exercises it will be necessary to join two ankle weights together lengthwise and use them as a waist weight. If the ankle weights have velcro straps and rings, join the weights together by using the velcro straps. Then loop a belt or heavy twine through the rings. If the weights attach with velcro straps alone, join the weights with the velcro straps or use a belt to wrap around the weights and hold them in place at your waist (Figure 6.3).

Constructing a Barbell

You will need a dowel at least 2 inches in diameter and 5 feet long. For small amounts of weight, a broom handle may be used, unless the length is too short to feel comfortable. Use duct tape or some other strong tape to attach the handle of an aluminum pail to each end of the dowel (Figure 6.3). Finally, put ankle weights, bags of salt, bags of sand, or other measurable weights in the aluminum pails. Be sure the weights are equal in each pail. Check periodically the dowel, tape, and handles of the pails for wear.

7

The Strength Conditioning Exercises

The number of repetitions of an exercise that you perform is an important consideration in strength conditioning programs. The following material describes how to determine the number of repetitions to perform, and contains information on resistance, tempo, adding variety to the program, and some words of caution.

Determining the Number of Repetitions

When you first begin a strength conditioning program, you will probably find that different muscle groups differ in strength. As a result, the number of repetitions you can perform will vary from one exercise to another. To determine how many repetitions you should perform of any given exercise, repeat the exercise until you feel the muscle reach a point of fatigue, but not exhaustion. If the feeling of fatigue goes away within an hour after exercise, you have performed the correct number of repetitions. Use this number as the starting point for that particular exercise.

If you experience soreness the next day, you may have done too many repetitions and pushed the muscle too hard. The comment "no pain, no gain" is not accurate; "no work, no gain" is the correct concept. If you do not work the muscle hard enough to become tired, you will not build strength. On the other hand, you can push the muscle too hard. The resulting muscle soreness can then cause your performance to suffer.

Increasing Your Repetitions

You can add a few more repetitions as soon as the muscle no longer feels tired at the end of the exercise. Increases should be in small, gradual steps. Your body will tell you if you are asking too much, too soon. Listen to it!

Generally speaking, sixteen repetitions of an exercise should be an appropriate number for older teen and adult dancers to perform. Exceptions to this rule will be noted in the descriptions for specific

31

exercises. If you are completing sixteen repetitions of an exercise but still need more strength, we suggest you increase the resistance.

Sets, or Repetition Groups

Many people like to divide the number of repetitions into groups, or sets, and rest for a few seconds between sets. For example, if your goal is sixteen repetitions, you could begin with two sets of six repetitions. When you are no longer fatigued by these repetitions, you can progress to two sets of seven repetitions, and finally work up to two sets of eight. Some dancers prefer to divide their repetitions into three sets. This provides one more pause for those who are working with greater resistance.

Repetitions and Resistance

As a general guideline, you should try working up to sixteen repetitions of a specific exercise without any added resistance. When you can do this without muscular fatigue, you can begin to add resistance. To increase resistance for the exercises suggested in this book, you can use more elastic resistance or additional weight. The elastics and weights should be added in small increments to avoid muscular injury. You should be able to complete at least half as many repetitions as you performed without the added resistance; if not, cut back on the resistance.

Once you have reached the level of strength necessary for dance, you will not need to increase your resistance further. For this reason, it is important to evaluate your dance technique periodically as you build strength. There is no universal, preset level of resistance to be used in these conditioning exercises. Each individual will need to evaluate their technique and decide when they have reached their strength goals. Dancers who are uncertain about their level of strength should check with their teacher.

Timing Patterns and Tempos

Working slowly will help you achieve your goal of improving strength. When you work slowly, you can be certain to work correctly and thoroughly. For these reasons, the strength conditioning exercises in this book are designed to be performed at a slow tempo. If at first an exercise seems too easy, try slowing down the tempo before you increase the difficulty in any other way. Different rhythmic patterns have been included for the sake of variety. The patterns are:

Timing pattern A

Move from the starting position through the action on counts 1 and 2.

Hold at the peak of the action for counts 3 through 6.

Return to the staring position on counts 7 and 8.

Timing pattern B

Move from the starting position through the action on counts 1 through 4.

Return to the starting position on counts 5 through 8.

Timing pattern C

Move from the starting position through the action on count 1.

Hold the peak of the action for counts 2 and 3.

Return to the starting position on count 4.

Timing pattern D

Lift on counts 1 and 2.

Rotate on counts 3 and 4.

Return to the center position on counts 5 and 6.

Lower on counts 7 and 8.

As you perform the strength building exercises you must move evenly and smoothly. Do not jerk up or drop down. It is very important that you perform the return to the starting position with control, utilizing all of the counts designated. The muscles will build strength during this part of the exercise, if you work correctly.

Generally speaking, timing patterns A, B, and C are to be used with all of the strength conditioning exercises. Timing pattern D is only used for a few of the exercises. The performance instructions for each individual exercise specify which timing patterns should be used.

When more than one timing pattern is suggested for an exercise, the patterns should be used on a rotation schedule. Chapter 22 gives examples of how to do this.

Variety in Your Exercise Program

There is a certain amount of necessary repetition to conditioning work. In order to increase your strength, the repetitions and the resistance must be increased. If you are committed to improving your dance technique, you will have to accept repetition as part of the process.

Exercising with a friend makes the repetition more fun, as does listening to your favorite music or watching television. The conditioning program presented in this book provides a variety of rhythms and tempos for each exercise. This also helps to relieve possible boredom.

Once you have become familiar with the exercises and material presented in this book, you will have a good foundation from which to evaluate other strength and flexibility programs. The exercises recommended in this book are by no means the only set of appropriate exercises. As you become aware of other programs, you can analyze their effectiveness and judge their contribution to your conditioning work. If you decide to incorporate additional exercises, you can alternate them with those that you are currently doing. This is another way in which you can keep your conditioning program from becoming stale.

Finding the Time

While you can do your daily conditioning work in one block of time, it is not necessary. You can divide the exercises up and do a few throughout the day, as long as you remember that the body should be warmed up. By taking a few minutes before and after dance class or rehearsal, or a few minutes after a hot bath or shower, you can make the time.

There is no use pretending that conditioning will not take additional time. If you want to improve your dance technique and be less susceptible to injury, you will have to find the time for a conditioning program.

Sessions per Week

Most experts recommend that a muscle group be conditioned for strength three times a week to produce gains in strength without chronic fatigue. Not all muscle groups need to be exercised on the same day. For example, you might want to concentrate on exercising the foot and ankle on Monday, Wednesday, and Friday and the upper leg on Tuesday, Thursday, and Saturday. You should be aware that it may take up to six weeks of strength training before you see a significant improvement.

Words of Caution

There are three points you should consider when beginning any strength conditioning program: (1) the correct way to breathe during the exercises; (2) the correct organization of a conditioning session; and (3) maintaining a balance.

Proper Breathing
Many strength training experts recommend that you exhale as you perform the action and inhale as you return to the staring position. Do

not hold your breath during the action. If you hold your breath during a contraction, an increase in pressure on the heart can occur, called the *Valsalva maneuver*. One way to prevent this is to exhale as you perform the motion. Another way is to talk or count out loud as you perform the muscular contractions. Because the resistance recommended for the exercises in this book is light, compared to competitive weight training, we do not expect a Valsalva maneuver to occur. As a precaution, however, we recommend that you remain aware of your breathing patterns as you exercise.

Correct Organization of a Conditioning Session
Some dancers prefer to do all of their conditioning work in one session. Others prefer to divide up the exercises and do some exercises before class or rehearsal and other exercises afterwards. No matter which system you follow, it is important to plan the sequence in which you perform your exercises. The following guidelines will help you correctly organize your conditioning session:

1. Strength conditioning in which the muscles are worked to the point of fatigue should not be done when the body is cold. It is better to perform a warm-up before starting a strength building session. This warm-up should include light intensity activities that begin to warm and stretch the muscles.
2. Strength conditioning exercises for one muscle group should be followed by flexibility exercises for that same muscle group. For example, strength conditioning work for the knee extensors should be followed by flexibility exercises for the knee extensors.

    In the chapters that follow, various "exercise prescriptions" will be given to help improve technique and prevent injury. Whenever a recommendation is made to strengthen a particular muscle group, the flexibility exercise for that muscle group will also be listed. This is to serve as a reminder to include flexibility work in your strength conditioning program.
3. Large muscle groups should be exercised before smaller muscle groups. For example, the muscles of the hip and knee should be conditioned before the muscles of the ankle and foot.
4. As you perform a series of exercises, it is important to listen to your body. It will provide important information as to what particular sequence of exercises "feels right" and works best for you.
5. A proper cool-down is an important part of any exercise session. In the cool-down process, you need to gradually decrease the intensity of the exercise, and stretch the muscle groups that have been conditioned for strength. If you follow the previous guidelines, you will have met the requirements for a proper cool-down. Exercise

intensity will have decreased as smaller muscle groups are exercised last, and the appropriate flexibility exercise will have been performed after each strength conditioning exercise.

Maintaining a Balance

Various "exercise prescriptions" will be suggested throughout the book. These will recommend strengthening or stretching specific muscle groups. As you work with these exercises, it is important to periodically evaluate your technique. Remember the importance of keeping an overall balance of strength and stretch in the muscle pairs throughout the body. If you do not keep this goal in mind, you could overcorrect a muscular imbalance and create a new problem.

The best way to maintain a balance of strength and stretch is to follow a regular conditioning program for the entire body. Chapter 22 presents examples of programs that may be designed by using the exercises in this book.

8

The Flexibility Exercises

When you perform the flexibility exercises in this book, you should think of four words: hold; relax; release carefully. You should *hold* the stretch position and *relax* the muscle group being stretched. When you have finished holding a stretch position, you should *release* the stretch *carefully*, then gently move the muscles and joints involved.

Two additional points can help you increase your flexibility. First perform the stretches when the muscles are warm, either after class or after a hot bath or shower. Second, do not use a bouncing type of stretch. Bouncing is not the best way to stretch because muscles will contract in response to a sudden stretch. This could lead to injury. More information on stretching, including the timing and intensity of the stretches is presented below.

Timing the Stretch

There is a difference of opinion about the length of time a stretch should be held. Some experts recommend thirty seconds, others advise one minute, or even longer. We suggest you begin with thirty seconds. If that does not seem sufficient, you can try holding your stretch for a longer period of time.

Intensity of the Stretch

The intensity of the stretch should be determined by the way your muscle "feels" during the stretch. You should feel the muscle stretching, but it should be a "friendly" stretch, not an "angry" one. Furthermore, the stretch should be felt in the middle of the muscle rather than at the ends of the muscle, where the tendons attach to the bones.

Flexibility is increased by working *with* your muscles, not *against* them. Easy does it. There is a difference between feeling the muscle stretch and feeling pain while the muscle is stretching. Listen to your body. Let it guide the intensity of your stretch.

Exercise Sessions per Week

Researchers have not yet determined how many times a week a dancer should train to gain the most flexibility. We suggest you stretch each muscle group three times per week in addition to the flexibility work that occurs during your dance classes. As in developing strength, you do not need to stretch all of your muscles on the same day. You might want to stretch the leg muscles on Monday, Wednesday, and Friday and the upper body on Tuesday, Thursday, and Saturday. You should be aware that it may take five to six weeks before you see significant improvement in flexibility.

There is one exception to the suggestion that you stretch a muscle group three times per week. If you use one particular muscle group a great deal in class or rehearsal, you should take time afterwards to stretch that muscle group. For example, if class includes a lot of *relevés*, *pointe* work, or jumps, you should stretch the ankle plantar flexors as well as the knee and hip extensors. A wise dancer makes a mental check at the end of each day to be certain that the muscle groups used the most often for strength have also been stretched.

Other Flexibility Exercises

Physical therapists often recommend a specific form of flexibility training called Proprioceptive Neuromuscular Facilitation (PNF) or Contract-Relax. This method is an effective way of stretching to increase flexibility. We do not advise PNF stretching in this book for the following reasons: (1) many PNF stretches require a partner; (2) the partner must be carefully trained or injury could result; and (3) training the partner requires on-site, personal guidance and cannot be adequately done by reading a book.

9
Starting Positions

The starting positions described in this chapter are used in the strength and flexibility exercises throughout the book. There are nine starting positions for the body, three for the feet, and four starting positions for the arms. These positions are identified by name only in the conditioning exercises. If you take a few minutes to learn the starting positions now, it will make it easier when you learn the conditioning exercises.

The nine starting positions for the body are identified by the position of the body and legs. For example, in the *Back horizontal* starting position, the dancer is lying horizontal, on the back. In the *Double-V horizontal* position, the dancer is lying horizontal, on the back, with both knees bent. (The shape formed by the knees gives the appearance of a double *V*, and thus the position is named *Double-V horizontal.*) In the *Single-V horizontal* starting position, the dancer is lying horizontal, on the back, with just one knee bent. In the *L-sitting* position, the dancer's body and legs form the shape of the capital letter *L*.

The three positions of the feet and the four positions of the arms are identified according to terminology used in ballet, modern dance, and jazz classes. For example, the starting position identified as *Turned-out first position of the feet* is the first position used for the feet in the ballet technique. The starting position identified as *Second arm position* is the second position used for the arms in the ballet technique and in many modern dance and jazz classes.

The Nine Starting Positions For the Body

1. Front Horizontal
The dancer is lying in a horizontal position, on the front. A small pillow, or towel folded to form a small pillow, should be placed between the pelvis and the ribs to protect the lower back. In this position the arms may be at the sides (Figure 9.1a) or folded so the forehead rests on the hands (Figure 9.1b). The face may be turned towards the floor (Figures 9.1a and b), or turned to one side (Figure 9.1c). Choose the head and

Figure 9.1 Starting positions for the body.

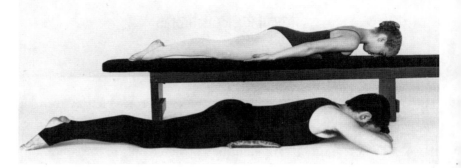

Dancer (a) is on the bench in the **Front horizontal** position with arms at the side and looking straight ahead. **Dancer (b)** is on the floor in the **Front horizontal** position, arms folded and looking straight ahead.

Dancer (c) is on the bench in the **Front horizontal** position with arms at the side and looking to the side. **Dancer (d)** is on the floor in the **Back horizontal** position.

arm positions that are most comfortable for you, unless an exercise gives other instructions.

2. Back Horizontal
The dancer is lying in a horizontal position, on the back (Figure 9.1d) In this position the spine should be correctly aligned. Dancers with hyperextended backs should use their abdominal muscles to prevent

Dancer (e) is on the bench in the **Side horizontal** position, elbow bent. **Dancer (f)** is on the floor in the **Side horizontal** position, elbow straight and one knee bent.

Dancer (g) is on the bench in the **Double-V horizontal** position. **Dancer (h)** is on the floor in the **Single-V horizontal** position.

the lower back from over arching. In this position the arms are at the sides and the back of the head rests on the floor.

3. Side Horizontal
The dancer is in a horizontal position, on the side. Care should be taken to stay positioned on the side of the body. Do not roll backward. In this

Figure 9.1 continued.

Dancer (i) is on the bench in the **Double-V sitting** position. **Dancer (j)** is on the floor in the **Single-V sitting** position.

position both legs may be straight (Figure 9.1e), or the bottom leg may be bent (Figure 9.1f). There are also two possible positions for the head and top arm. The arm can be bent, and the head can rest on the hand (Figure 9.1e), or the arm may be extended, and the head can rest on the upper arm (Figure 9.1f). You may choose the most comfortable head, arm, and leg positions, unless an exercise gives other instructions.

4. Double-V Horizontal
The dancer is lying horizontal, on the back, with both knees bent (Figure 9.1g). The arms are at the sides, and the back of the head rests on the floor.

5. Single-V Horizontal
The dancer is lying horizontal, on the back, with one knee bent (Figure 9.1h). The other leg is extended in a straight line from the hip. The arms are at the sides, and the back of the head rests on the floor.

Dancer (k) is on the bench in the **Cross-sitting** position. **Dancer (l)** is on the floor in the **L-sitting** position.

6. Double-V Sitting

The dancer is sitting, with both knees bent, feet flat on the floor (Figure 9.1i). The feet should be a comfortable distance from the seat, and the back should be straight. The arms are at the sides, with the face looking straight ahead.

7. Single-V Sitting.

The dancer is sitting with one knee bent, foot flat on the floor, and the other leg extended (Figure 9.1j). The foot should be a comfortable distance from the seat, and the back should be straight. The arms are at the sides, with the face looking straight ahead.

8. Cross-Sitting

The dancer is sitting with both knees bent, and the ankles crossed (Figure 9.1k). The back should be straight, and the arms at the sides. The face should look straight ahead.

9. L-Sitting
The dancer is sitting with both legs extended and the back straight (Figure 9.1l). The arms rest at the sides, and the face looks straight ahead.

Three Starting Positions for the Feet

1. Parallel First Position of the Feet
The dancer stands with the feet slightly apart, and the toes pointing straight ahead (Figure 9.2a). The weight should be evenly divided between the heel and the ball of the foot.

Figure 9.2 Two starting positions for the feet. **Dancer (a)** is on the left in **Parallel first** position. **Dancer (b)** is on the right in **Turned-out first** position.

2. Turned-out First Position of the Feet

The dancer stands with the inner legs touching, and the toes pointing diagonally outward (Figure 9.2b). The weight should be evenly divided between the heel and the ball of the foot. The degree to which the legs turnout should be determined by outward rotation at the hip. The dancer must not force turnout from the knee and ankle. When correctly turned out, the knee will align with the center of the foot.

3. Second Position of the Feet

The dancer begins in a parallel or turned-out first position, then moves the feet apart a comfortable distance (Figure 9.3).

Figure 9.3 Third starting position of the feet and four starting positions for the arms. **Dancer (a),** on the left, demonstrates **Second** position of the feet and the **Right-angle** arm position. **Dancer (b),** on the right, demonstrates **Second** position of the feet and the **Second** arm position.

Figure 9.3 continued.

Dancer (c), on the left, demonstrates **Second** position of the feet and the **Diagonal fifth** arm position. **Dancer (d),** on the right, demonstrates **Second** position of the feet and the **Fifth** arm position.

Four Starting Positions for the Arms

1. Right-Angle Arm Position
The arms are raised to the side until they reach shoulder height. The elbows are bent 90 degrees, forming a right angle (Figure 9.3a). The palms should face forward.

2. Second Arm Position
The arms are raised to the side until they are just below shoulder height. The elbows are slightly bent, and the palms face each other (Figure 9.3b). The elbows should face the back, not point down to the floor.

3. Diagonal Fifth Arm Position
The arms are raised above shoulder height in a forward, diagonal direction (Figure 9.3c). The shoulders should be kept down, and the palms should face forward.

4. Fifth Arm Position
The arms are raised above shoulder height in a forward, diagonal direction. The elbows are bent slightly, and the palms face the floor (Figure 9.3d). There should be enough space between the finger tips to accommodate the width of your face, and you should be able to see your fingers with your peripheral vision.

III

The Foot, Ankle, and Lower Leg

Dancers must be able to flex and extend the ankle fully, balance on half-toe or full pointe, *and to jump and move quickly. To perform these basic dance movements, the muscles of the foot and ankle must be strong and flexible. In this part of the book, we discuss these muscles and describe ways in which dancers can improve their technique and prevent injury to the foot, ankle, and lower leg.*

10

The Major Muscles of the Foot, Ankle, and Lower Leg

The Structure of the Foot, Ankle, and Lower Leg

The foot has twenty-six bones. These are divided into three groups known as the *tarsals, metatarsals,* and *phalanges* (Figure 10.1). The bones of the foot are connected by a complex network of 117 ligaments. There are two additional bones called *sesamoid* (floating) bones located under the ball of the foot at the base of the big toe. The two arches of the foot are the transverse arch and the longitudinal arch. The *transverse arch* extends from the medial to the lateral side of the foot. The *longitudinal arch* extends along the medial border of the foot. It is commonly referred to as the "instep."

The bones of the lower leg are the *tibia* and *fibula* (Figure 10.1). They attach to the rear bone of the ankle, which is the *talus*. The *talus* sits on top of the *calcaneus,* or heel bone. The majority of muscles that flex and extend the toes or ankle have their origin on the *fibula* or *tibia* and run over the ankle onto specific bones of the foot.

This chapter does not include a description or discussion of all bones, ligaments, and muscles of the foot and ankle. We will concentrate instead on those muscles primarily involved in producing the basic dance movements.

Movements of the Toes, Foot, and Ankle

There are two primary categories of movement of the toes, two of the ankle, and two of the foot. The toes either *extend* (lift upwards toward the knee) or *flex* (point or, in the extreme case, curl under). The ankle can *dorsiflex* (flex the foot) and *plantar flex* (point the foot). Various joints in the foot allow movements in the lateral and medial directions. The foot can move toward the little toe or toward the big toe. It is also possible to lift the outer border of the foot and to lift the inner border of the foot. The terms *eversion* or *pronation* will be used to describe a combination of moving the foot toward the little toe and raising the

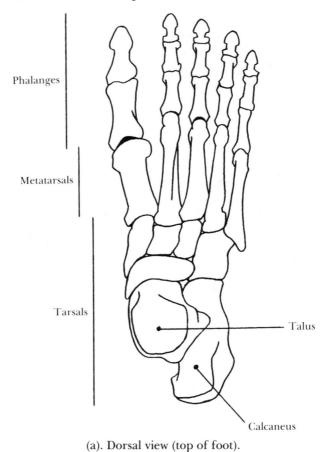

Phalanges

Metatarsals

Tarsals

Talus

Calcaneus

(a). Dorsal view (top of foot).

Figure 10.1 Dorsal and lateral views of right foot and lower-leg bones.

outer border of the foot. The terms *inversion* or *supination* will be used to describe a combination of moving the foot toward the big toe and raising the inner border of the foot.

Movements at the ankle and foot can occur simultaneously. For example, "sickling out" is produced by a combination of ankle plantar flexion, and foot eversion. "Sickling in" is produced by the simultaneous actions of ankle plantar flexion and foot inversion.

Extension of the Toes
The muscles that extend the toes are the *extensor hallucis longus*, the *extensor digitorum longus*, and the *extensor digitorum brevis*. The *extensor*

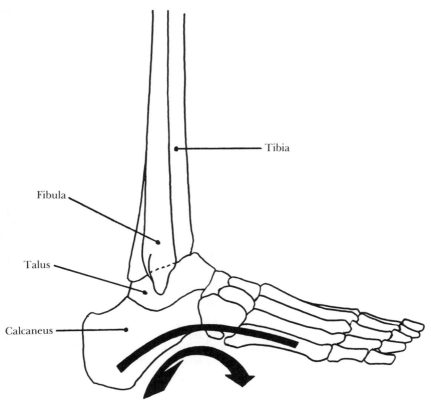

(b). Lateral view. Wide arrow indicates transverse arch; wide bar indicates longitudinal arch.

hallucis longus lifts up the big toe. The *extensor digitorum longus* and *brevis* muscles lift up the four outer toes. These muscles are located on the anterior side of the lower leg or on the top of the foot. Their more exact location is described below.

The *extensor hallucis longus* is attached to the *fibula* on one end, and to the top of the big toe on the other end (Figures 10.2 and 10.3). The easiest way to feel the tendon of this muscle is to place your fingers on the top of the foot at the base of the big toe and then extend the big toe.

The *extensor digitorum longus* is attached to both the *tibia* and the *fibula* at one end, and to the tops of the four outer toes at the other end (Figures 10.2 and 10.3).

The *extensor digitorum brevis* is attached below the ankle joint (Figure 10.3).

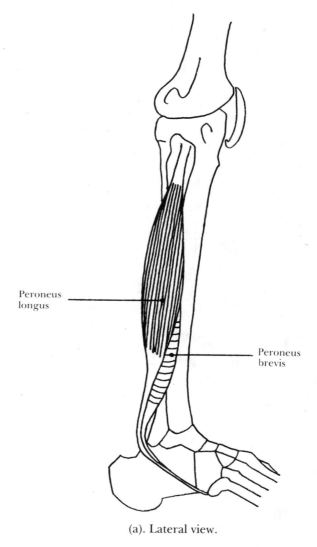

Peroneus
longus

Peroneus
brevis

(a). Lateral view.

Figure 10.2 Lateral and anterior views of lower-leg muscles.

Flexion of the Toes

The three muscles that flex the toes are the *flexor hallucis longus,* the *flexor digitorum longus,* and the *flexor digitorum brevis.* The *flexor hallucis longus* flexes the big toe, while the four outer toes are flexed by the *flexor digitorum longus* and *brevis.* These muscles are located on the

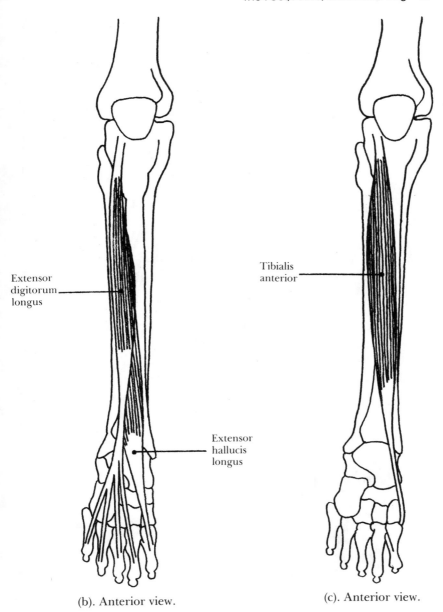

Extensor
digitorum
longus

Tibialis
anterior

Extensor
hallucis
longus

(b). Anterior view.

(c). Anterior view.

posterior side of the lower leg and on the bottom of the foot. Their
more exact location is described below.

The *flexor hallucis longus* is attached to the posterior side of the *fibula*
on one end, and to the bottom of the big toe on the other end (Figure
10.4).

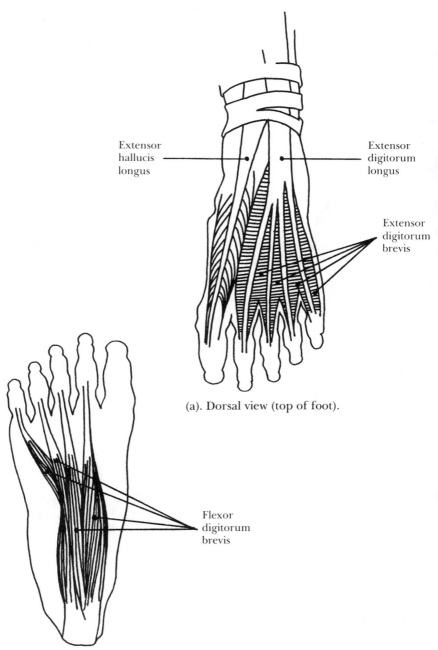

Extensor
hallucis
longus

Extensor
digitorum
longus

Extensor
digitorum
brevis

(a). Dorsal view (top of foot).

Flexor
digitorum
brevis

(b). Plantar view (sole of foot).

Figure 10.3 Dorsal and plantar views of foot muscles.

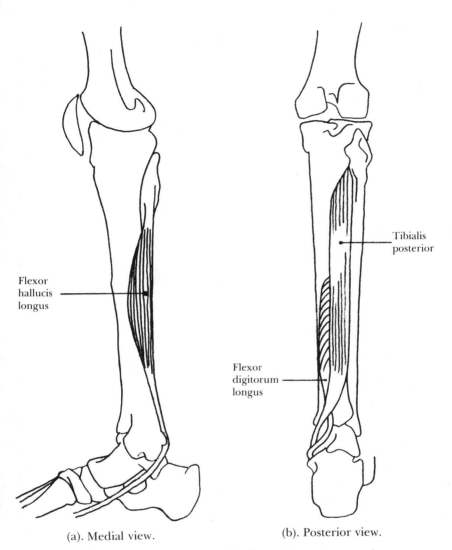

Flexor
hallucis
longus

Tibialis
posterior

Flexor
digitorum
longus

(a). Medial view.   (b). Posterior view.

Figure 10.4 Posterior and medial views of lower-leg muscles.

The *flexor digitorum longus* is attached to the posterior side of the *tibia* on one end, and to the bottom of each of the four outer toes at the other end (Figure 10.4). This muscle cannot be easily palpated, or felt.

The *flexor digitorum brevis* is located on the sole of the foot. It is attached to the *calcaneus* on one end, and to the outer four toes at the other end (Figure 10.3).

Figure 10.4 continued.

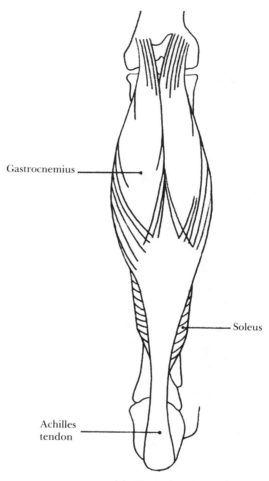

Gastrocnemius

Soleus

Achilles
tendon

(c). Posterior view.

Dorsiflexion of the Ankle

The primary muscles that dorsiflex the ankle are the *tibialis anterior,* the *extensor digitorum longus,* and the *extensor hallucis longus.* These three muscles are located on the anterior side of the lower leg. The *extensor digitorum longus* and the *extensor hallucis longus* have been described in the previous paragraphs. The more exact location of the *tibialis anterior* is described below.

The *tibialis anterior* is attached to the *tibia* on one end, and to the bones of the foot on the other end (Figure 10.2). To feel this muscle in action, place your fingers on the front of your lower leg as you dorsiflex the ankle.

Plantar Flexion of the Ankle
The primary muscles that plantar flex the ankle are the *gastrocnemius* and the *soleus* muscles. These two muscles are located on the posterior side of the lower leg. Other muscles assist the *gastrocnemius* and the *soleus* muscles. Two of these, the *flexor hallucis longus* and the *flexor digitorum longus,* have been described. (The *peroneus longus* and the *tibialis posterior* muscles, which also contribute to plantar flexion of the ankle, are described shortly under *Eversion of the Foot* and *Inversion of the Foot*.)

The *gastrocnemius* is attached to the *femur* (the upper leg bone) on one end and to the *calcaneus* (the heel bone) on the other end (Figure 10.4). The tendon connecting the *gastrocnemius* to the *calcaneus* is known as the *Achilles tendon*. Because the *gastrocnemius* originates on the upper leg bone, it can also bend the knee when the foot is not bearing weight. Its primary action is to plantar flex the ankle, however. The *gastrocnemius,* generally referred to as the "calf muscle," can be visually or tactually identified by plantar flexing the ankle.

The *soleus* is attached to both the *tibia* and the *fibula* on one end. Like the *gastrocnemius,* it is attached to the *calcaneus* by way of the Achilles tendon on the other end (Figure 10.4), but because it is located under the *gastrocnemius* muscle, it cannot be easily palpated.

Eversion of the Foot
The muscles that cause the foot to evert are the *peroneus longus,* the *peroneus brevis,* and the *extensor digitorum longus* (described previously). The *peroneus longus* and *brevis* are located on the lateral side of the lower leg.

The *peroneus longus* is attached at one end to the *fibula*. On the other end it is attached to the under surface of some of the foot bones (Figure 10.2). The *peroneus longus* may be identified by placing the hand on the lateral side of the lower leg and everting the foot.

The *peroneus brevis* is attached to the *fibula* on one end and to the under surface of one of the foot bones at the other end (Figure 10.2). It is not easily palpated.

Inversion of the Foot
The muscles that cause the foot to invert are the *tibialis posterior,* the *tibialis anterior,* the *flexor hallucis longus,* and the *flexor digitorum longus*. With the exception of the *tibialis posterior,* which is located on the

posterior side of the lower leg, these muscles have already been described.

The *tibialis posterior* is attached at one end to the *tibia* and the *fibula*. At the other end it is attached to the bones of the foot (Figure 10.4). In addition to inverting the foot, the *tibialis posterior* helps to maintain the longitudinal arch.

Intrinsic Muscles of the Foot

On the bottom surface of the foot are four layers of intrinsic muscles. These muscles are attached at both ends to the bones within the foot. All the intrinsic muscles of the foot function to move the toes and are important for rising on the toes and for propulsion. According to some experts they also prevent the toes from "clawing" or curling under when the foot is pointed (Howse & Hancock, 1988, p. 33.)

11

Questions and Answers

Note: The questions and answers that follow concern improvement of dance technique and the prevention of injuries to the foot, ankle, and lower leg.

1. What is the correct alignment of the foot and ankle?

Correct alignment of the foot and ankle can be described in several ways. One important consideration is the way in which the body's weight is distributed along the surface of the foot. When the foot and ankle are properly aligned with the lower leg, the weight of the body is transmitted through the *tibia* to the *talus* and *calcaneus* and then distributed across the ball of the foot with more weight falling on the first *metatarsal*. The body's weight is equally supported by the heel and ball of the foot, allowing the toes to relax. The toes should be in contact with the floor for balance, but they should not "claw" the floor. The longitudinal arch should be in a neutral position. It should not be depressed by excessive rolling in, nor unnaturally elevated by excessive rolling out.

One way to evaluate the position of the longitudinal arch is to look at the Achilles tendon as it runs down the back of the heel. If the tendon bows medially, the dancer is rolling in. If the tendon bows laterally, the dancer is rolling out.

The relationship of the foot to the knee is another important consideration. The middle of the foot should be centered under the middle of the knee. This is true in parallel as well as in turned-out positions. One way to check this alignment is to stand in parallel first position *demi-plié.* If you look down at your feet, you should be able to see your big toe. If you can see only your knees, your foot-knee alignment is incorrect. You need to move your knees wider apart until they are centered over the midline of your feet.

Next, you should try the same test in a turned-out first position *demi-plié.* If you cannot see your big toe, you can correct your knee-foot alignment in one of two ways. Either you can increase the external rotation of your legs at the hip, which will cause the knees to move

63

laterally, or you can decrease the turnout of the foot and ankle, which will cause the feet to move medially.

It is important to recognize that some alignment problems may be due to structural deviations. Structural deviations cannot be changed by improving technique or performing conditioning exercises. If you suspect your problem is structural and not due to poor technique, you may want to consult a physician for an evaluation.

2. Why is correct alignment of the foot and ankle important?

Correct alignment of the foot and ankle is an important factor in both improving technique and preventing injury. Proper placement allows the muscles of the foot and ankle to work efficiently, while improper placement jeopardizes the structural component of both the foot and ankle. Because the entire weight of the body is transmitted to the ankle and foot, even a small deviation in placement can place a great deal of stress on the foot and ankle structure.

Ligaments are primarily responsible for holding the bones of the ankle and foot together, and these ligaments can become permanently stretched if they are subjected to the continual pressure of incorrect alignment. It is important to understand that ligaments do not have the same elastic property that muscles have. Once a ligament is over-stretched, it remains elongated and is no longer able to hold the bones in their proper place. As a result, the correct architecture of the foot and ankle can no longer be maintained. This leaves the foot and ankle vulnerable to further injury.

Jumps are performed frequently both in dance classes and choreography. These jumps further increase the problems associated with incorrect alignment of the foot and ankle. Every time you land from a jump, the force of gravity increases the weight of your body. This extra weight is transmitted to the ankle and foot. If they are not properly aligned, the ligaments, tendons, and sometimes even the muscles can be badly injured.

3. I understand that some dancers wear orthotics *(molded arch supports) in their dancing shoes. Why do they do this?*

Orthotics can be placed inside the shoes to hold the foot in better alignment. In certain situations they might be of benefit to dancers with problems in foot alignment. Some dancers, for example, are born with an alignment problem in the bone structure of their feet. No matter how correct their dance technique, they are vulnerable to all of the injuries associated with poor alignment of the foot and ankle. Sometimes these dancers may be helped by wearing a regular, firm orthotic in their street shoes, and a lightweight, flexible orthotic in their dancing shoes.

There can be problems with orthotics. It may be difficult to find an orthotic that fits satisfactorily in a dance shoe. In addition, some shoes may not be strong enough to support an orthotic. Not all dancers like the appearance of an arch support. Some ballet dancers, for example, feel orthotics destroy the line of the foot.

If you believe that you have a congenital problem in foot structure, and are interested in orthotics, you should consult a medical professional. Do not attempt to construct your own orthotics.

4. My dance teacher tells me I am forcing my turnout from the foot and ankle. What's wrong with this?

Turnout should come from the hip socket. When turnout is performed properly, the upper leg, knee, lower leg, ankle, and foot are turned out equally. When you try to increase your turnout by pulling your feet into greater rotation than the hip allows, you run the risk of injuring not only your feet and ankles, but the rest of your body as well. In addition, you reduce the efficiency of your muscular system, and your technique suffers.

When turnout is forced at the foot and ankle, the body's weight can no longer be properly transmitted through the center of the *talus* and *calcaneus* to the ball of the foot. In forced rotation, the weight falls to the medial side of the ankle and foot. This stress makes the ankle, longitudinal arch, and big-toe joint vulnerable to injury. If the stress on the arch continues over a period of time, the ligaments can become overstretched and the bones can actually shift position. This can cause the arch to fall and can be very painful. *Pointe* dancers who force turnout at the foot and ankle often develop bunions.

Forcing rotation also affects the muscles, tendons, and bones. Not only does it decrease muscular efficiency, it can also contribute to tendonitis, shinsplints, and stress fractures of the lower leg bones. Forcing can also cause a dancer to excessively grip, or "claw," the toes.

When turnout is forced at the foot and ankle, the effects are registered throughout the body. Excessive rotation, for example, can strain the medial side of the knee or lead to a condition called *chondromalacia*. In some dancers, forcing turnout at the foot and ankle causes the pelvis to tilt forward and the back to hyperextend. This posture can weaken the abdominal muscles and lead to lower back injury. Forcing can also cause a dancer to "sit" in the standing hip. This limits technique and creates an unpleasing aesthetic line. Chapters 14 and 17 explain further the problems related to incorrect alignment of the knee, hip, and spine.

Related information can be found in the answers to questions 15, 17, and 18, below; questions 2, 15, and 24 in Chapter 14; and questions 2 and 5 in Chapter 17.

5. *Whenever I stand in a turned-out position, my feet roll-in. What can be done about this?*

The term most often used to describe rolling-in is "pronation." If your feet pronate whenever you stand in a turned-out position, you are probably forcing your turnout from the knee and ankle rather than correctly turning out from the hip.

If your turnout is correctly controlled and your feet still pronate, then the problem may be a weakness in the muscles that lift and support the arch. When these muscles are weak, gravity can cause the foot to pronate. Strengthening the muscles that lift the arch will help to solve this problem

Some experts also recommend strengthening the foot everters as part of a conditioning program to correct foot pronation (Fitt, 1988, pp. 135, 310.) This is because some of the muscles that lift and support the arch are also responsible for inverting the foot. If these muscles were to become stronger than the muscles that evert the foot, they might cause the foot to invert or supinate as you jump in the air. Landing from a jump with the foot supinated could result in an ankle sprain.

Related information can be found in the answer to question 4, above.

Recommended exercises are found in Chapter 12 to strengthen the muscles that lift and support the arch (12.A), flex the toes (12.B), invert the foot (12.C), and evert the foot (12.D). These muscles are difficult to stretch. Massage can help relax the muscles that lift and support the arch; massage and gentle hand manipulation in the direction of toe extension can help relax the toe flexors; massage, gentle hand manipulation in the directions of inversion and eversion as well as performing ankle circles can help relax the foot inverters and everters.

6. *When some of my students try to point their feet, the feet sickle in toward the midline of the body. Are there exercises I can give them to help correct this problem?*

Yes, and it is important to begin correcting this problem immediately. A sickled foot is not only aesthetically unpleasing, but it can lead to injuries such as tendonitis and ankle sprains. Strengthening the everters of the foot will help to balance the pull of the inverters and allow the foot to point in alignment with the lower leg.

Recommended exercises to strengthen the foot everters are found in Chapter 12 (12.D). These muscles are difficult to stretch. Massage, gentle hand manipulation in the direction of inversion as well as performing ankle circles can help to relax the foot everters.

7. *I have heard that everting the foot (sickling out, beveling, or flagging) when the leg is in back* attitude *or* arabesque *can lead to injury. Is this true?*

There is a difference of opinion about this matter. Some experts believe this position might strain the ankle (Benjamin, 1981, p. 84.) If you choose to work this way, you must be careful not to evert the foot in weight bearing positions. This could lead to problems associated with pronation.

Related information can be found in questions 4 and 5, above.

8. *When I try to balance on half-toe or full* pointe, *my feet wobble from side to side. What can I do to improve my balance?*

Sometimes problems in balance are caused by a poor sense of joint-angle position *(proprioception)*. If this is the case, you may need to work on a wobble board or other equipment designed to improve proprioception. In other situations, a lack of balance may be due to inadequate strength. Conditioning the foot inverters and everters can help to stabilize your balance.

Good balance depends on more than just strong feet, however. One very important factor is correct alignment of the torso over the legs and strong torso muscles to maintain this alignment. Information concerning the torso is found in Chapter 17.

Related information can be found in the answer to question 1, Chapter 17.

Recommended exercises are given in Chapter 12 to strengthen the foot inverters (12.C) and everters (12.D). These muscles are difficult to stretch. Massage, gentle hand manipulation in the directions of inversion and eversion, as well as performing ankle circles can help to relax the foot inverters and everters.

9. *Is it correct to stand with your weight shifted onto the balls of the feet?*

Many styles of dance require the weight to be shifted slightly toward the ball of the foot so that it is easier to move. If you choose to work this way, it is important that you do not shift the weight so far forward that the heels lose contact with the floor. When this happens, all of your weight is pressed onto the metatarsal heads instead of being partially distributed to the heels. This could put undue stress on the ball of the foot and overwork the ankle plantar flexors. In some cases it might also lead to shinsplints.

10. Why is it important to keep my heels down in the demi plié *that proceeds and follows a jump?*

There are several reasons why it is important to press your heels down. One is to prevent injury. If you do not press your heels down when you land from a jump you might develop tendonitis or shinsplints. (Double heel strikes can also cause shinsplints. These occur when a dancer lands from a jump with the heels pressed down, momentarily releases the heels, then presses them down again before the next movement occurs.)

Another reason for keeping your heels down is to improve the height of your jump. A muscle can exert greater force when it contracts from a slightly stretched position. When you press your heels down in *demi plié,* you stretch the ankle plantar flexors. This stretched position allows them to generate greater force as they contract and plantar flex the ankle.

If you have trouble keeping your heels down, it could be that your ankle plantar flexors are tight and need to be stretched.

A *recommended exercise* to stretch the ankle plantar flexors may be found in Chapter 12 (12.H).

11. Is there something I can do to improve the strength of my relevé *and jump?*

Yes. First of all, you want to be sure your ankle plantar flexors are flexible enough to permit a good *demi-plié.* In addition to being flexible, the ankle plantar flexors must be strong enough to plantar flex the ankle when lifting the body's weight. Exercises to stretch and strengthen the ankle plantar flexor muscles are listed below.

There are other muscle groups that must also be conditioned for a good *relevé* and jump. You need strong toe flexors to help you rise to the toes and propel the body into the air. You also need strong foot everters and inverters to prevent wobbling from side to side as you *relevé* or push-off for a jump. Finally, the ankle dorsiflexors and toe extensors should be flexible so they will not limit plantar flexion and toe flexion. We also recommend strengthening the dorsiflexors so as to maintain a balance of strength around the ankle joint.

To have a strong jump and good *relevé* you will need to condition the muscles at the knee and hip as well as those of the ankle and foot. In Part 4, we explain the major hip and knee muscles and their part in producing *relevé* and jump movements.

Related information can be found in question 10, above, and question 17 in Chapter 14.

Recommended exercises are found in Chapter 12 to strengthen and stretch the ankle dorsiflexors (12.E, 12.G), and plantar flexors (12.F, 12.H). Chapter 12 also contains exercises to strengthen the toe flexors (12.B), foot inverters (12.C), and foot everters (12.D). The toe flexors, foot inverters, and foot everters are difficult to stretch. Massage and gentle hand manipulation in the direction of toe extension can help relax the toe flexors. Massage, gentle hand manipulation in the direction of inversion and eversion, as well as performing ankle circles can help relax the foot inverters and everters.

12. *What can I do to improve the depth of my* demi-plié?

The depth of your *demi-plié* may be limited by the skeletal system. In some individuals, the bones of the lower leg and ankle are shaped and positioned in such a way as to limit the depth of the *plié*. However, if your ankle plantar flexor muscles are tight, they will also restrict the depth of your *demi-plié*.

A *recommended exercise* to stretch the ankle plantar flexors may be found in Chapter 12 (12.H).

13. *When should a dancer go* en pointe? (on point)

There are many factors to consider before a dancer is allowed to go *en pointe*. One important consideration is the physical development of the bones in the ankle and foot. The bones must be sufficiently mature to accommodate the additional demands of *pointe* work. Usually this physical development takes place around the age of 12. Another factor is the dancer's muscular strength. For example, if the muscles are weak and the dancer wobbles on *demi-pointe*, she will have increased difficulty on full *pointe*, and the danger of injury is increased.

In addition to muscular strength, alignment must be evaluated. If the dancer cannot perform the basic ballet vocabulary while maintaining correct alignment, she will not be able to do well *en pointe*. In fact, errors in alignment and technique are exaggerated *en pointe* and, once again, the danger of injury is increased.

Because each dancer develops at an individual rate, the decision to go *en pointe* should be based on the dancer's development. It should not be arbitrarily determined by chronological age or years of dance training.

14. What is the correct alignment of the foot when a dancer is en pointe?

When a dancer is correctly placed *en pointe,* the line of gravity will pass through the *tibia,* ankle, foot, and toes. Inside the point shoe, the toes will be extended and straight. If one of the four lesser toes is longer than the others, it will have to be curled under, but at no time should all five toes curl or knuckle under. It is also incorrect for the toes to hyperextend or curve back toward the sole of the shoe. Knuckling under or hyperextending the toes can stress the joints and make them vulnerable to injury.

Correct placement further requires that the weight of the body be distributed across the entire *pointe* surface. It is incorrect for a dancer to pronate, or roll in. This sends the dancer's weight toward the big toe and medial edge of the *pointe* surface. Pronation can aggravate bunions and lead to injuries such as tendonitis and shinsplints.

It is also incorrect for a dancer to roll out. This sends the weight of the body toward the little toe and the lateral edge of the *pointe* surface. Rolling out stresses the lateral structure of the foot and ankle, as well as the muscles on the lateral side of the leg.

Furthermore, it is very important that a dancer be "all the way up" when assuming the *pointe* position. This places the dancer in the position of greatest mechanical stability. If the dancer does not reach the full *pointe* position, her weight is primarily supported along the rear edge of the *pointe* surface. This causes compensatory changes in body alignment. It also puts excessive strain on the ankle plantar flexors which must contract with considerable force to maintain the position. This can lead to tendonitis and muscular tightness.

Just as it is important to get all the way up *en pointe,* it is equally important not to exaggerate the *pointe* position so the weight shifts to the front of the *pointe* surface. Dancers with flexible feet and ankles need to control their plantar flexion so they do not roll toward the front of the *pointe* shoe. Rolling over can stress the ligaments of the foot as well as the muscles and tendons along the anterior surface of the foot and lower leg.

Pointe dancers who have been working with improper placement over a period of time may need to correct certain muscular imbalances before they can achieve proper alignment. Those who have been working with the toes hyperextended may need to strengthen the toe flexors, while those who knuckle under may need to strengthen the intrinsic muscles of the foot. Dancers who have been rolling in or out may need to strengthen the inverters and everters of the foot. Those who have not achieved the full *pointe* position may need to strengthen and stretch the ankle plantar flexors and stretch the ankle dorsiflexors.

Others who have been rolling over may need to strengthen the ankle dorsiflexors. They may also find it helpful to use a *pointe* shoe with a longer vamp.

Related information can be found in questions 2 and 11, above.

Recommended exercises are found in Chapter 12 to strengthen and stretch the ankle dorsiflexors (12.E, 12.G), and plantar flexors (12.F, 12.H). Chapter 12 also contains exercises to strengthen the muscles that lift and support the arch (12.A), the toe flexors (12.B), the foot inverters, (12.C), and the foot everters (12.D). This last group of muscles are difficult to stretch. Massage can help relax the muscles that lift and support the arch; massage and gentle hand manipulation in the direction of toe extension can help relax the toe flexors; massage, gentle hand manipulation in the directions of inversion and eversion, as well as performing ankle circles can help relax the foot inverters and everters.

15. I notice that many ballet dancers have bunions. What causes them and are there conditioning exercises that can help with this problem?

The tendency to form bunions is inherited. Faulty technique such as forcing turnout and rolling in, as well as narrow *pointe* shoes can exacerbate the situation. A wider *pointe* shoe box, slitting the part of the box that presses on the bunion, and a pad around the bunion can be of help in managing this problem. A careful evaluation of technique is also important. Someone with painful bunions should see a physician for immediate relief. Generally, it is not recommended that bunions be surgically treated until after a dance career is over. This is because surgery may limit the range of motion in the big toe joint.

Related information can be found in question 5, above, and in question 24, Chapter 14.

16. Some of my students continually sprain the same ankle. Are there any exercises they can do to prevent this from happening?

When an ankle is sprained, the surrounding ligaments can be over-stretched or even torn. Because ligaments are not elastic, this trauma can leave them permanently overstretched and unable to firmly hold the bones in the correct alignment. In addition, serious ankle sprains may damage some of the surrounding nerve fibers. This can make it difficult for a dancer to accurately judge the position of the foot when jumping in the air. If a dancer should land with the foot supinated, the weakened ankle can be resprained, and a chronic problem begun. This need not be the case if proper treatment is received. It is possible to strengthen the surrounding muscles, improve joint proprioception, and thus increase joint stability.

Dancers who sprain an ankle should immediately consult a physician. Those who have chronic problems with ankle injury should also be under the care of a specialist. By working with medical professionals, these dancers will be guided in rehabilitation programs developed to meet their individual needs. These programs may include training on a wobble board to develop proprioception as well as training for strength and flexibility.

Once the injury has been rehabilitated, it is important that you carefully evaluate your student. Errors in technique or alignment should be immediately addressed.

Dancers can help prevent ankle sprains by strengthening all of the muscle groups around the ankle. Those who have suffered previous ankle sprains should pay particular attention to strengthening the muscles that evert the foot. The exercises listed below will help your students condition all of these muscles.

Recommended exercises are given in Chapter 12 to strengthen and stretch the ankle dorsiflexors (12.E, 12.G), and the plantar flexors (12.F, 12.H). Chapter 12 also presents strength conditioning exercises for the foot inverters (12.C) and the foot everters (12.D). The foot inverters and everters are difficult muscles to stretch. Massage, gentle hand manipulation in the directions of inversion and eversion, as well as performing ankle circles can help relax these two muscle groups.

17. Is there anything I can do to help my students who suffer with ankle tendonitis?

Tendonitis, an inflammation of a tendon or tendon sheath, is a problem dancers frequently encounter. At the ankle, it usually occurs in the tendon sheath of the *flexor hallucis longus,* or in the Achilles tendon. In either case, the dancer experiences pain at the back of the ankle during *demi-plié* or *relevé.*

Tendonitis is often caused by faulty technique as well as other factors. Teachers should check to see if their students are forcing turnout at the ankle, rolling in, rolling out, or sickling. All of these can lead to tendonitis, as can failure to get the heels down, or jumping on hard floors. Other factors include a sudden increase in class or rehearsal schedule; prolonged, unaccustomed *pointe* work; or choreography that makes unaccustomed demands on the ankle and foot muscles. Finally, tendonitis can be caused by continually contracting a muscle group without properly stretching it out. Teachers should check to see if their students are gripping or clenching any of the muscles of the foot or ankle, and they should be certain that their students are regularly stretching after class and rehearsal.

Dancers with mild tendonitis can try aspirin, ice, rest, and careful stretching. If pain continues, a physician should be consulted. Once the immediate symptoms have been controlled, and any muscle imbalances have been corrected, you can work to change other factors that lead to the problem. Teaching your students to regularly stretch the ankle plantar flexors can help them avoid one cause of tendonitis.

Related information can be found in the answers to questions 4–7, 9, and 10, above.

A *recommended exercise* may be found in Chapter 12 to stretch the ankle plantar flexors (12.H).

18. *Sometimes the front of my shins hurt when I perform a series of jumps, and I develop* shinsplints. *Is there something I can do to prevent this from happening?*

The term *shinsplints* is often used to describe any pain in the lower leg. More specifically it refers to pain along the anterior lateral or posterior medial lower leg. The muscles often involved are the *anterior* and *posterior tibialis*, the *flexor digitorum longus*, as well as the *peroneals*.

Shinsplints can be brought on by a variety of factors. Some dancers develop shinsplints when they return to dance after a layoff. A sudden or excessive increase in jumps or leaps can also cause the problem. In other cases, tightness in the ankle plantar flexors can result in foot pronation, and pronation leads to the injury.

If the cause is muscular weakness or muscular imbalance, you can perform conditioning exercises to help correct this problem. We recommend strengthening and stretching all of the muscle groups around the ankle. Where pronation is involved we also recommend strengthening the muscles that help support the arch. Dancers who develop shinsplints each time they return from vacation are advised to do conditioning exercises during their layoff.

Shinsplints can also be caused by other factors. Forcing turnout at the foot and ankle can precipitate shinsplints. Another possible cause is failure to press and keep the heels down when you land from a jump. You should also be certain that you are dancing on a floor that is specially constructed for dance. If you are dancing on concrete or another nonresilient surface, you are vulnerable to shinsplints and other injuries.

Dancers with mild shinsplints can try aspirin, rest, and careful stretching. Some experts also recommend using heat (Arnheim, 1980,

p. 204.); others recommend using ice (Fitt, 1988, p. 311.) Dancers with severe and/or chronic shinsplints should consult a physician. Many times the necessary conditioning work is more complex than the strengthening and stretching exercises recommended here. In these cases it is important to have an expert prescribe a conditioning program that is specifically tailored for the individual.

A final word of caution is needed at this point. Pain in the lower leg may be caused by problems other than shinsplints. For example, unaccustomed exercises may cause the lower leg muscles to swell. This can lead to a condition known as *anterior compartment syndrome.* Sometimes pain on the front of the shin can be caused by a stress fracture. You should consult a physician regarding pain in your lower leg if it occurs when you are in good shape, if the pain persists during activity as well as at rest, or if it lasts for more than one week.

Recommended exercises can be found in Chapter 12 to strengthen and stretch the ankle dorsiflexors (12.E, 12.G) and the plantar flexors (12.F, 12.H). Chapter 12 also presents strength conditioning exercises for the muscles that lift and support the arch (12.A), the toe flexors (12.B), the foot inverters (12.C), and the foot everters (12.D). This last group of muscles is difficult to stretch. Massage can help relax the muscles that lift and support the arch; massage and gentle hand manipulation in the direction of toe extension can help relax the toe flexors; massage, gentle hand manipulation in the directions of inversion and eversion, as well as performing ankle circles can help relax the foot inverters and everters.

12

Strength and Flexibility Exercises

Note: Be sure to read Part II before performing the following exercises.

12.A Strength Conditioning Exercise for the Muscles That Lift and Support the Arch

Equipment
Chair

Starting position
Sit with the feet flat on the floor.

Part 1.

Action
1. Keep your toes relaxed and lift the arches of your feet so they make a dome shape (Figure 12.1a). All five toes must stay in contact with the floor. Do not curl your toes under. Do not evert your ankles.
2. Return to the starting position.
3. Complete all repetitions for Part 1 before going further.

Part 2.

Action
1. Spread your toes apart as far as possible without lifting them off the floor (Figure 12.1b).
2. Return to the starting position.

Repetitions
8 of each part.

Timing patterns
A, B, C.

Increasing the difficulty
Perform the exercise in a standing position.

Exercise 12.A adapted from: Alter (1986b), pp. 180–81; Como (1964), p. 57; Daniels and Worthingham (1977), p. 93; Hobby and Hoffmaster (1986), p. 34; Howse and Hancock (1988), pp. 162–63; Kisner and Colby (1985), p. 388; Molnar (1987), p. 317.

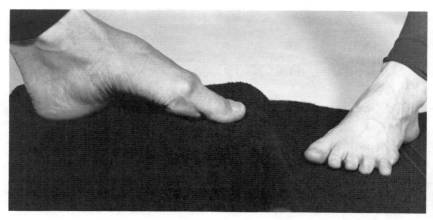

Figure 12.1 Strengthening the muscles that lift and support the arch. **Dancer (a)** is on the left. **Dancer (b)** is on the right.

12.B   Strength Conditioning Exercise for the Toe Flexors

Equipment
   Chair or bench, and hand towel

Starting position
   Sit on a chair with your legs parallel, toes pointed straight ahead. Place the hand towel on the floor in front of your feet.

Action
   1. Grasp the edge of the hand towel with your toes and pull the towel toward you. Do not let the foot sickle.
   2. Relax your toes.
   3. Grasp the towel again (Figure 12.2) and pull it toward you, then relax your toes.
   4. Continue this action until the far end of the towel is under your toes.
   5. Straighten the towel and begin again.

Repetitions
   Repetitions for this exercise are counted by the number of times your toes grasp the towel and pull it toward you.

Timing pattern
   No set pattern.

Increasing the difficulty
   Place a weight on the far end of the towel. You can also alternate, pulling on the towel first with the toes of one foot then with the toes of the other foot.

Exercise 12.B adapted from: Arnheim (1980) Dance Injuries, p. 100; Bachrach, (1984); Como (1964), p. 56; Hobby and Hoffmaster (1986), p. 34; Kisner and Colby (1985), p. 388; Teitz (1982), p. 1414; Roy (1983), p. 395.

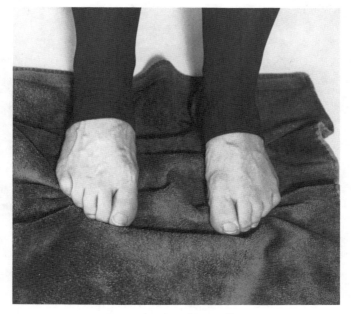

Figure 12.2 Strengthening the toe flexors.

12.C Strength Conditioning Exercise for the Foot Inverters

Equipment
Elastic resistance attached to the leg of a heavy piece of furniture.

Part 1.

Starting position
1. L-sit with your right side facing the piece of furniture. Place the tube-sock loop or *Thera-band* around the ball of your right foot at the base of your toes. Move far enough away from the furniture that the elastic is taut and can offer resistance to the action.
2. Plantar flex your right ankle as much as possible. Do not let the toes "claw" or curl under excessively. Evert your foot.

Action
1. Keep the ankle plantar flexed and invert your foot (Figure 12.3a). The elastic should provide resistance. If there is not enough resistance, sit further away from the piece of furniture.
2. Return to the starting position.
3. Complete all repetitions before going further.

Part 2.

Starting position
1. Sit as in Part 1.
2. Dorsiflex the ankle.

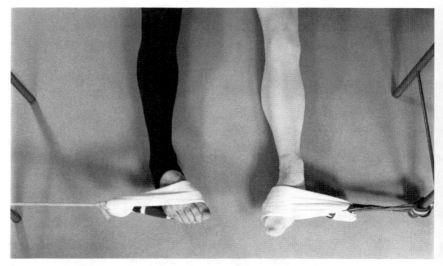

Figure 12.3 **Dancer (a),** on the left, is performing part of the exercise to strengthen the foot inverters. **Dancer (b),** on the right, is performing part of the exercise to strengthen the foot everters.

Action
   1. Maintain dorsiflexion as you invert against the resistance.
   2. Return to the starting position.
   3. Complete all repetitions before going further.

Part 3.

Starting position
   Sit as in Part 2.

Action
   1. Change from dorsiflexion to plantar flexion as you invert against resistance.
   2. Return to the starting position.
   3. Complete all repetitions on the first side before changing sides.

Repetitions
   5 of each part.

Timing patterns
   A, B, C.

Increasing the difficulty
   Sit further from the furniture, add more elastic resistance, or both.

Comments
   Performing this exercise will not cause you to sickle in when you point the foot in dance class. Strengthening these muscles so that they are

equal in strength to the foot everters will help you achieve a correct *pointe* position. It is possible to combine this exercise with the strength conditioning exercise for the foot everters (Exercise 12.D) that follows.

Exercise 12.C adapted from: Barnes and Crutchfield (1971), p. 22; Fitt (1988), p. 338; Kisner and Colby (1985), p. 389; Molnar (1987), pp. 311–12; Teitz (1982), p. 1414.

12.D Strength Conditioning Exercise for the Foot Everters

Equipment
Elastic resistance attached to the leg of a heavy piece of furniture.

Part 1.

Starting position
1. L-sit with your left side to the furniture. Put the tube sock loop or *Thera-band* around the ball of your right foot at the base of your toes. Move far enough away from the furniture that the elastic is taut and can offer resistance to the action.
2. Plantar flex your right ankle as much as possible, then invert your foot. Do not let the toes "claw" or curl under excessively.

Action
1. Evert your foot as far as possible while keeping your ankle plantar flexed (Figure 12.3b). The elastic should offer resistance. If there is not enough resistance, sit further away from the piece of furniture.
2. Return to the starting position.
3. Complete all repetitions before going further.

Part 2.

Starting position
1. Sit as in Part 1.
2. Dorsiflex your ankle.

Action
1. Maintain dorsiflexion as you evert against the resistance.
2. Return to the starting position.
3. Complete all repetitions before going further.

Part 3.

Starting position
Sit as in Part 2.

Action
1. Move from dorsiflexion to plantar flexion as you evert against the resistance.
2. Return to the starting position.
3. Complete all repetitions on the first side before changing sides.

Repetitions
5 of each part.

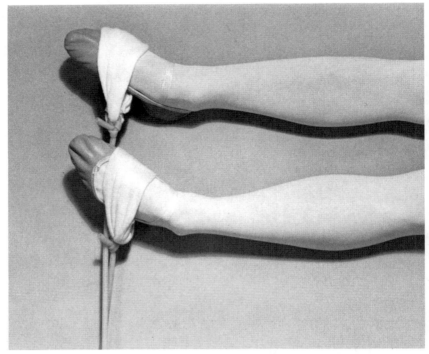

Figure 12.4 Combining exercises 12.C and 12.D.

Timing patterns
A, B, C.

Increasing the difficulty
Sit further from the furniture, add more elastic resistance, or both.

Comments
It is possible to combine this exercise with Exercise 12.C. With two elastics, you can perform Exercise 12.C with one ankle while you perform this exercise with the other ankle. Figure 12.4 illustrates this combination.

Dancers often need a great deal of strength in the foot everters in order to recover from or help prevent additional ankle sprains. Those who try this exercise and find they still need to build additional strength may want to try the following exercise.

Alternate Strength Conditioning Exercise for the Foot Everters

Equipment
Ankle Weights, Tube Sock, Small Shopping Bag, and Bed or Bench.

Starting position

1. Strap one weight around the instep of your right foot. Put a sock on over your foot and the weight if you have trouble holding the weight in place during the exercise.

2. Lying side horizontal on your left side, extend your right ankle over the edge of the bed or bench. Let your left leg flex at the hip and knee.

3. Plantar flex your right ankle as much as possible, then invert your foot. Do not let your toes "claw" or curl under excessively.

Action

1. Keeping your ankle plantar flexed, evert your foot as far as possible (Figure 12.5a).

2. Return to the starting position.

3. Complete all repetitions on the first side before changing sides.

Timing patterns

A, B, C.

Increasing the difficulty

Add additional weight. One alternative to wrapping additional weight around your foot is to place the weights in a small shopping bag and hang the handles over your instep. Tying the handles together will keep the bag from slipping off of your foot (Figure 12.5b).

Exercise 12.D adapted from: Bachrach (1984); Barnes and Crutchfield (1971), p. 22; Hamilton (1982b), p. 48; Molnar (1987), pp. 310–13; Teitz (1982), p. 1414.

Figure 12.5 Strengthening the foot everters, alternate exercise. **Dancer (a)** is on the left. **Dancer (b)** is on the right.

12.E   Strength Conditioning Exercise for the Ankle Dorsiflexors

Equipment
Elastic resistance attached to the leg of a heavy piece of furniture.

Starting Position
1. L-sit facing the heavy piece of furniture. Place the tube-sock loop or *Thera-band* around the ball of your right foot at the base of your toes. Move far enough away that the elastic is pulled taut and can offer resistance to the action.
2. Plantar flex your right ankle and foot as much as possible without having the loop slip off. Do not let the toes "claw" or curl excessively.

Action
1. Dorsiflex your right ankle and foot as much as possible (Figure 12.6). The elastic should provide resistance. If there is not enough resistance, sit further away from the piece of furniture.
2. Return to the starting position.
3. Complete all repetitions on the first side before changing sides.

Timing patterns
A, B, C.

Increasing the difficulty
Sit further from the furniture, add more elastic resistance, or both.

Comment
By using two sets of elastic resistance, you can exercise both ankles at the same time.

Exercise 12.E adapted from: Barnes and Crutchfield (1971), p. 21; Kisner and Colby (1985), p. 389.

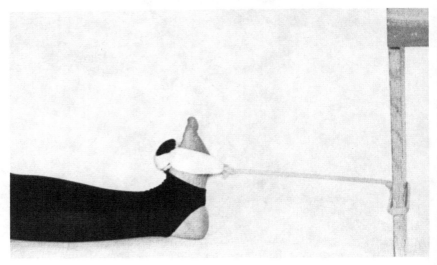

Figure 12.6 Strengthening the ankle dorsiflexors.

12.F   Strength Conditioning Exercise for the Ankle Plantar Flexors

Equipment
   Barre or chair.

Part 1.

Starting position
   Stand in parallel first position. Lightly hold onto a *barre* or the back of a chair for balance.

Action
   1. Rise to half toe (Figure 12.7a).
   2. Return to the starting position.
   3. Complete all repetitions of Part 1 before going further.

Part 2.

Starting position
   Stand in parallel first position *demi-plié*.Lightly hold onto a *barre* or the back of a chair for balance.

Action
   1. Rise to half toe.
   2. Return to the starting position.
   3. Complete all repetitions of Part 2 before going further.

Part 3.

Starting Position
   Stand in turned-out first position. Lightly hold onto a *barre* or the back of a chair for balance.

Action
   1. Rise to half toe (Figure 12.7b).
   2. Return to the starting position.
   3. Complete all repetitions of Part 3 before going further.

Part 4.

Starting position
   Stand in turned-out first position *demi-plié*. Lightly hold onto a *barre* or the back of a chair for balance.

Action
   1. Rise to half toe.
   2. Return to the starting position.

Repetitions
   4 of each part.

Timing patterns
   A, B, C.

Increasing the difficulty
   Perform the exercise while standing on one leg. You can also add waist weights.

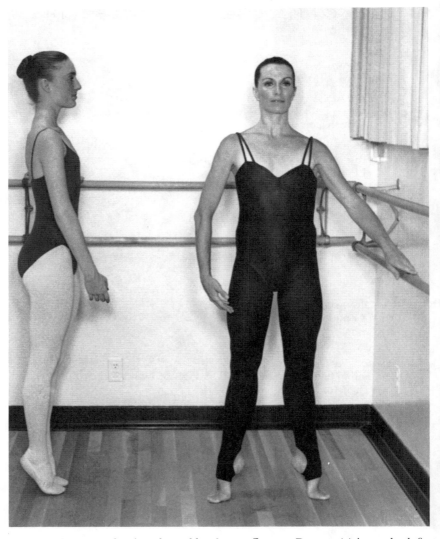

Figure 12.7 Strengthening the ankle plantar flexors. **Dancer (a)** is on the left. **Dancer (b)** is on the right.

Another way to increase the difficulty is to perform all of your repetitions while standing on stairs in parallel first position. To do this, stand backwards on the stairs and let your heels hang off the edge of the steps. Use the hand rails for balance as you rise to half toe and return to the starting position. Keep your knees straight throughout the exercise. This exercise can also be done standing on one leg.

Comments
It is very important that you maintain correct alignment of your torso and legs while performing this exercise.

To develop the power necessary for an explosive jump, it is important to include speed as part of your strength training. If you are using this exercise to improve your jump, we suggest you perform timing pattern C at a faster tempo. If you do this, you must be careful to maintain proper alignment. You must also be careful not to move so fast that you lose control and let momentum take over. Use all of the counts, and pay particular attention to correctly controlling the one count return to the starting position.

Exercise 12.F adapted from: Alter (1986b), p. 172; Arnheim (1985) p. 468; Fitt (1988), p. 362; Roy (1983), p. 396; Teitz (1982), p. 1413.

12.G Flexibility Exercise for the Ankle Dorsiflexors and Toe Extensors

Starting position:
1. L-sit, leaning your back against a wall if that is more comfortable. Keep your right leg straight and lift it up toward your chest.
2. Grasp both hands around your right heel.
3. Plantar flex your right foot at the same time you pull down on your heel, pulling it down toward your hip.

Action
1. Hold the stretch (Figure 12.8a). Feel the stretch across the top of your foot and ankle. Some people feel an additional stretch in the front of the shin.
2. Stretch the other side.

Figure 12.8 Stretching the ankle dorsiflexors and toe extensors. **Dancer (a)** is on the left. **Dancer (b)** is on the right.

Increasing the difficulty

Instead of pulling down on your heel with both hands, release the left hand (if you are stretching the right dorsiflexors), and use your left hand to gently push your toes into an increased *pointe* position (Figure 12.8b). Be certain you are increasing your *pointe* in a straight line with your leg. Do not push the *pointe* toward your big or little toe.

Comment

This exercise may be combined with Exercise 15.G (in Chapter 15).

Exercise 12.G adapted from an interview with S. Anthony and M. Calitri, physical therapists, in June 1985. At the time of this interview, Ms. Anthony and Ms. Calitri were affiliated with the Center for Health and Sports Medicine of the National Hospital for Orthopaedics and Rehabilitation.

12.H   Flexibility Exercise for the Ankle Plantar Flexors

Equipment

Wall or *Barre*.

Starting position

1. Stand approximately two feet from the wall or *barre* with your feet in parallel first position. Do not turn out.

2. Step forward with your left leg and *demi-plié* on your left leg. Lean your hands against the wall or *barre*. Your right knee must be straight, and your right heel must be touching the floor. In order to get the best stretch, the right foot must be absolutely parallel, toes pointing straight ahead. If you are accustomed to dancing in a turned-out position, this parallel position may feel turned in. Be sure to maintain the longitudinal arch; do not let your right foot pronate. It is also important to contract your abdominal muscles so your lower back does not over arch.

Part 1.

Action

Hold the stretch (Figure 12.9a). Feel the stretch in your right calf muscle, closer to your knee than to your ankle.

Part 2.

Action

1. *Demi-plié* your right knee. Be sure your right foot is absolutely parallel, and your right heel is touching the floor. It is also important to maintain the right longitudinal arch so that your right knee is over the middle of your right foot. Do not allow your lower back to over arch.

2. Hold the stretch (Figure 12.9b). Feel the stretch in your right calf muscle, closer to your ankle than your knee.

3. Repeat Parts 1 and 2 on the other side.

Comments: Part 1 stretches the *gastrocnemius* muscle. Part 2 stretches the *soleus* muscle.

It is possible that these muscles will be very tight if you have been doing a lot of *relevés*, jumps, or *pointe* work without stretching this muscle

Figure 12.9 Stretching the ankle plantar flexors. **Dancer (a)** is on the left. **Dancer (b)** is on the right.

group. If so, you will have a very small step forward and a very small *demi-plié*. Do not be frustrated with this limited range of movement and force the stretch into an "angry" stretch. Tight muscles can be stretched if you work regularly and listen to your body. Remember you want to feel a "friendly" stretch, not a painful one.

Sometimes a limited range of motion during ankle dorsiflexion may be caused by structural limitations rather than tightness in the ankle plantar flexors. If you suspect this is the case, consult a physician. The exercise may not be appropriate for you.

Exercise 12.H adapted from: Alter (1986b), pp. 167–68; Arnheim (1980), p. 86; Daniels and Worthingham (1977), p. 97; Fitt (1988), p. 341; Howse and Hancock (1988), p. 163; Kisner and Colby (1985), p. 386; Roy and Irvin (1983), p. 43; Ryan and Stephens (1988), p. 182.

IV

The Knee, Upper Leg, and Hip

Both the knee joint and the hip joint are discussed in this part of the book because many muscles that affect movement of the knee also affect movement of the hip. These muscles originate at the pelvis and end below the knee on the bones of the lower leg. They are often called "two-joint muscles" because they cause movements at two joints, the hip and knee. In contrast, the ankle joint has very few two-joint muscles. Most of the muscles that move the ankle originate on the bones of the lower leg, cross only the ankle joint, and end on the bones of the foot.

13

The Major Muscles of the Knee, Upper Leg, and Hip

The Structure of the Knee Joint

The knee joint is the largest joint in the body and the most complex. The *femur* (thigh bone) has two enlarged processes called *condyles* at the lower end of the bone (Figure 13.1). These condyles articulate (fit together) with the enlarged surfaces of the *tibia* which are also called condyles.

The other bone associated with the knee is the *patella*, commonly known as the knee cap. It is classified as a sesamoid (floating) bone because it does not articulate with any other bone (Figure 13.1). Tendons from the four knee extensor muscles encase the *patella* and are attached to the front of the *tibia* by way of the *patellar ligament* (Figure 13.1). This system allows the knee extensor muscles to produce greater force during knee extension than would be possible without the *patella*.

Cartilage forms a cushion between the bones of the knee joint. Ligaments and tendons provide strength and support. Some of the knee ligaments include the *cruciate* and the *collateral ligaments* (Figure 13.1). The cruciate ligaments "cross" within the knee joint between the *tibia* and the *femur*. These ligaments provide internal stability for the knee joint. The collateral ligaments are found on the medial and lateral sides of the knee and provide an external support for the knee joint.

Movements of the Knee Joint

Movements at the knee include *flexion* (bending the knee) and *extension* (straightening the knee). A slight degree of *inward* and *outward rotation* accompanies the movements of flexion and extension. Inward and outward rotation can only occur when the knee is bent. Rotation is not possible once the knee is fully extended and straight.

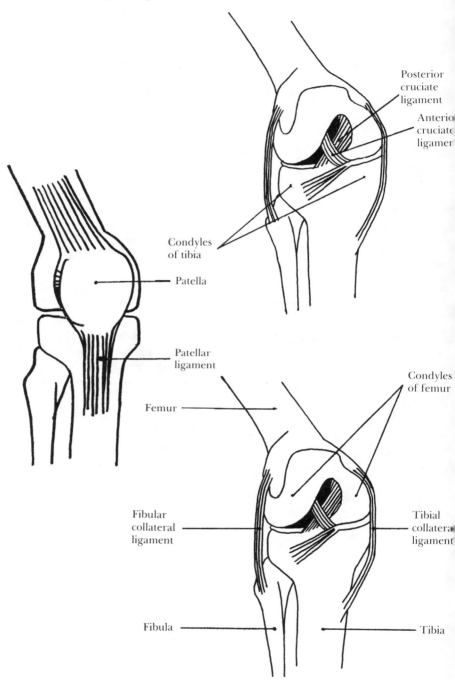

Figure 13.1 Anterior view of right knee bones and ligaments. In the drawings on the right the patella has been removed.

Flexion of the Knee

The muscles responsible for knee flexion include the *hamstrings*, the *popliteus*, the *sartorius*, and the *gracilis*. The hamstrings and *popliteus* are found on the posterior side of the thigh; the greater part of the *sartorius*, on the anterior side; and the *gracilis*, on the medial side. The *gastrocnemius* (described in Chapter 10) is attached to the *femur* and can also assist with knee flexion when the lower leg is not bearing weight.

The hamstrings consist of the *biceps femoris*, the *semitendinosus*, and the *semimembranosus*. The *biceps femoris* has two heads (Figures 13.2 and 13.3). The long head is attached to the pelvis and the short head to the *femur*. Both muscles are attached on the other end to the lateral side of the *fibula* as well as to the lateral condyle of the *tibia*. You can feel the *biceps femoris* on the lateral side of the posterior thigh, near the knee.

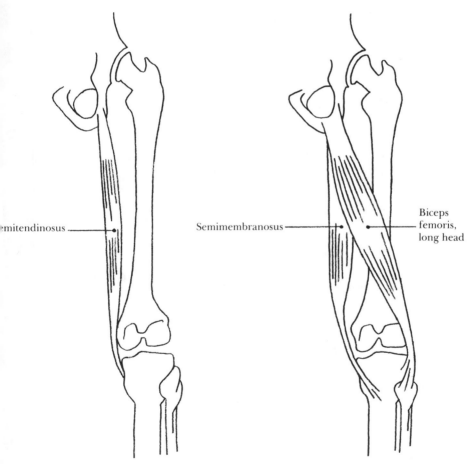

Figure 13.2 Posterior view of knee and hip muscles.

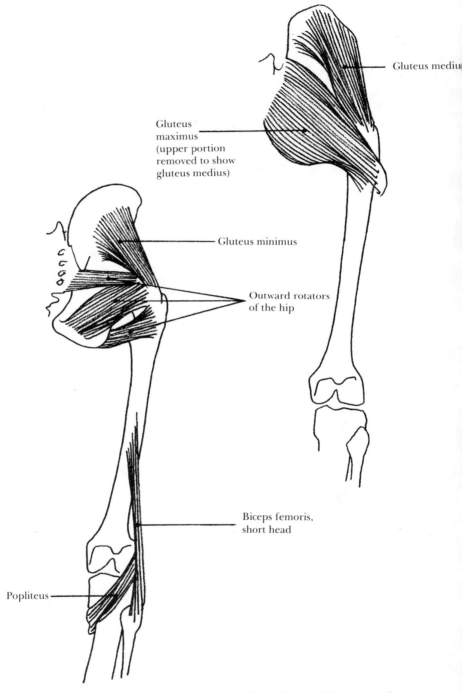

Gluteus mediu

Gluteus
maximus
(upper portion
removed to show
gluteus medius)

Gluteus minimus

Outward rotators
of the hip

Biceps femoris,
short head

Popliteus

Figure 13.3 Posterior view of additional hip and knee muscles.

The *semimembranosus* and the *semitendinosus* are attached at one end to the pelvis and at the other end to the medial side of the *tibia* (Figure 13.2). You can feel these muscles on the medial side of the posterior thigh, near the knee.

The *popliteus* is a small muscle that is attached to the lateral condyle of the *femur* at one end and to the *tibia* at the other (Figure 13.3). It is a deep muscle and cannot be palpated. The *popliteus* serves to flex the knee and is the only one-joint muscle that performs this function. It also acts with the cruciate ligaments to stabilize the knee.

The *sartorius* is a slender muscle that is attached on one end to the anterior side of the pelvis (Figure 13.4). On the other end it is attached to the anterior and medial surface of the *tibia*. It may be visually identified as the slender muscle running diagonally across the front of the thigh.

The *gracilis* is another long slender muscle located on the inner thigh. It is attached on one end to the pelvis and on the other end to the medial surface of the *tibia* (Figure 13.4). To feel this muscle in action, place your hand on the medial side of the thigh, two to three inches below the *pubic* bone as you flex the knee.

Extension of the Knee

The *quadriceps* muscle group, located at the front of the thigh, is responsible for knee extension. It is comprised of four muscles: the *rectus femoris*, the *vastus lateralis*, the *vastus intermedius*, and the *vastus medialis*, all of which are shown in Figure 13.4. Of these, only the *rectus femoris* is a two-joint muscle. The lower tendons of all four muscles encase the *patella* and then form the patellar ligament, which inserts on the anterior surface of the *tibia* just below the knee joint.

The *rectus femoris* is attached at one end to the pelvis and at the other end to the *tibia* by way of the patellar ligament (Figure 13.4). Of the four quadriceps muscles, it is closest to the surface and can be easily palpated on the front of the thigh. If you have been told by your instructor that you are "gripping your thigh muscle" when performing a *développé*, the muscle that is gripping is the *rectus femoris*.

The *vastus lateralis, vastus intermedius,* and *vastus medialis* muscles are attached on one end to the *femur* and on the other end to the *tibia* by way of the patellar ligament (Figure 13.4). The *vastus lateralis* is the largest and can be palpated on the lateral, mid-thigh. The *vastus intermedius* is located beneath the *rectus femoris* and cannot be palpated. The *vastus medialis* may be palpated on the medial side of the anterior thigh near the knee.

Inward and Outward Rotation of the Knee

A small degree of inward and outward rotation can occur when the knee is bent. Inward rotation is performed mainly by the *semimembranosus* and the *semitendinosus*.

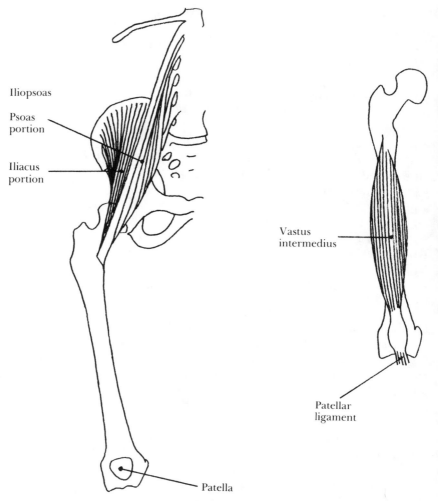

Iliopsoas

Psoas
portion

Iliacus
portion

Vastus
intermedius

Patellar
ligament

Patella

Figure 13.4 Anterior view of knee and hip muscles.

Outward rotation is performed mainly by the *biceps femoris*. All of these muscles have been described above.

The Structure of the Hip Joint

The bones of the hip joint include the *femur* and the *pelvis* (Figure 13.5). The *femur* is comprised of the head, a short neck, a prominent bony projection called the *greater trochanter*, a smaller bony projection

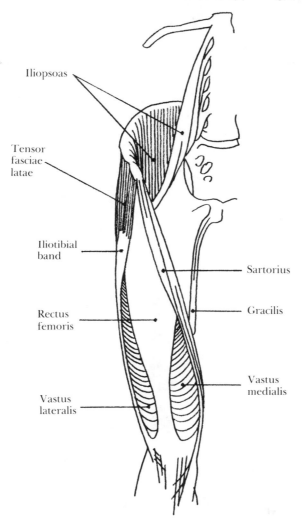

Iliopsoas

Tensor
fasciae
latae

Iliotibial
band

Rectus
femoris

Vastus
lateralis

Sartorius

Gracilis

Vastus
medialis

called the *lesser trochanter*, and the shaft with its condyles at the knee joint. The head of the *femur* articulates with the pelvis at the *acetabulum*, or hip socket.

Three bones—the *ilium, ischium,* and *pubis*—are fused together to form the pelvis (Figure 13.5). The right and left sides of the *ilium* form the upper portion of the pelvis. The right and left sides of the *ischium* form the posterior and lower portion, while the right and left sides of the *pubis* form the anterior and lower portion.

The *ilium* is the largest bone. On the front of the *ilium* are the bony

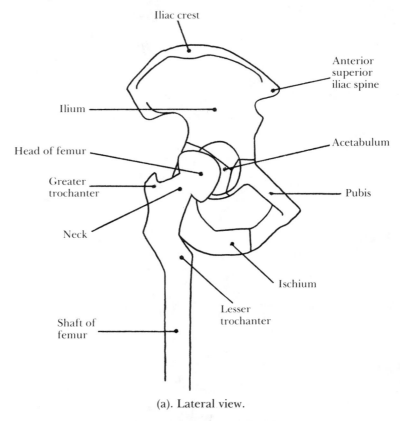

Iliac crest

Anterior
superior
iliac spine

Ilium

Acetabulum

Head of femur

Greater
trochanter

Pubis

Neck

Ischium

Lesser
trochanter

Shaft of
femur

(a). Lateral view.

Figure 13.5 Lateral and anterior views of right hip joint and ligaments.

projections commonly referred to as the "hip bones." Anatomically they are referred to as the *anterior superior iliac spines*. The crest of the *ilium* is the top ridge of hip bone just below the waist. If you carry books or packages in one arm and let them rest on your "hip," they are resting on the crest of the *ilium*. The *sacrum,* or lowest part of the spine, fits between the right and left portions of the posterior *ilium*.

The "sitting bones" are found on the *ischium* and they are referred to as the *ischial tuberosities*. They bear the weight of the body when sitting.

Several ligaments attach the *femur* to the hip socket. Two of these ligaments, the *iliofemoral* and *pubofemoral,* are of great interest to dancers (Figure 13.5). They are located at the front of the hip socket, and their names indicate the bones they connect. The iliofemoral ligament joins the *ilium* and the *femur*. The pubofemoral ligament joins the *pubis* and the *femur*. If these ligaments are short and tight they can

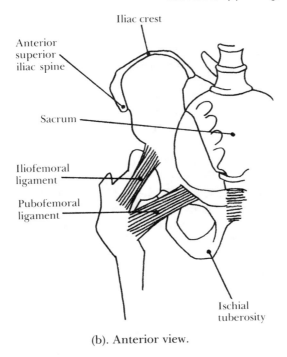

Iliac crest

Anterior
superior
iliac spine

Sacrum

Iliofemoral
ligament

Pubofemoral
ligament

Ischial
tuberosity

(b). Anterior view.

limit outward rotation of the leg at the hip. For a dancer this can mean a reduced ability to turn out.

Movements of the Hip Joint

Movements at the hip include *flexion* (bending at the hip) and *extension* (straightening of the hip). There is a difference of opinion among experts as to whether *hyperextension* (a continuation of extension beyond 180 degrees) is possible at the hip joint. Some experts believe a small degree of hyperextension is possible (Luttgens & Wells, 1982, p.152). An example of this would be a *tendu* back. Other experts believe that all posterior movement, from *tendu* back to *arabesque,* is more correctly classified as hyperextension of the spine, rather than hyperextension of the hip (Fitt, 1988, p. 56). For the purpose of this book we will simply use the term hyperextension when referring to movements such as *tendu* back, back *attitude,* and *arabesque.*

Other movements at the hip include *abduction* (sideward movement of the leg away from the midline of the body), *adduction* (sideward movement of the leg toward the midline of the body), and *inward* and *outward rotation.* An example of abduction is the lifted leg in a modern dance or jazz front layout position (Figure 13.6). Adduction would occur if the lifted leg moved to parallel first position. Inward and outward rotation refer to turning in and turning out.

Movement of the hip usually involves a combination of the actions just described. For example, a ballet dancer's *grand battement* front would involve hip flexion and outward rotation. If the same dancer were to lift the leg in a forward diagonal direction, as usually occurs in a *grand battement* to the side, movements at the hip would include flexion, abduction, and outward rotation.

Just as there can be a complex interaction of movement occurring at the hip, there can also be a complex interaction of the muscles that produce this movement. Many of the muscles at the hip are involved in more than one action. Sometimes different parts of the same muscle are active in producing entirely different actions. In the material that follows we will only discuss those muscles that are primarily involved in producing a certain movement. Understanding this simplified discussion will give you the general background you need to proceed with the questions and exercises that follow.

Flexion of the Hip
Some of the muscles responsible for hip flexion are the *iliopsoas*, the *pectineus*, the *sartorius* and the *rectus femoris* (both already described), and

Figure 13.6 Hip abduction while performing a front layout.

the *tensor fasciae latae*. These muscles are located on the anterior side of the thigh and pelvis, except for the *tensor fasciae latae*, which is located on both the anterior and lateral sides of the thigh.

The *iliopsoas* is the most important hip flexor muscle. It is actually composed of two muscles, the *iliacus* and the *psoas* (Figure 13.4). The *iliopsoas* is attached on one end to the lower vertebra and the *ilium*. On the other end it is attached to the *femur* at the lesser trochanter. The *iliopsoas* is a powerful muscle. If its strength is not balanced by the abdominal muscles, the *iliopsoas* can pull down on the front of the pelvis, flexing the hip and tilting the pelvis forward. When the pelvis tilts forward, the spine often hyperextends or overarches. This tipping action and the balancing role of the abdominal muscles will be discussed in Part V.

The *pectineus* is a small muscle attached on one end to the *pubic* bone, and on the other to the medial side of the *femur* (Figure 13.7). Like the *iliopsoas*, the *pectineus* tends to pull the pelvis downward in front, thereby flexing the hip and tilting the pelvis forward.

The *tensor fasciae latae* is another small muscle (Figure 13.4). It is attached on one end to the *ilium*, and on the other end to the *iliotibial band* (connective tissue) of the lateral thigh. The iliotibial band runs the length of the lateral leg, crosses the lateral side of the knee joint and inserts on the lateral condyle of the *tibia*. Not only does the *tensor fasciae latae* flex the hip, it also exerts a pull on the iliotibial band. In this way it stabilizes the knee joint in weight-bearing positions.

Extension of the Hip

Some of the muscles responsible for hip extension include the hamstrings (already described) and the *gluteus maximus*. These muscles are located on the posterior side of the body. They are also responsible for lifting the leg in *arabesque*, back *attitude*, and other hyperextended positions.

The *gluteus maximus* is attached to both the *ilium* and *sacrum* at one end. At the other end it is attached to the *femur* and along the iliotibial band (connective tissue) of the lateral thigh (Figure 13.3). The *gluteus maximus* muscle is a powerful hip extensor against resistance. For example, it is very active in stair climbing or coming up from a deep lunge. It also assists with outward rotation when the hip is extended. This muscle can easily be palpated in the wide area of the buttocks.

Abduction of the Hip

Some of the muscles responsible for hip abduction are the *gluteus medius*, the *gluteus minimus,* and the *tensor fasciae latae* (already de-

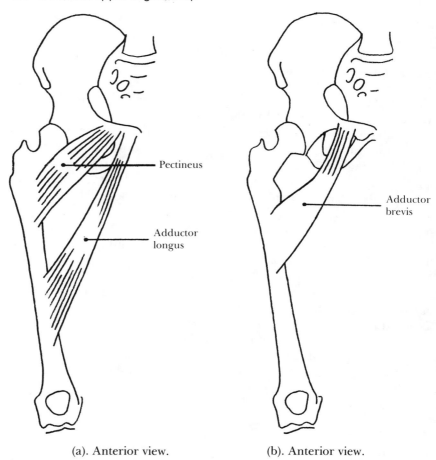

Pectineus

Adductor
longus

Adductor
brevis

(a). Anterior view.   (b). Anterior view.

Figure 13.7 Anterior and posterior views of hip muscles.

scribed). The *gluteus medius* and *minimus* are located on the lateral side
of the hip.

The *gluteus medius* is a small muscle that lies under the *gluteus
maximus*. It is attached on one end to the lateral surface of the *ilium*,
and on the other end to the top of the greater trochanter (Figure 13.3).
It is the chief abductor of the thigh at the hip and is also important in
stabilizing the standing leg.

The *gluteus minimus* is another small muscle that lies under the *gluteus
medius*. It is attached to the lateral side of the *ilium* and on the top of the
greater trochanter (Figure 13.3).

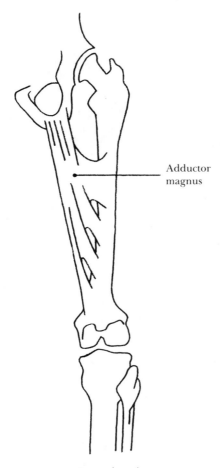

Adductor
magnus

(c). Posterior view.

Adduction of the Hip

The muscles generally classified as hip adductors are the *adductor longus*, the *adductor brevis*, the *adductor magnus*, as well as the *gracilis* and the medial hamstrings (described previously). These muscles are located on the medial side of the thigh.

The *adductor longus, adductor brevis,* and *adductor magnus* are attached on one end to the *pubic* bone or *ischium,* and on the other end to the medial or posterior aspect of the *femur* (Figure 13.7). The *adductor magnus* is attached to the largest area of the *femur* and can be palpated midway down the thigh on the medial surface. The *adductor brevis* cannot be palpated. The *adductor longus* can be felt by placing your hand just below the *pubic* bone on the medial side of the thigh as you adduct the thigh against resistance.

Inward Rotation of the Hip

The primary inward rotators are the *gluteus medius* and *minimus*, the *minimus* being the most effective. Other muscles that assist in inward rotation are the *semimembranous, semitendinosus, gracilis, tensor fasciae latae,* and some of the adductors. All of these muscles have been described previously.

Outward Rotation of the Hip

Some of the muscles responsible for outward rotation are the *six outward rotators,* the *gluteus maximus, sartorius, biceps femoris,* and the adductors. With the exception of the six outward rotators, these muscles have been described previously.

The six outward rotators are very short muscles that attach on one end to the posterior surface of the *sacrum, ilium,* and *ischium* (Figure 13.3). On the other end they attach to the greater trochanter. These muscles are very deep and cannot be palpated.

14

Questions and Answers

Note: The questions and answers that follow concern improvement of technique and prevention of injuries in the knee, upper leg, and hip.

1. What is correct alignment of the knee?

In order to understand the correct alignment of the knee, we need to view it from three different perspectives. When viewed from the front or back, the knees should be horizontally level, and the knee caps should face straight ahead. They should not "knock" together, nor should they "bow" with unusual space between them.

The position of the knee when viewed from the side is another key to good alignment. When a dancer stands in parallel first position, a plumb line should pass through the center of the hip, continue behind the patella, passing slightly forward of the center of the knee, and finish in front of the ankle bone. If the plumb line passes through the front of the knee, the knee is considered to be hyperextended. If the plumb line passes through the back of the knee, the knee is said to be hyperflexed.

The third perspective is knee alignment in relation to the foot. In all dance positions, the knee should be in line with, or centered over, the middle of the foot. One common mistake in knee-foot alignment is to force turnout from the knee and ankle rather than turning out the entire leg from the hip. When this happens, the foot is pulled backward and the knee falls forward. The knee is then aligned with the floor in front of the foot rather than being centered over the middle of the foot.

Problems in knee-foot alignment are easy to see in the *demi-plié* position. In Figure 14.1a, the dancer has obviously forced turnout and allowed the knees to roll forward. Note that the knees are positioned over the floor in front of his feet, instead of being centered over the middle of his feet. In Figure 14.1b, the alignment problem is more subtle. The knee is still not centered over the middle of the foot, although it is in a better position than in Figure 14.1a. The overall degree of outward rotation is better, but it has been achieved by allowing the pelvis to tilt forward slightly. As a result, the back is slightly overarched. This stresses the lower back, as we shall see in Part V.

The problem of knee-foot alignment demonstrated in Figure 14.1a is

Figure 14.1 Poor knee-foot alignment. **Dancer (a)** is on the left. **Dancer (b)** is on the right.

often seen in the beginning levels of dance training. The more subtle problem shown in Figure 14.1b is more often seen in advanced levels of training. In each case, the knee is being stressed by improper alignment, and the problem needs to be corrected.

Related information can be found in questions 2, 12, 13, and 24, below.

2. *The anatomy section of this chapter lists outward rotation as one of the movements possible at the knee joint. The answer to question 1 indicates that turning out from the knee causes knee injury. How can both statements be true?*

To answer this question, it is important to understand the role of the collateral and cruciate ligaments. When the knee is fully extended and straight, the collateral ligaments are pulled taut. Neither inward nor outward rotation is possible. When the knee is bent, however, the collateral ligaments are slack. This allows a slight degree of inward and outward rotation to take place. This rotation is controlled by the cruciate ligaments. They act to limit rotation when the knee is bent.

Unfortunately, many dancers misuse the slight degree of outward rotation possible in the bent knee position. This occurs when they *demi-plié*, force their lower legs into an exaggerated turnout, and then maintain the forced position as they straighten their knees. This practice puts improper stress on both the cruciate and collateral ligaments, and can lead to serious knee injury.

In a position of forced outward rotation, the body's weight can no longer be directed through the center of the knee and foot. Instead, the weight is directed toward the medial side of the leg. This stresses not only the medial knee ligaments, but the cartilage of the knee as well as the medial side of the ankle and foot.

Ligaments do not have the elastic capability that muscles have. This makes them susceptible to being torn or permanently stretched. If knee ligaments are overstretched, their ability to stabilize the joint is impaired. Furthermore, when a medial collateral ligament is torn, the knee cartilage may be torn as well. Some experts believe that if dancers would stop forcing turnout at the knee, the cause of most cartilage tears would be eliminated (Silver & Campbell, 1985, p. 79).

3. I have heard that teachers of young children should be particularly careful to see that they do not force turnout from the knee. Why?

It is particularly important that young children be taught correct alignment from the beginning of their dance experience. Bad habits learned early in training are difficult to correct in later years. Furthermore, these habits subject the developing musculoskeletal system to improper stress. For example, young children who continually force turnout from the knee and ankle may develop tibial torsion (Arnheim, 1980, pp. 46–7, 59). *Tibial torsion* is a twisting of the *tibia* so the foot no longer aligns with the knee.

In the most common form of tibial torsion, the knee faces inward when the foot points straight ahead. Dancers with this malalignment find it imposible to *demi-plié* correctly with the knee centered over the foot. This can stress the knee. In addition, dancers who have developed tibial torsion may also have problems with a lowered or fallen longitudinal arch.

Related Information can be found in the answers to questions 1 and 2, above.

4. *Some people say that* grand pliés *are not good for the knees. Is this true?*

Many orthopedists and physical therapists who work with dancers, as well as dance kinesiologists, find the *grand plié* to be extremely taxing on the knee. Some believe it is an appropriate movement if it is executed correctly, but express concern that the majority of dancers may not perform the movement correctly. Dancers with problem-free knees are advised to be extremely careful in executing *grand pliés,* and dancers with bad knees are advised to avoid performing them.

Most of these experts agree that the *grand plié* should be regarded as an advanced skill, and taught only when dancers have sufficient strength to control the alignment of the torso, hip and leg throughout the entire movement. Even then, *grand pliés* should be practiced with moderation and their placement in the class structure should be considered. Many experts recommend that *grand pliés* occur late in the warmup, so that the body is prepared before this exacting work begins.

Considerable stress is placed on the knee during a *grand plié.* On the downward movement of the *plié,* the quadriceps function in an eccentric muscle action. On the upward movement of the *plié* the quadriceps are again active, but this time they function in a concentric muscle action. The pull of these knee extensors in both the downward and upward movements creates a compressive force in which the *patella* is pressed against the condyles of the *femur.* If there is any deviation in the pull of the extensors, the compressive force can damage the *patella,* leading to a condition called *chondromalacia.*

Gravity is another force that taxes the knee during a *grand plié.* As the body is lowered and raised during the movement, gravity requires the knee joint to control more than three times the body's weight. When this stress is accumulated over a period of time it can lead to knee injury, especially if the body is not strong enough to maintain the proper alignment of the knee during the *plié.*

Related information can be found in questions 5, 6, and 15 below.

5. *My advanced dance class performs the* grand plié. *How can I be certain I am doing it properly and thereby avoiding knee injury?*

There are four parts of a *grand plié* that require particular attention in order to protect the knee. A dancer should first check the starting position. The torso must be correctly aligned and this alignment must be maintained throughout the *grand plié.* If the trunk muscles are not strong enough to maintain proper placement, the weight of the body will not be transferred through the center of each joint. This can stress the entire structure and be particularly harmful to the knee.

In addition to the alignment of the torso, the alignment of the knee and foot must be carefully checked in the starting position. If a dancer begins a *grand plié* from a turnout position that is forced, the knees will not be properly centered over the feet. They will be aligned with the floor in front of the feet, and the weight of the body will be shifted to the medial side of the knee joint. This can strain the ligaments and possibly damage the cartilage.

The second part of the *plié* that needs careful execution is at the moment when the heels leave the floor. It is very easy at this point to press the heels in a forward direction beyond the turnout capability of the hip joint. Once again, this can place increased and improper force on the medial side of the knee and foot.

The transition between going down and coming up from a *grand plié* is the third factor that warrants consideration. Relaxation should not occur at the end of the downward movement. If a dancer allows the knees to flex fully, or "sits" at the bottom of the *plié*, the cartilage can be pinched between the *femur* and the *tibia*. This position of extreme flexion can also stretch the cruciate ligaments of the knee, particularly if the dancer has large, muscular thighs or forcefully allows the body's weight to drop into the position. Further injury can result should any rotation or forcing of the turnout occur at this point. A dancer must also be careful to keep the weight properly centered over the feet once the upward movement begins. Actively pressing against the floor will facilitate the upward movement.

The fourth part of the *plié* that needs careful attention is the moment when the heels return to the floor. If a dancer forces turnout at this point, the collateral ligaments may be injured as the knees continue to straighten.

Related information can be found in questions 2 and 4 in this chapter, and in question 1 in Chapter 17.

6. If I reduce the number of grand pliés *given in my classes, should I replace them with other exercises?*

Grand pliés are often used to warm up the hip and knee joints. They are also used to strengthen muscle groups such as the knee extensors, hip extensors, and the outward rotators, and to stretch muscle groups such as the adductors and ankle plantar flexors. It is possible, however, to achieve these same results by other means. *Demi-pliés* should provide a good warm up without unnecessary stress to the knees. They also provide a stretch for the ankle plantar flexors. Other dance and conditioning exercises that are not taxing to the knee could be performed to strengthen and stretch the other muscle groups.

Recommended exercises are found in Chapter 15 to strengthen and stretch the hip extensors (15.A, 15.G), knee extensors (15.B, 15.H), and outward rotators (15.F, 15.L, 15.M). Chapter 15 also includes an exercise to stretch the adductors (15.K).

7. *There are several dancers in my modern and jazz classes who complain of pain in the back knee when they perform a hurdle position or the hurdle layback position (Figure 14.2). Their back knees also hurt when they sit on the floor in fourth position (Figure 14.3a). As their teacher, I would like to know if there are exercises I could recommend to prevent this pain.*

The hurdle position and the seated fourth position are essentially the same position in terms of the back knee. Some dancers with laxity or looseness in the ligaments of the knee may not experience knee pain in these positions. Many dancers do encounter knee pain and should not try to endure and work through it.

In Figure 14.3a, you will see that the *femur* is rotated in one direction while the lower leg is rotated in another. If your students are experiencing knee pain in the hurdle or seated fourth position, it is probably because they do not have enough natural rotation in the knee to accommodate the position of the thigh and lower leg. Should they continue to work through the pain, they could injure their knee ligaments. When the medial collateral ligament is seriously injured, it can often damage the medial knee cartilage as well. This is why movement experts recommend these positions not be used by anyone experiencing pain.

Figure 14.2 Hurdle layback position.

Many dancers have enough natural rotation to be comfortable in the hurdle or seated fourth position as long as the back hip is off the floor. When these dancers try to place the back hip on the floor, however, they experience pain. It would be a mistake for these dancers to believe their knee pain will eventually go away if they continue to "work hard" by placing the back hip on the floor.

There is a variation of the hurdle and seated fourth position in which the back leg is realigned. In this position, the lower leg is brought closer to the back thigh and buttock. Dancers may find this position a useful alternative to the hurdle or the seated fourth position. In this adjustment, distance between the back thigh and the back heel should feel comfortable. It will vary from one dancer to another and will also be influenced by the movement required in the position. Figure 14.3b illustrates a possible adaptation of the seated fourth position. The dancer is most comfortable with the heel quite close to the thigh and buttock.

Related information can be found in question 2, above.

8. *When I try to stretch my inner thighs by putting one leg on the* barre *and sliding into a wide second position split, I feel pain on the inside of the supporting knee. Should this happen?*

Figure 14.3 **Dancer (a),** on the left, is in the seated fourth position. **Dancer (b),** on the right, is in an adaptation of that position.

No. You probably have allowed your supporting leg to turn in, and most of your weight is being shifted to the medial side of your supporting knee. To correct the problem, you need to keep the supporting leg turned out. Some dancers find this difficult to do as they reach the full stretch position. An alternative is to *demi-plié* on the supporting leg as you slide the other leg down the *barre*. This allows many dancers to reach a position of stretch without losing control of their turnout and placement. The muscles that you are stretching when you do this exercise at the *barre* are the hip adductors.

A *recommended exercise* can be found in Chapter 15 to stretch the hip adductors (15.K).

9. *I am having trouble performing knee hinges (Figure 14.4a) and back hinge falls (Figure 14.4b) in my modern dance and jazz classes. How can I improve my performance of these movements?*

If you look closely at the knee hinge and the back hinge fall, you will see that the knees flex about as much as they do in a *grand plié*. The stress that *grand pliés* can place on the knee is discussed in question 4, above. Many of those concerns also apply to knee hinges and back hinge falls.

Figure 14.4 **Dancer (a),** on the left, is performing a knee hinge. **Dancer (b),** on the right, is performing a back hinge fall.

To prevent knee injury while performing knee hinge movements, keep the hips extended or "lifted up" and the torso in straight alignment. The descent in the knee hinge must be controlled. At no time should the weight be allowed to drop. Dancers who do not have the necessary control to perform a back hinge fall, can bruise the shoulder structure and forcefully jam the knee into a fully flexed position.

Teachers should regard knee hinges and back hinge falls as advanced techniques. These movements should be introduced only when the dancer has the necessary strength to execute every phase of the movement properly. It is also important to place knee hinges and back hinge falls late enough in the class that the body is prepared to perform these taxing movements.

Both the knee hinge and back hinge fall require strong and flexible knee extensors. In addition, the hip extensors must be strong enough to prevent the hip from flexing, and the trunk muscles must be strong enough to maintain the alignment of the torso. The exercises listed below will help you condition the knee and hip muscles. Part V discusses strength conditioning for the trunk.

Related information can be found in the answer to question 4, above, and in question 17, Chapter 17.

Recommended exercises can be found in Chapter 15 to strengthen and stretch the hip extensors (15.A, 15.G), and knee extensors (15.B, 15.H).

10. If I perform movements that go to the kneeling position, or kneel very much in my modern or jazz classes, my knees swell and hurt. Is there something I can do to prevent this from happening?

A *bursa,* or fluid-filled "pillow," lies between the knee cap and the skin. Constant kneeling can irritate this bursa and cause an inflammation and swelling. The swelling generally occurs over the knee cap and causes considerable pain during movement. Physicians recommend ice, rest, and elevation as an immediate treatment. If the swelling does not disappear, a specialist should be consulted.

Dropping into the kneeling position rather than controlling the body's descent may be another cause of this problem. Strong knee and hip extensors are needed to control the kneeling movement. Conditioning these muscles may help.

If you are controlling the kneeling movement, then it may simply be the pressure of kneeling that irritates the bursa. Knee pads can help to relive this pressure, but it is important that these pads do not become a crutch. Sometimes dancers who wear knee pads control their descent into the kneeling position until they are close to the floor. At that point they allow their weight to fall onto the knee because the knee pad cushions the impact. When performance time comes and the dancer cannot wear knee pads, the knee can be injured. Check with your teacher to be sure it is appropriate for you to wear knee pads in class.

Recommended exercises can be found in Chapter 15 to strengthen and stretch the hip extensors (15.A, 15.G) and knee extensors (15.B, 15.H).

11. Several of my students do not straighten their knees when they go en pointe. I know they are trying to straighten their knees, but they are not successful. What is wrong?

Anatomical structure could be one cause of this problem. If one of a dancer's legs is longer than the other, the longer leg will flex slightly when the weight is supported on both feet. The problem may have other causes, however. For example, students with weak knee extensors will have difficulty straightening their knees. This is often true of beginning *pointe* dancers. For these dancers, a program to strengthen the knee extensors may be helpful in preventing bent knees.

More advanced students usually have sufficient strength in their knee extensors. In these dancers, the bent knee may reflect a deviation in alignment elsewhere in the body. These students may need to condition the trunk muscles to achieve a stronger "center" and thereby help to correct alignment problems in the torso. Correct alignment of the torso is discussed in Chapter 17.

The importance of correcting bent knees while *en pointe* goes beyond aesthetic considerations. The bent knee actually creates an unstable knee joint and an unstable placement. You may have already noticed that dancers with bent knees have trouble with their balance and turns. This is because bent knees cannot provide the same solid foundation for *pointe* work that straight knees can provide.

Related information can be found in the answer to question 1, Chapter 17.

Recommended exercises can be found in Chapter 15 to strengthen and stretch the knee extensors (15.B, 15.H).

12. Several of my students have hyperextended knees. What causes this condition, and should I be concerned about it?

The knee is said to be hyperextended when the joint straightens beyond 180 degrees. This can be the result of laxity or looseness in the knee ligaments as well as muscular imbalances. Hyperextended knees can be recognized by their curved or bowed appearance when viewed from the side. Figure 14.5 illustrates a slight degree of hyperextension.

Figure 14.5 Hyperextension of the knee.

Some experts regard a slight degree of hyperextension as aesthetically advantageous for women who dance *en pointe.* Nevertheless, it would be unwise to assume that hyperextended knees present no problem. Many dancers have a hyperextension that goes beyond being "slight," and there are anatomical repercussions from this alignment that can lead to injury.

When a dancer "locks back" into the hyperextended position, the weight of the body is no longer transferred through the center of the knee joint. Instead, it is directed towards the back of the knee joint. This can further stretch the knee ligaments and weaken the stability of the joint. When the dancer's weight falls toward the back of the hyperextended knee, it may be transferred to the heels rather than the center of the ankle and foot. This can make it more difficult to *relevé*, or jump.

Because the body is a closed system, it is not surprising that other problems may also occur in connection with hyperextended knees. These include weak forefeet, patellar instability, and hyperextended backs. All of these conditions can lead to further injury and limit technique.

Some experts express concern that knee deviation and the related problems may increase if hyperextension is not corrected (Howse & Hancock, 1988, p. 181). Dancers who are used to hyperextending their knees may find it a difficult habit to change, however. Dancers and teachers should be aware that it takes time and patience.

If a student has a serious problem with hyperextended knees, we recommend that he or she sees a physician or physical therapist who specializes in dance. These experts can identify the extent of the specific problem, the related body compensations, and recommend the proper rehabilitation program. These programs may include exercises to improve proprioception as well as strength and flexibility work for muscles of the foot, ankle, lower leg, knee, hip and spine.

13. My knees are always bent, even in the standing position. Are there exercises I can do to help with this problem?

Bent knees can be caused by tight knee flexors. Stretching these muscles should help to alleviate the problem.

A *recommended exercise* to stretch the knee flexors is given in Chapter 15 (15G).

14. Can conditioning exercises help knock knees and bow legs?

Problems in structure or posture can precipitate the conditions commonly called "knock knees" and "bow legs." Dancers with structural knock knees or bow legs cannot change their structure by performing corrective exercises. They need to work with these deviations and make whatever technical adjustments are necessary. For example, dancers with knock knees should not try to bring their heels together in turned-out first position. Their parallel first position will also need to be slightly changed. In both cases there should be enough space between the feet so the knees do not have to overlap or hyperextend. Because dancers with knock knees are susceptible to pronation, they must be particularly careful to turn out from the hip and not force turnout at the knee or ankle.

Sometimes knock knees and bow legs are a postural problem that is caused by a combination of hyperextended knees and femoral rotation. If the knees hyperextend and the *femur* is allowed to rotate inwardly, the dancer will appear to have bow legs. On the other hand, if the knees hyperextend and the *femur* is allowed to rotate outwardly, knock knees will be the result.

Knock knees and bow legs caused by postural deviations usually precipitate problems in foot and ankle alignment. Early detection of these alignment problems is particularly important. If they are recognized soon enough, a specialist can recommend corrective shoes and/or corrective exercises. These exercises may include work for the hip, knee, and ankle.

15. I've heard that dancers often have a knee problem called chondromalacia. *What is it, and can I prevent it?*

The *patella* is a sesamoid bone that is encased by the tendons of the knee extensors. When properly aligned, the *patella* fits in a grove formed by the two condyles of the *femur*. This is called the *intercondylar groove*. Sometimes the *patella* is not properly aligned, and it does not sit in the center of the intercondylar groove. When this happens, it sits off center and rubs against the femoral condyle each time the knee moves. This causes a softening or splitting on the posterior surface of the *patella;* this condition is called *chondromalacia.*

The pain from chondromalacia is felt directly behind the knee cap or just above it. It is experienced in dance movements that require flexion and extension of the knee as well as in daily activities such as stair climbing. Dancers with chondromalacia often experience discomfort if they sit with their knees bent for long periods of time. Chondromalacia must be treated because it can result in a severe deterioration of the kneecap. If you think you might have this condition, see a physician as soon as possible.

One cause of chondromalacia is a slightly lateral attachment of the patellar ligament to the *tibia*. This can create a lateral pull that positions the *patella* toward the lateral side of the intercondylar groove, rather than allowing it to sit in the center of the groove. Another cause of chondromalacia is forced turnout from the knee. When the lower leg is forced into excessive lateral rotation, the patellar ligament is pulled laterally. This stress can pull the *patella* off center.

Chondromalacia can also be caused by an imbalance in the strength of the knee extensors. When these muscles are balanced in strength, they pull evenly on the *patella*, and the *patella* is correctly located in the center of the intercondylar groove. If one of these muscles is weak, however, the pull on the *patella* will not be balanced. The *patella* will be pulled off center, toward the side of the stronger muscle. The weak muscle is generally the *vastus medialis,* and the *patella* is usually pulled to the lateral side of the intercondylar groove.

To help prevent this muscular imbalance, dancers can strengthen the entire quadriceps muscle group, paying particular attention to the *vastus medialis.* This muscle comes into action during the last 15 degrees of knee extension. In order to strengthen the *vastus medialis,* you should either keep the knee straight as the leg is raised and lowered, or extend the knee fully from a flexed position. (This does not mean to hyperextend the knee). Exercises to strengthen the knee extensors will help you strengthen the *vastus medialis* as well as the other knee extensors.

It has also been recommended that dancers strengthen the adductor muscles in addition to strengthening the *vastus medialis.* When strong adductors assist in controlling the *plié,* there is less compressive force on the *patella.* Compression occurs when the knee extensors contract and pull the *patella* against the *femur.* Alleviating some of this force can lessen the possibility of harmful friction between the *patella* and the femoral condyles.

Recommended exercises can be found in Chapter 15 to strengthen and stretch the knee extensors (15.B, 15.H) and hip adductors (15.E, 15.K). Do not attempt to perform them if you suspect that you have chrondomalacia and you have not seen a physician. These exercises are to help prevent the condition from occurring, not to be used as a self-prescribed treatment.

16. Sometimes during and after class my knees ache and generally hurt. What can I do about this?

If you are experiencing chronic pain in your knees, you should speak with your teacher and see a physician. Improper use of the knee may lead to numerous conditions that could cause knee pain, including chondromalacia, swelling and inflammation of the knee joint, straining or damaging the knee ligaments, and damaging the cartilage. These conditions all require medical attention to deal with the immediate problem, as well as reevaluation of technique to identify and correct the source of the problem.

Related information can be found in questions 1, 2, 10, 12, and 15, above.

17. Is there something I can do to improve the strength of my relevé *and jump?*

In Chapter 11, we explained the role of strong ankles and feet in producing a good *relevé* or jump. These movements also require strength in the knee and hip extensors. The exercises recommended below will help you to strengthen your knee and hip extensors. In addition, strong torso muscles are needed to maintain proper trunk alignment throughout each movement (see Chapter 17).

Related information is in question 11, Chapter 11, and questions 1 and 17, Chapter 17.

Recommended exercises can be found in Chapter 15 to strengthen and stretch the hip extensors (15.A, 15.G) and knee extensors (15.B, 15.H).

18. *I would like to improve my front and side* attitudes *as well as my front and side leg extensions. What can I do to perform them better in both the parallel and turned-out positions?*

One important limitation of a turned-out front *attitude* or turned-out side *attitude* is the outward rotation of the thigh. Those dancers who have poor turnout generally have a poor *attitude*. To increase turnout in these positions, you should stretch the inward rotators and strengthen the muscles that produce outward rotation. Exercises to help you do this are recommended below. Tight ligaments at the front of the hip socket can also restrict turnout. The consequence of stretching these ligaments is discussed in question 24, below.

If turnout is not the problem and you want to hold either a parallel or turned-out *attitude* in higher position, then you need to condition other muscles at the hip. The hip flexors should be strengthened, and the hip extensors should be stretched. Exercises to help you condition these muscles are recommended below.

Many dancers have no problem holding a high parallel or turned-out *attitude*, but when they try to extend the knee in a *développé*, the leg drops lower. This may be the result of a weakness in the hip flexors, a tightness in the hip extensors, or a combination of both. Strengthening the hip flexors and stretching the hip extensors should help you perform a *développé* without dropping the leg.

In many modern and jazz classes, the leg is lifted to the side while held in a parallel or turned-in position. To increase the height of the leg in this position, it is necessary to strengthen the hip abductors. The hip adductors should also be stretched. Exercises to do this are recommended below.

Finally, proper alignment of the torso is crucial to the successful execution of these leg positions. Strong abdominal muscles are needed to stabilize the pelvis and maintain correct torso alignment. Chapter 17 discusses this concept in greater detail.

Related information is in Chapter 17, questions 1 and 5.

Recommended exercises can be found in Chapter 15 to strengthen and stretch the hip flexors (15.C, 15.I), abductors and inward rotators

(15.D, 15.J, 15.M), adductors (15.E, 15.K), and outward rotators (15.F, 15.L, 15.M). Chapter 15 also presents an exercise to stretch the hip extensors (15.G).

19.   I want my arabesque *as well as my parallel and turned-out back* attitudes *to be higher. What conditioning work will improve those positions?*

The height of an *arabesque* or back *attitude* is determined by several factors. Some of these involve the spine and muscles of the torso, others involve muscles at the hip. Part V will discuss spinal structure as it relates to *arabesque* and back *attitude* as well as the muscles of the torso that help achieve these positions.

At the hip socket, a high *arabesque* or back *attitude* position requires strength in the hip extensors and flexibility in the hip flexors. Turnout in these positions can be improved by strengthening the outward rotators of the hip and stretching the inward rotators. Exercises for these muscle groups are listed below.

Sometimes dancers try to achieve a higher *arabesque* or turned-out back *attitude* by allowing the hip to raise and the pelvis to twist. This stresses the lower back and is not advisable. Chapter 17 discusses this alignment problem and explains the potential for injury.

Related information can be found in Chapter 17, question 11.

Recommended exercises can be found in Chapter 15 to strengthen and stretch the hip extensors (15.A, 15.G) and outward rotators (15.F, 15.L, and 15.M). Chapter 15 also presents flexibility exercises for the hip flexors (15.I), and inward rotators (15.J, 15.M).

20.   I have difficulty sitting on the floor in second position. My knees bend and my legs do not open very far. What can I do?

Sitting in second position requires flexibility in the knee flexors and hip extensors as well as the adductors. The exercises recommended below will help you stretch these muscle groups. In addition, you may need to strengthen the trunk extensors if your back is rounded in this position. These trunk muscles are discussed in Chapter 17.

Related information can be found in Chapter 17, question 12.

Recommended exercises can be found in Chapter 15 to stretch the knee flexors and hip extensors (15.G) and adductors (15.K).

21.   I am too tight to do the splits. What is the best way to develop this kind of flexibility?

One way to increase this range of motion is to assume a partial split position, with the hands supporting the body weight. This stretch position is then held for the required length of time. Many dancers find this to be an effective way of improving their flexibility in the split position.

Some dancers, however, should not try to use this stretch. It is not recommended for dancers with weak arm muscles, for example. These dancers could injure themselves if their arm muscles become too tired to offer support, and the weight of the body falls onto the tight leg muscles. Other dancers find the partial split too painful to hold for even a short length of time. Dancers who experience this kind of pain should not try to stretch by using this position. As an alternative to performing the partial split, dancers can stretch each of the muscle groups individually.

Recommended exercises can be found in Chapter 15 to stretch the knee flexors and hip extensors (15.G), hip flexors (15.I), and adductors (15.K).

22. *I can do the splits on the floor, but I can't reach the split position when I leap in the air. What's wrong?*

You are experiencing the difference between a passive and an active stretch. A *passive stretch* is possible when you are relaxed and no other movement is occurring. An *active stretch* is the stretch when you actually dance; this stretch depends on several factors, one of which is strength. To have as much active stretch as passive stretch, you must develop strength to control and use your passive flexibility.

Conditioning work can help you perform a better split leap. To reach the split position in the air, you probably need to strengthen the hip flexors and extensors in order to lift the legs into the split position. Exercises for these muscle groups are recommended below. You may also need to improve the height of your jump. A strong jump will allow you to stay in the air long enough to reach the split position.

Related information can be found in question 17, above.

Recommended exercises can be found in Chapter 15 to strengthen and stretch the hip extensors (15.A, 15.G) and hip flexors (15.C, 15.I).

23. *I am always pulling my hamstring muscle. Is there a way to prevent this from happening?*

A pulled hamstring muscle is generally referred to as a hamstring strain. Muscles that cross more than one joint, like the hamstrings, are particularly susceptible to muscle strains. These strains can result from a variety of causes. An explosive movement can strain the muscle, especially if the dancer is not warmed up or has recently returned from vacation or another absence. Hamstring strains can also be caused by incorrect stretching techniques, especially if performed when the body is cold.

Some experts find improper warm-up apparel to be another cause of hamstring strain (Howse & Hancock, 1988, p. 138). They caution dancers against wearing warm-up pants made of nonporous fabric. This fabric can make the skin feel warm before the muscles are thoroughly warm, thus giving the dancer a false sense of confidence when stretching or performing explosive choreography. Furthermore, these pants do not allow sweat to evaporate. Consequently, there is a noticeable cooling effect when they are taken off and the sweat finally evaporates. This change in temperature could lead to injury if these pants are taken off just before performance or the last part of a technique class.

Other factors that can contribute to hamstring strain include incorrect technique and muscle imbalance. If dancers work incorrectly with their weight back, they will probably pull off the supporting leg when performing a *grand battement* to the back or an *arabesque penchée*. This could injure the hamstrings on the supporting leg. Strains can also occur if dancers have very tight or weak hamstrings or very strong quadriceps.

Mild hamstring strains may be treated with ice, rest, and careful stretching. Dancers who sustain a more serious injury, or those with chronic problems, should consult a physician.

As is true with any injury, treatment and rehabilitation are only part of the process. Unless you identify the cause of your injury and correct the underlying fault, you will continue to face chronic problems.

To help prevent strain related to muscle imbalance, you should be sure the hamstrings are both strong and flexible. If your quadriceps are tight they should be stretched.

Recommended exercises can be found in Chapter 15 to strengthen and stretch the knee flexors (15.A, 15.G). Chapter 15 also presents a flexibility exercise for the knee extensors (15.H).

24. Several of my students have a very poor turnout. Are there exercises that I can recommend to increase their turnout?

Turnout is determined by the shape of the bones that form the hip socket, as well as the looseness or tightness of the ligaments at the front of the hip. Other factors that also affect turnout include the strength and flexibility of the muscles acting on the hip joint. Exercise can affect turnout to some extent, but much of the body's architecture is determined by heredity. A dancer with structural factors that limit turnout will never be able to match the turnout of another who was born with an anatomy favoring turnout. As dancers work to increase their turnout, they should realize that ultimately there are structural limitations that may limit their performance. Furthermore, structural limitations differ from one dancer to another.

Before the age of 11, it is easier for the body to develop turnout. At this time, the ligaments in the body are more easily stretched. Young dancers probably begin to develop turnout by stretching the ligaments of the hip socket and strengthening the muscles responsible for outward rotation. In addition, some dance activities may help to shape the developing femoral neck so as to maximize turnout.

After age 11, it is more difficult for the body to increase turnout. The shape of the femoral neck has been established by that time and cannot be changed. Furthermore, the ligaments become less flexible.

Teen and young-adult dancers who try to increase turnout by forcefully stretching hip ligaments may experience problems. Painful forcing for turnout can strain the ligaments and soft tissues surrounding the hip, injure cartilage inside the hip, and may cause small growths of bone to form on the head and neck of the *femur*. It may also lead to medial snapping of the hip as the iliopsoas tendon rides over the prominent femoral head.

For these reasons, we do not recommend exercises that forcefully try to alter the ligamentous structure of the hip. Instead, we suggest you help your students stretch and strengthen the muscles related to turnout. This will help them realize the maximum turnout possible within their anatomical structure. Exercises to do this are listed below.

As you help your students improve turnout, it is important to caution them against two common errors in technique. Sometimes dancers try to increase turnout by letting the pelvis tilt forward. This action relaxes the iliofemoral ligament at the front of the hip socket, making some increase in turnout possible. Unfortunately, the action also puts stress on the lower back, and is not an advisable practice (see Chapter 17). At other times dancers try to increase turnout by forcing rotation at the knee, ankle, and foot. This can lead to many problems throughout the body.

It is especially important for directors of ballet companies, choreographers, teachers, and students to understand and accept individual differences in turnout. This does not mean structure should be an excuse for lazy work habits. Each ballet dancer should be concerned with achieving his or her anatomical potential for turnout. They should not, however, be obsessively concerned with achieving a perfect 180 degree turnout of the feet, "no matter what the consequences." The consequences may well be pain and injury throughout their dance career and the rest of their lives.

Related information can be found in the answers to questions 2 and 27 in this chapter; questions 2, 4, and 5 in Chapter 11; questions 2 and 5 in Chapter 17.

Recommended exercises can be found in Chapter 15 to strengthen and stretch the hip extensors (15.A: parts 2 and 4, 15.G), hip flexors (15.C: parts 2 and 4, 15.I), adductors (15.E, 15.K), and outward rotators (15.F, 15.L, 15.M). Chapter 15 also presents flexibility exercises for the inward rotators (15.J, 15.M).

25. *The majority of my dance training has been in ballet. When I take a modern or jazz class I have difficulty achieving the proper line in positions where the legs are parallel. What can I do about this?*

Your previous ballet training may have caused an imbalance between the outward and inward rotators of your hip. If this is the case, you will probably find an improvement in parallel positions by stretching the outward rotators of the hip and strengthening the inward rotators. Your line may be further improved by strengthening the hip flexors and extensors as they work in parallel positions.

Recommended exercises can be found in Chapter 15 to strengthen and stretch the hip extensors (15.A: parts 1 and 3, 15.G); flexors (15.C: parts 1 and 3, 15.I), inward rotators (15.D, 15.J and 15.M), and adductors (15.E, 15.K). Chapter 15 also presents flexibility exercises for the outward rotators (15.L, 15.M).

26. *My teacher is always telling me to stop "sinking" into the standing hip. I try to "get up on my leg," but I am not successful. What's wrong?*

First you should check your foot position. Forcing turnout at the foot and ankle can sometimes cause a dancer to "sink" or "sit" in the standing hip. If this is not the problem, then you may need to strengthen your hip abductors. These muscles play an important role in stabilizing the standing hip. The lateral muscles of the torso also help with alignment when you stand on one leg (see Chapter 17).

Related information can be found in the answer to question 15 in Chapter 17.

Recommended exercises can be found in Chapter 15 to strengthen and stretch the hip abductors (15.D, 15.J, 15.M).

27. *Some of my students complain of a "snapping" or "popping" in the hip when they land from a jump, lower the leg from a* développé, *or perform a* rond de jamb. *Why does this happen?*

The snap is thought to be caused by a ligament or a tendon sliding over the *femur* or hip capsule. The location of the snap indicates the probable cause. A snap at the side of the hip may be due to the iliotibial band sliding over the greater trochanter of the *femur*, especially when landing from a jump. A snap at the front of the hip may be caused by one of the hip flexor tendons, often the iliopsoas tendon sliding over the hip capsule or neck of the *femur*. The iliofemoral ligament may also slide over the head of the *femur* and cause a snap.

28. Is there anything that can be done to correct a snapping hip?

When the snapping hip is caused by muscular imbalance, stretching and strengthening specific muscle groups is recommended. If the snap is at the side of the hip, the abductors generally need stretching and strengthening. The hip extensors may also need to be strengthened and stretched. If the snap is at the front of the hip, various conditioning programs may be recommended. In some cases, experts recommend stretching then strengthening the hip flexors (Fitt, 1988, p. 312). In other situations, experts suggest stretching the outward rotators and strengthening the inward rotators, adductors, and extensors (Micheli, 1988, p. 204). Exercises to help with this conditioning work are recommended below.

Careful observation of the dancer's technique may reveal that subtle deviations in alignment are occurring simultaneously with the snap. For example, the anterior snap has sometimes been reported to be accompanied by a forward tilt of the pelvis (Clippenger-Robertson, 1985, p. 12). A program that combines strengthening the muscles controlling pelvic tilt along with correcting any other faulty technique may be the solution to this particular problem. Appropriate exercises to help correct a forward tilt of the pelvis are discussed in Chapter 17.

It has also been reported that the snap may occur in dancers with slightly uneven legs (Alter, 1986a, pp. 6–7). The snap is usually in the hip of the longer leg. A physician or podiatrist may suggest that a slight heel lift be added to the shoe of the shorter leg.

Related information can be found in Chapter 17, question 5.

Recommended exercises can be found in Chapter 15 to strengthen and stretch the hip flexors (15.C, 15.I); extensors (15.A, 15.G); abductors and inward rotators (15.D, 15.J, 15.M); and adductors (15.E, 15.K). Chapter 15 also presents a flexibility exercise for the outward rotators (15.L, 15M).

29. My hip hurts when it snaps. What should I do about it?

If a snapping hip causes pain, you should consult a physician. In some cases the snapping tendon can become irritated and tendonitis may develop. Underlying many tendons are bursa. Snapping tendons sometimes irritate the bursa, and the result is bursitis.

Some dancers develop a nervous habit of snapping the hip. Because this can eventually cause pain and further problems, dancers should avoid this practice.

30. I have heard that dancers often get arthritis in the hip. Why is this?

There are many forms of arthritis. Two forms are of particular interest to dancers. *Fibrositis syndrome,* which can occur in younger dancers, is thought to be related to improper training and joint overuse, as well as repeated stretching before the body has been properly warmed up. *Osteoarthritis,* usually occurring in older dancers, results from aging as well as overuse and abuse. This is the type of arthritis often found in the hip. In fact, arthritis of the hip occurs in older dancers more frequently than in the general population. Some experts suggest osteoarthritis may be caused by forcing turnout at the hip (Fitt, 1988, p. 62).

Male dancers suffer from osteoarthritis more than female dancers. This may be due to the fact that men usually start dance training later than women. Consequently, men may over work the hip in an effort to improve technique quickly.

Arthritis begins with a feeling of stiffness, ache, or loss of mobility in one of the joints. It can occur at any age. Dancers who have arthritis or suspect that they have it should see a physician. In addition, dancers with arthritis should monitor and correct their technique, pay particular attention to adequate warm-up, and avoid forced, painful positions.

31. I have known several dancers who have had either tendonitis or bursitis of the hip. Can this be prevented?

Tendonitis often occurs in the iliopsoas tendon and can be caused by tightness in the *iliopsoas* muscle and tendon unit. It is felt as a pain during performance of a *développé*. Flexibility exercises can help prevent tendonitis. Dancers who suspect they already have tendonitis of the hip should see a physician. Treatment for this condition may include medication to reduce the inflammation as well as special conditioning exercises to stretch and strengthen various muscles acting at the hip.

Bursitis is a serious problem in which the protective bursa of the hip joint become irritated by excessive muscular exertion. The lateral hip is one common site for bursitis. In this situation, the bursa found between the greater trochanter and the iliotibial band is irritated by excessive action of the iliotibial band. Another common location for bursitis is the anterior hip. In this case the bursa found between the anterior hip and the iliopsoas tendon is irritated by excessive action of the iliopsoas tendon. When either situation occurs, the bursa become inflamed and swell so that all movement at the hip is painful.

Bursitis can develop from inadequate warm-up, a sudden increase in the level of dance activity, returning to a full schedule of dance after lack of activity during a layoff, or poor technique. Once bursitis occurs, a physician should be consulted. Treatment may include physical therapy techniques such as ultrasound and hot packs along with conditioning the muscles affecting the area of irritation.

A recommended exercise can be found in Chapter 15 to stretch the hip flexors (15.I).

15

Strength and Flexibility Exercises

Note: Be sure to read Part II before performing these exercises.

15.A Strength Conditioning Exercise for the Knee Flexors and Hip Extensors

Equipment
Small pillow, or bath towel folded to make a small pillow.

Part 1.

Starting position
1. Begin front horizontal with a small pillow placed under your abdominals between your pelvis and your ribs. Place your arms in the right-angle position, your forehead on the floor, and your legs parallel.
2. Flex the working knee 90 degrees.

Action
1. Lift the working leg in parallel back *attitude*. Maintain a feeling of lengthening the leg as you lift it. Keep both hip bones on the floor (Figure 15.1).
2. Return to the starting position.
3. Complete all repetitions on the first side before changing sides.

Part 2.

Starting Position
1. Begin front horizontal as in Part 1, number 1.
2. Turn out both legs.
3. Flex the working knee so the leg is in a crossed *passé* position.

Action
1. Lift the working leg in turned-out back *attitude*. Maintain a feeling of lengthening the leg as you lift it. Keep both hip bones on the floor.
2. Return to the starting position.
3. Complete all repetitions on the first side before changing sides.

Part 3.

Starting position
Front horizontal as in Part 1, number 1.

Action
1. Lift the working leg in parallel *arabesque*. Maintain a feeling of lengthening the leg as you lift it. Keep both hip bones on the floor.

Figure 15.1 Performing part of the exercise to strengthen the knee flexors and hip extensors.

    2. Return to the starting position.
    3. Complete all repetitions on the first side before changing sides.

Part 4.

Starting position
    1. Begin front horizontal as in Part 1, number 1.
    2. Turn out both legs.

Action
    1. Lift the working leg in turned-out *arabesque*. Maintain a feeling of lengthening the leg as you lift it. Keep both hip bones on the floor.
    2. Return to the starting position.
    3. Complete all repetitions on the first side before changing sides.

Repetitions
    4 of each part.

Timing patterns
    A, B, C.

Increasing the difficulty
    Complete all parts on one side before changing sides. You can also add ankle weights. If there is any discomfort in the knee, place the ankle weight around the thigh, just above the knee. Adult dancers may want to work up to a ten-to-fifteen-pound weight resistance. As you strengthen the muscles around your knee, it will be helpful to keep in mind the recommended relationship in strength between your knee flexors and knee extensors. The strength in your knee flexors (hamstrings) should equal approximately 67 percent of the strength in your knee extensors (quadriceps). This is a ratio of 2 to 3, hamstrings to quadriceps. If you work up to a ten-pound resistance with your knee flexors in this exercise,

you will want to work up to fifteen-pounds resistance with your knee extensors in the strengthening exercise for that muscle group.

Comment
Ballet, modern, and jazz dancers should perform this exercise in both the parallel and turned-out leg positions. Working this way will help keep a balance of strength in the muscles that make up the knee flexor-hip extensor group. Remember that keeping a muscular balance will help maintain your range of motion and can help prevent injury.

Exercise 15.A adapted from: Arnheim (1985), p. 567; Barnes and Crutchfield (1971) p. 32; Daniels and Worthingham (1977), p. 85; Fitt (1988), p. 352; Howse and Hancock (1988), pp. 160–61; Kisner and Colby (1985), p. 339; Molnar (1987), p. 309; Roy and Irvin (1983), p. 351.

15.B Strength Conditioning Exercise for the Knee Extensors

Part 1.
Equipment
Chair or Bench.

Starting position
Sit and let your feet rest lightly on the floor. Both legs should be parallel and your torso should be held in good dance alignment.

Action
1. Completely straighten both knees, but do not lock them or hyperextend them (Figure 15.2a).
2. Return to the starting position.
3. Complete all repetitions of Part 1 before going further.

Part 2.
Starting position
Single-V horizontal.

Action
1. Raise your extended leg in parallel position until it reaches the mid-shin of your bent leg. Maintain a feeling of lengthening your leg as you lift it. Contract your abdominals to keep your lower back in contact with the floor (Figure 15.2b).
2. Return to the starting position.
3. Complete all repetitions on the first side before changing sides.

Part 3.
Starting Position
Single-V horizontal with the extended leg turned out.

Action
1. Raise the turned-out leg as in Part 2.
2. Return to the starting position.
3. Complete all repetitions on the first side before changing sides.

Figure 15.2 Performing part of the exercise to strengthen the knee extensors. **Dancer (a)** is on the bench. **Dancer (b)** is on the floor.

Repetitions
  8 of Part l; 4 of Parts 2 and 3.

Timing patterns
  A, B, C.

Increasing the difficulty
  Complete Parts 2 and 3 on the same leg before changing sides. You can also add ankle weights. Adult dancers may want to work up to a fifteen-to-twenty-pound weight resistance. As you strengthen the muscles around your knee, it will be helpful to keep in mind the recommended relationship in strength between your knee flexors and knee extensors. The strength in your knee flexors (hamstrings) should equal 67 percent of the strength in your knee extensors (quadriceps). This is a ratio of 2 to 3, hamstrings to quadriceps. If you work up to 15 pounds of weight resistance with your knee extensors in this exercise, you will want to work up to ten pounds with your knee flexors in the strengthening exercise for that muscle group.

Comment

Parts 2 and 3 of this exercise use the knee extensors in an isometric muscle action as they hold the knee straight while the hip flexes. This is what the knee extensors have to do whenever you lift a straight leg to *arabesque, grand battement* in any direction, or perform any other lifting movement with the leg held straight.

Exercise 15.B adapted from: Arnheim (1980), p. 107; Arnheim (1985), p. 567; Barnes and Crutchfield (1971), p. 29; Como, Ed., (1964), p. 42; Fitt (1988), p. 352; Hamilton (1978g), p. 85; Howse and Hancock (1988), pp. 154–55; Kisner and Colby (1985), p. 359; Roy and Irvin (1983), p. 350.

15.C Strength Conditioning Exercise for the Hip Flexors

Equipment
Chair

Part 1.

Starting position

1. Sit so your pelvis is tucked under. Your lower back will be slightly rounded and your weight will be directed toward your *coccyx,* or tail bone, rather than centered on the ischial tuberosities. This position is called a *posterior pelvic tilt.* Let your upper back lightly rest against the back of the chair. Your hands can rest on the sides of the chair seat.

2. Maintain a contraction of the abdominal muscles to stabilize the posterior pelvic tilt.

3. Both legs should be parallel, side by side, and your feet should rest on the floor.

Action

1. Flex one hip and bring the bent knee toward your clavicle, or collar bone, in a parallel front *attitude* position (Figure 15.3a).

2. Lower your leg until the back of your thigh lightly touches the chair seat.

3. Complete all repetitions on the first side before changing sides.

Part 2.

Starting position

1. Sit in the posterior pelvic tilt position as in Part 1.

2. Turn out both legs. Your feet will be in a turned-out first position.

Action

1. Flex one hip and lift the bent knee toward your clavicle in a turned-out front *attitude* position (Figure 15.3b).

2. Lower the leg until the back of your thigh lightly touches the chair seat.

3. Complete all repetitions on the first side before changing sides.

Part 3.

Starting Position

1. Sit in the posterior pelvic tilt as in Part 1.

2. Keep your legs parallel and open them as far as possible.

Figure 15.3 Performing part of the exercise to strengthen the hip flexors. **Dancer (a)** is on the left. **Dancer (b)** is on the right.

Action
  1. Flex one hip and bring the bent knee toward your shoulder in a parallel side *attitude* position.
  2. Lower the leg until the back of your thigh lightly touches the chair seat.
  3. Complete all repetitions on the first side before changing sides.

Part 4.

Starting position
  1. Sit in the posterior pelvic tilt with your legs apart, as in Part 3.
  2. Turn out both legs.

Action
  1. Flex one hip and lift the bent knee toward your shoulder in a turned-out side *attitude* position.
  2. Lower the leg until the back of your thigh lightly touches the chair seat.
  3. Complete all repetitions on the first side before changing sides.

Repetitions
  4 of each part.

Timing patterns
A, B, C.

Increasing the difficulty
You can perform these exercises on one side before changing sides. You can also add ankle weights. If ankle weights cause any discomfort in the knee, place the weights around your thigh, just above the knee.

Comments
If you find you are overusing the *rectus femoris,* (gripping your thigh muscle), you can increase the pelvic tilt and concentrate on relaxing the thigh muscle. You can also allow your lifted knee to bend a little more. When done correctly, this exercise will strengthen the hip flexors without overusing the *rectus femoris.*

Ballet, modern, and jazz dancers should perform this exercise in both the parallel and turned-out leg positions. Working this way will help maintain a balance of strength in the muscles involved, maintain range of motion, and can help to prevent injury.

Exercise 15.C adapted from: Clippenger-Robertson (1986), p. 10.

15.D   Strength Conditioning Exercise for the Hip Abductors and Internal Rotators

Starting position
1. Begin side horizontal.
2. Turn in the top leg as much as possible. Be sure this rotation comes from the hip. Do not sickle your foot and think you have turned in your leg.

Action
1. Raise the top leg as high as possible while maintaining the turned-in position (Figure 15.4a). If you allow your top leg to turn out, it will go higher, but you will not be strengthening the hip abductors and internal rotators. Maintain a feeling of lengthening the leg as you lift it.
2. Return to the starting position.
3. Complete all repetitions for the first side before changing sides.

Timing patterns
A, B, C.

Increasing the difficulty
Add ankle weights.

Exercise 15.D adapted from: Alter (1986b), p. 151; Arnheim (1980), p. 104; Arnheim; (1985), p. 604; Fitt (1988), p 334; Howse and Hancock (1988), pp. 158–59; Kisner and Colby (l985), p. 339; Roy and Irvin (1983), p. 350.

15.E   Strength Conditioning Exercise for the Hip Adductors

Equipment
Bench or chair.

Figure 15.4 **Dancer (a),** on the bench, is strengthening the hip abductors. **Dancer (b),** on the floor, is strengthening the hip adductors.

Optional Equipment
  Small pillow.

Starting position
  1. Begin side horizontal and let one leg rest on top of a bench or chair seat. You may want to put a small pillow under your leg. The other leg will extend underneath the bench or chair.
  2. Your body should be in a straight line and both legs should be parallel.

Action
  1. Lift the bottom leg. Maintain a feeling of lengthening the leg as you lift it (Figure 15.4b).
  2. Return to the starting position.
  3. Complete all repetitions on the first side before changing sides.

Timing patterns
  A, B, C.

Increasing the difficulty
  Add ankle weights.

Comment

If low chair rungs preclude raising and lowering the bottom leg, move the chair so it is across from your waistline. Rest the ankle of the top leg on the chair. Your top leg will be at right angles to your body. The bottom leg will be in a straight line with the body.

Exercise 15.E adapted from: Alter (1986b), pp.144–45; Arnheim (1980), p. l05; Arnheim (1985), p. 605; Fitt (1988), p. 334; Howse and Hancock (1988), pp. 156–58; Roy and Irvin (1983), p. 351.

15.F   Strength Conditioning Exercise for the Outward Rotators of the Hip

Starting Position

1. Begin side horizontal with the bottom leg extended.
2. Flex the hip and knee of the top leg and let the knee rest on the floor. The top leg will be in a parallel *passé* position (Figure 15.5a).

Action

1. Turn out the top leg until the knee reaches the turned-out *passé* position. For most dancers the knee will be pointing slightly forward into the diagonal, rather than pointing directly up to the ceiling. The toes of your working leg should be pointed and lightly touching the bottom leg at the knee (Figure 15.5b).

Figure 15.5 Strengthening the outward rotators of the hip. **Dancer (a)** is on the floor. **Dancer (b)** is on the bench.

2. Return to the starting position.

3. Complete all repetitions on the first side before changing sides.

Timing patterns
A, B, C.

Increasing the difficulty
Add weights. These should be placed around the thigh.

Exercise 15.F adapted from an interview with S. Anthony and M. Calitri, physical therapists, in June 1985. At the time of this interview, Ms. Anthony and Ms. Calitri were affiliated with the Center for Health and Sports Medicine of the National Hospital for Orthopaedics and Rehabilitation; Dowd (1984b), p. 100.

15.G Flexibility Exercise for the Knee Flexors and Hip Extensors

Equipment
Bench, or 2 or 3 chairs placed side by side to make a bench.

Starting Position
1. Sit at one end of the bench, facing the length of the bench.

2. Put one leg in front of you along the length of the bench. The foot of the opposite leg should be on the floor. Both legs should be parallel.

3. Bend forward at the hip and try to touch your pelvis to your thigh. Do not round your back. Keep your knee straight, but do not lock or hyperextend it.

Action
1. Hold the stretch (Figure 15.6). Feel the stretch along the back of your thigh and buttock.

2. Stretch the other side.

Comments
This exercise is to be used in addition to Exercise 15.M.

An adaptation of the flexibility exercise for the ankle dorsiflexors and the toe extensors (12.G) can be performed by some dancers at the same time they perform this exercise. Figure 15.7 illustrates this combination of exercises. Dancers with short arms should not try to combine these exercises if reaching the foot causes them to round their back.

Increasing the difficulty
Sometimes dancers have more flexibility in one hamstring muscle than in another. If there is a difference in flexibility, it may be beneficial to stretch the muscles individually. The medial hamstrings may be stretched along with the adductors in Exercise 15.K. The lateral hamstring may be stretched with the following exercise.

Flexibility Exercise for the Lateral Hamstrings

Starting Position
1. Begin single-V horizontal with your right leg extended and your left arm out to the side.

2. Flex your right hip approximately 90 degrees and inwardly rotate the right leg as much as possible.

Figure 15.6 Stretching the knee flexors and hip extensors.

3. Bring the right leg across the body as far as possible, maintaining inward rotation.

4. Use your right hand to help position the right leg.

Action

1. Hold the stretch position (Figure 15.8). Feel the stretch along the back of your thigh, on the lateral side.

2. Stretch the other side.

Exercise 15.G adapted from: Daniels and Worthingham (1977), p. 89; Fitt (1988), p. 353; Kisner and Colby (1985), p.333; Myers (1983a), p. 68.

15.H   Flexibility Exercise for the Knee Extensors

Equipment
   Barre or chair.

Starting position
   1. Use a *barre* or the back of a chair for balance.
   2. Standing with your legs parallel, flex your right knee and hold your right ankle behind your body with your right hand. Your right ankle

Figure 15.7 Combining exercises 12.G and 15.G.

must be in line with your right thigh, and your right knee should lightly touch or almost touch your left knee. Do not let your right hip flex.

3. Maintain a contraction of the abdominal muscles to prevent your back from over arching. Bend slightly forward from the waist if you need to.

Action
1. Hold the stretch (Figure 15.9a). Feel the stretch in the front of your thigh, between your knee and your hip.
2. If you are feeling an "angry" stretch because your arm is too short or your thigh is too tight, wrap a hand towel or leg warmer around your ankle and hold onto it.
3. Stretch the other side.

Increasing the difficulty
Pull your thigh further back. Do not pull the foot up until it touches the buttock. This can stress the knee joint.

Comment
Be careful as you move into the stretch position. It is possible to put stress on the medial part of the knee joint if you swing the lower leg out and up, grasp it, and pull it back into position. A good suggestion for safely assuming the stretch position is as follows: (1) bring your knee to your chest; (2) grasp your ankle as in (Figure 15.9b); and (3) move your

Figure 15.8 Stretching the lateral hamstrings.

knee down, back, and into position. Do not let the knee swing out to the side as you move into position.

Exercise 15.H adapted from: Alter, J. (1986b), p. 127; Arnheim (1980), p. 89; Arnheim (1985), p. 605; Fitt (1988), p. 342; Myers (1983a), p. 67; Ryan and Stephens (1988), p. 182; Sammarco (1987), p. 226.

15.I   Flexibility Exercise for the Hip Flexors

Equipment
   Table, bench, or firm bed.

Part 1.

Starting position
   1. Begin on a table, bench, or firm bed in the double-V horizontal position. Bring your knees up to your chest. Your hips should be at the edge of the supporting surface.
   2. Clasp your hands around one thigh and extend the other leg toward the floor. Keep the knee of the extended leg straight. If your lower back begins to arch and lose contact with the supporting surface, pull your thigh a little closer to your chest.
   3. If you do not have enough space to extend your leg beyond the end of the supporting surface, you can position yourself in the middle of the table, bench, or bed and let your leg hang off the side.

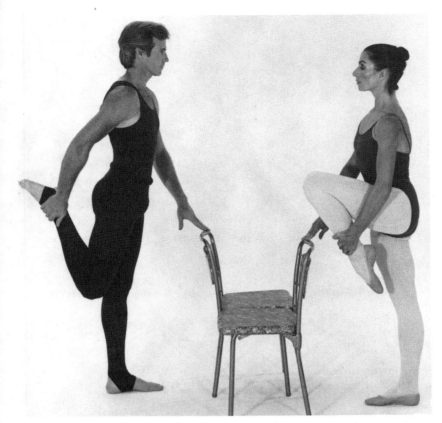

Figure 15.9 **Dancer (a),** on the left, is stretching the knee extensors. **Dancer (b),** on the right, is protecting the knee as she assumes the stretch position.

Action
1. Hold the stretch (Figure 15.10). Feel the stretch across the front of your hip socket.
2. Stretch the other side.

Part 2.
Starting Position
1. Begin as you did in Part 1, number 1.
2. Clasp your hands around one thigh and extend the other leg toward the floor. Let the knee of the extended leg bend. If your foot touches the floor, you need to work on a higher surface.

Action
1. Hold the stretch. Feel the stretch across the front of your thigh and hip socket.
2. Stretch the other side.

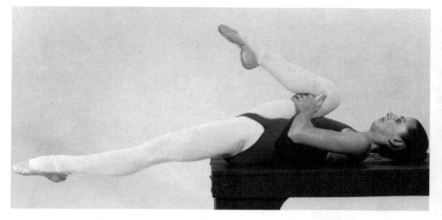

Figure 15.10 Performing part of the exercise to stretch the hip flexors.

Comment
   Part 1 stretches the *iliopsoas* muscle. Part 2 stretches the *rectus femoris*.

Exercise 15.I adapted from: Arnheim (1985), p. 642; Bachrach (1987), pp. 260–61; Kendall and McCreary (1983), p. 289; Kisner and Colby (1985), p. 331; Molnar (1987), p. 308; Roy and Irvin (l983), p. 285.

15.J   Flexibility Exercise for the Hip Abductors and Internal Rotators

Equipment
   Wall.

Starting Position
   1. Stand with your right side approximately one foot from the wall, and your weight on your right leg. Your right leg should be parallel and the knee straight.
   2. Rest your right hand and forearm on the wall. Your hand should be approximately head height.
   3. Cross your left leg in front of your right and lift the left heel. Shift part of your weight onto the ball of the left foot.
   4. Allow your right hip to lean toward the wall. Keep your right knee straight.

Action
   1. Hold the stretch position (Figure 15.11a). Feel the stretch along the right side of your body from your waistline to your upper thigh.
   2. Stretch the other side.

Comments
   You may need to adjust the position of the leg that crosses over in order to increase hip lean and stretch. Some dancers prefer to keep the crossed leg quite close to the straight leg, while others prefer to move the

Figure 15.11 **Dancer (a),** on the left, is stretching the hip abductors. **Dancer (b),** on the right, is stretching the hip adductors (with outward rotation).

crossed leg slightly forward. In some cases dancers find an increased stretch if they keep the crossed leg parallel rather than turned out. Others prefer to keep both legs side by side in parallel first position and not cross one leg over at all.

This exercise is to be used in addition to Exercise 15.M.

Exercise 15.J adapted from: Arnheim (1980), p. 96; Bachrach (1984).

15.K Flexibility Exercise for the Hip Adductors (with Outward Rotation)

Starting Position

1. Assume the double-V horizontal position and place your hands under your *sacrum,* one hand on top of the other. Bring your thighs toward your chest and straighten your knees.

2. Turn out your legs. Slowly and carefully open your legs.

Action

Hold the stretch (Figure 15.11b). Feel the stretch along your inner thighs, between your knee and hip.

Comment

This exercise also stretches the medial hamstrings. If you want to increase the stretch for these hamstring muscles, grasp your ankles and gently pull your legs down toward the floor.

Exercise 15.K adapted from an interview with S. Anthony and M. Calitri, physical therapists, in June 1985. At the time of this interview, Ms. Anthony and Ms. Calitri were affiliated with the Center for Health and Sports Medicine of the National Hospital for Orthopaedics and Rehabilitation; Benjamin (1980b), p.88; Daniels and Worthingham (1977), p. 87; Fitt (1988), p. 353; Kisner and Colby (1985), p. 334.

15.L   Flexibility Exercise for the Outward Rotators of the Hip

Starting position

1. Begin cross-sitting with your right ankle on top.

2. Continue to cross your legs until your right thigh is completely crossed over your left thigh. The sole of your right foot will be on the floor beside your left thigh, and your right hip will be off the floor. Your upper body and both knees will face the left-front diagonal.

3. Wrap your left arm around your right knee and thigh and pull your right thigh toward your chest.

4. Twist your upper body to face the right side while maintaining the relationship of your thigh to your chest.

5. Pull your right hip back and down until it touches the floor. It is important to pull your hip back as well as down. There should be some space between your right hip and your left heel.

Action

1. Hold the stretch (Figure 15.12). Feel the stretch across the lower portion of the buttock and deep inside the hip.

2. Cross your other leg on top and stretch the other side.

Figure 15.12 Stretching the outward rotators of the hip.

Comment

This exercise is to be used in addition to Exercise 15.M.

Exercise 15.L adapted from: Fitt (1988), p. 355.

15.M Flexibility Exercise for Some of the Hip Abductors, Extensors, and Outward Rotators

Starting Position

1. Cross-sit with your ankles directly in front of your midline.
2. Bend forward at your hip joints, keeping your back straight.
3. Adjust the space between your ankles and body to the position that provides the best stretch. Some dancers find a better stretch if they place their hands on the floor in front of them. Others prefer to place their hands beside their hips.

Action

1. Hold the stretch (Figure 15.13a). Feel the stretch across the top and lateral side of your buttock and thigh.
2. Cross the other ankle in front and stretch the other side.

Figure 15.13 Stretching some of the hip abductors, extensors, and outward rotators. **Dancer (a)** is on the bench. **Dancer (b)** is on the floor.

Increasing the difficulty

Turn your upper body to face each diagonal. You can also use the alternative exercise described below.

Comment

This exercise is to be used in addition to the other exercises that stretch the hip abductors, extensors, and outward rotators.

Alternative Flexibility Exercise for Some of the Hip Abductors, Extensors, and Outward Rotators

Starting Position

1. Begin cross-sitting, ankles directly in front of your midline.

2. Cross your thighs until the top knee rests as directly as possible over the bottom knee. Both knees should be in line with the center of your body.

3. Flex the ankle of the top leg.

4. Bend forward at your hip joints and allow your back to round over.

Action

1. Hold the stretch (Figure 15.13b). Feel the stretch across the top and lateral side of your buttock and thigh.

2. Cross the other leg on top and stretch the other side.

Increasing the difficulty

Turn your upper body to face the flexed foot.

Exercise 15.M adapted from: Alter (1986b), pp.115–16; Bachrach (1984).

PART

V

The Trunk and Neck

The neck is formed by the first seven bones in the spinal column, while the trunk is formed by the rest of the spinal column and the pelvis. Neck muscles are responsible for moving the head. Trunk muscles move the torso and are either directly or indirectly involved in all dance movement. No matter which movement you execute, trunk muscles will either produce the movement, or act to control, stabilize, or support it.

A strong trunk is a strong "center." When the spine and pelvis are correctly aligned, the muscles of the upper and lower extremities have a stable foundation from which to operate.

While it may be easy to see that you have weak ankles, knees, or arms, it is not so easy to determine weakness in the trunk. Of course, there are obvious weaknesses such as a sway back or depressed chest. Many times, however, a weak trunk will show up as an inability to execute a turn, a fall, a jump, or a leap. For this reason we recommend that every dancer incorporate conditioning exercises for the trunk into their workouts.

The head also plays an important role in dance movement. Correct head alignment contributes to the successful execution of many dance movements, and head position is often used choreographically to convey subtle expression. Unfortunately, the neck muscles that control movement of the head are often ignored in many warm-up sequences. Weak neck muscles are vulnerable to injury and unable to accurately control head alignment. The exercises in Chapter 18 will help to strengthen and stretch the muscles of the neck. Greater range of motion in this area can contribute to many aspects of dance performance.

16

The Major Muscles of the Trunk and Neck

The Structure of the Trunk and Neck

The main skeletal structure in the trunk and neck is the spine. The spinal column is made up of twenty-four vertebrae that are held together by a complex system of ligaments. These vertebrae can be classified into five categories: (1) *cervical;* (2) *thoracic;* (3) *lumbar;* (4) *sacral;* and (5) *coccyx* (Figure 16.1). The cervical vertebrae form the neck, while the other vertebrae form the trunk. The ribs articulate with the thoracic vertebrae, and the pelvis articulates with the *sacrum.*

The vertebrae in each category differ in shape and size. The smallest vertebrae are in the cervical region, and the larger vertebrae are in the lumbar region. The thoracic vertebrae are unique in the fact that they are attached to the ribs. Vertebrae in the sacral region differ greatly from those in the cervical, thoracic, and lumbar categories: these vertebrae have been "fused" together to form the *sacrum.*

Cartilage cushions called *intervertebral disks* separate the vertebrae in the cervical, thoracic, and lumbar areas of the spine. These cushions are made up of a rubber-like ring surrounding a jelly-like center. The intervertebral disks function as shock absorbers for the spine.

The pelvis serves as a link between the spine and legs. It makes up part of the hip joint and forms part of the trunk. The specific bones of the pelvis are discussed in Chapter 13.

Movements of the Trunk and Neck

Although the spine and pelvis are both part of the trunk, they can move independently of each other, and their movements are described differently. The spine is capable of *flexion* (bending of the spine forward), *extension* (return of the spine from the flexed position), *hyperextension* (backward bend of the spine beyond 180 degrees), *lateral flexion* (bending the spine to the side), and *rotation* (twisting of the spine).

The pelvis can tilt forward (*ilium* moves forward, *pubis* moves

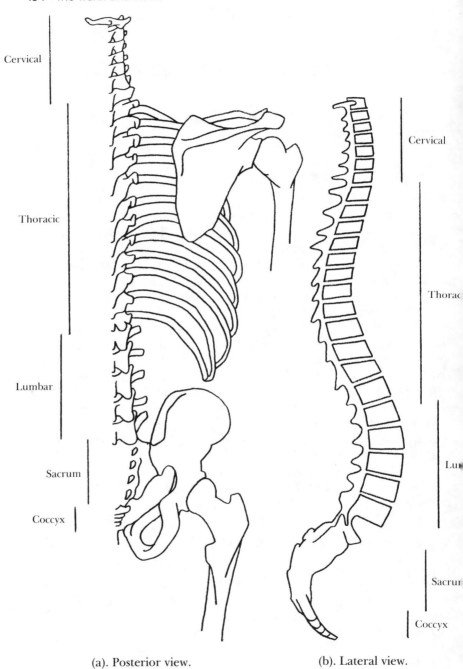

Cervical

Thoracic

Lumbar

Sacrum

Coccyx

Cervical

Thorac

Lu

Sacrur

Coccyx

(a). Posterior view.   (b). Lateral view.

Figure 16.1 Posterior and lateral views of the spine.

backward). Anatomically this is referred to as an *anterior pelvic tilt;* it is commonly referred to as "sticking the seat out." The pelvis can also tilt backward (*ilium* moves backward, *pubis* moves forward). Anatomically this is referred to as a *posterior pelvic tilt;* many dancers refer to this action as "tucking under." Finally, the pelvis can tilt laterally (*ilium* drops down on one side of the body and raises on the other side of the body). Anatomically this is referred to as *lateral pelvic tilt.*

Movements of the spine and pelvis often occur in combination. For example, an anterior pelvic tilt is usually accompanied by hyperextension of the spine. This combined movement is commonly referred to as "hyperextending" or "overarching" the back. Posterior and lateral pelvic tilts may also be accompanied by spinal action. A posterior pelvic tilt may be associated with flexion of the spine, while a lateral tilt of the pelvis may involve lateral flexion of the spine.

The neck, or cervical spine, can produce the same range of movement as the lower spine. It can flex, extend, hyperextend, laterally flex, and rotate.

Movement of the spine is controlled by muscles of the trunk and neck, while movement of the pelvis is controlled by trunk and hip muscles. The hip muscles are primarily responsible for tilting the pelvis anteriorly. The trunk muscles are primarily responsible for tilting the pelvis posteriorly. The muscles of both the hip and trunk are responsible for tilting the pelvis laterally.

The muscles that move the trunk and neck are generally *bilateral* (located on both sides of the body). When these bilateral pairs contract simultaneously, they produce either flexion, extension, or posterior pelvic tilt, depending upon the muscles involved. If the muscles on only one side of the trunk or neck contract, then lateral flexion is produced. When various muscles on the right side of the trunk contract simultaneously with various muscles on the left side, rotation is produced.

Anterior Pelvic Tilt
The primary muscles that tilt the pelvis forward are the *iliopsoas* and *pectineus*. These muscles also flex the hip. The are described in Chapter 13 with the other hip muscles.

Flexion of the Spine and Posterior Pelvic Tilt
There are four abdominal muscles, three of which serve to flex the spine and posteriorly tilt the pelvis. These muscles are the *rectus abdominis*, the *internal obliques*, and the *external obliques*. The abdominal muscles come into play primarily when the spine is being flexed from a lying down position, as in a sit-up. They are most active in the

beginning of the sit-up before the hips begin to flex. Once the hips flex, the abdominals serve to stabilize the pelvis.

The abdominal muscles are of particular importance to dancers because of their contribution to correct alignment. They are crucial in preventing a forward tilt of the pelvis and the resulting hyperextended or swayback posture problem.

There is some discussion among experts as to the role of the *psoas* muscle in producing movement of the lumbar spine. (Fitt, 1988, p. 183; and Luttgens & Wells, 1982, pp. 239–40.) In some situations the *psoas* is thought to flex the lumbar spine. In other situations it is thought to hyperextend the lumbar spine. This dual possibility is referred to as the *psoas paradox*. The *psoas,* part of the *iliopsoas* muscle, is discussed in Chapter 13 as one of the hip flexors (Figure 13.4).

The *rectus abdominis* muscle runs up the front of the body and can be easily palpated on the anterior surface of the abdomen near the midline (Figure 16.2). It is attached to the *pubic* bone on one end and, on the other, to the *sternum* and cartilage that connect some of the ribs to the *sternum.* The *rectus abdominis* is encased in a sheath, or envelope, of

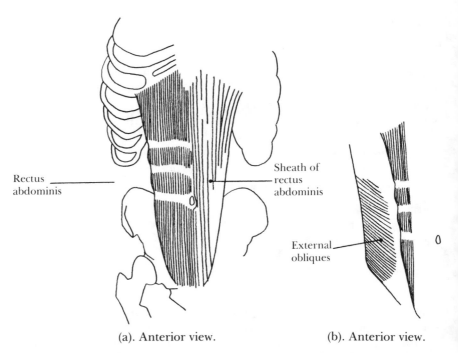

Rectus abdominis

Sheath of rectus abdominis

External obliques

0

(a). Anterior view.   (b). Anterior view.

Figure 16.2 Anterior view of trunk muscles; posterior view of trunk and neck muscles.

connective tissue called *fascia*. In addition to encasing the *rectus abdominis*, this envelope of fascia provides a place for the attachment of the other abdominal muscles.

Parts of the *external obliques* (Figure 16.2) are attached to the fascia of the *rectus abdominis*. Other parts are attached along the crest of the *ilium*. As a whole, the muscle runs diagonally upward and outward, and at the other end is attached laterally along the lower ribs. The *external obliques* may be palpated on the lateral side of the abdomen.

The *internal obliques* are attached to the crest of the *ilium*, and run diagonally upward and inward to attach to some of the ribs and fascia of the *rectus abdominis* (Figure 16.2). The *internal obliques* lie beneath the *external obliques*.

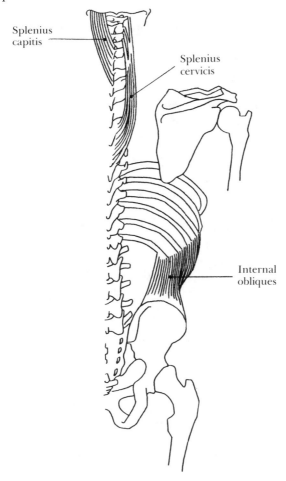

(c). Posterior view.

Extension and Hyperextension of the Spine

Although there are deep posterior muscles that contribute to the extension of the spine, the two major muscle groups responsible for this action are the *erector spinae* muscles and the *semispinalis* muscles. More specifically, it is the lumbar and thoracic portions of the *erector spinae* that work with the thoracic portions of the *semispinalis* to extend the spine.

These muscles are also active when the spine is hyperextended against resistance. An example of hyperextension against resistance occurs when you begin in the front horizontal position and then try to lift your chest off the floor.

The *erector spinae* is a complex muscle system illustrated in Figure 16.3. From its large attachment at the lumbar sacral region it branches as it moves upward with multiple attachments all along the ribs and vertebrae. A portion of this muscle can be palpated at the lower lumbar region on either side of the spine.

The *semispinalis* is another complex muscle system that runs along the thoracic and cervical vertebrae. It is composed of three sections: the *capitis, cervicis,* and *thoracis.* These muscles lie close to the vertebrae beneath the *erector spinae* (Figure 16.3).

Lateral Flexion of the Spine and Lateral Pelvic Tilt

Lateral flexion is brought about when the muscles on one side of the body contract. Many of the muscles involved in spinal flexion and extension are active during lateral flexion of the spine. When combined with muscles of the hip, they contribute to produce lateral pelvic tilt. The lateral flexors of the trunk include the *erector spinae,* the *internal* and *external obliques,* the *semispinalis thoracis,* the *rectus abdominis,* the deep posterior spinal muscles, and the *quadratus lumborum.* With the exception of the *quadratus lumborum,* all of the muscles have been described.

The *quadratus lumborum* is a relatively short back muscle attached at one end to the iliac crest and at the other end to the lower vertebrae (Figure 16.4).

Rotation of the Trunk

Rotation is brought about when certain muscles on one side of the trunk contract simultaneously with certain muscles on the other side. Muscles that produce rotation include the *internal* and *external obliques,* the thoracic and lumbar areas of the *erector spinae,* the *semispinalis,* and the deep posterior spinal muscles. All of these have been described previously.

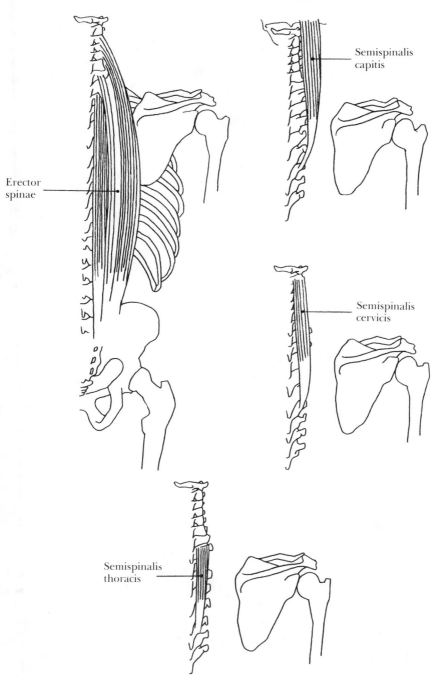

Figure 16.3 Posterior view of spinal muscles.

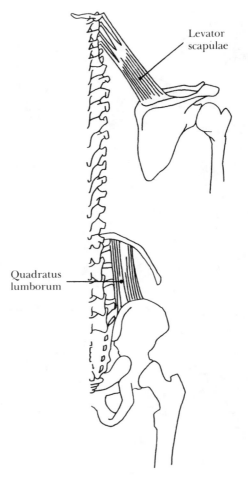

Figure 16.4 Posterior view of trunk and neck muscles.

Flexion of the Neck

The primary neck flexors are the *sternocleidomastoid* and the three *scalenes*. They are located on the anterior side of the spine.

The *sternocleidomastoid* has two heads, one attached to the *sternum* and the other to the *clavicle* (Figure 16.5). They come together and attach to the skull below and behind the ear. To feel these muscles in action, place your fingers on your neck, from the ear down to the center front of the neck, then flex your neck against resistance.

The *scalenus anterior, posterior, and medius* are attached at one end to one of the two upper ribs and at the other end to the cervical vertebrae (Figure 16.5). They are not easily palpated.

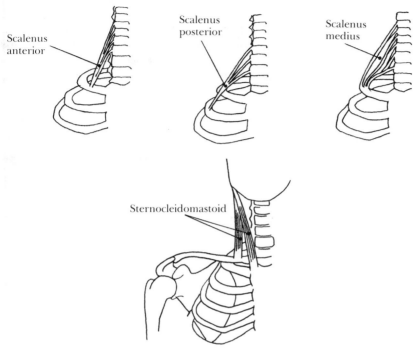

Figure 16.5 Anterior view of neck muscles.

Extension and Hyperextension of the Neck

Many muscles work together to produce extension of the neck. These include the *splenius capitis* and *cervicis,* the upper portions of the *erector spinae* and *semispinalis,* the *levator scapulae,* the deep posterior spinal muscles, and the *suboccipital* muscles. These muscles are also active whenever the neck is hyperextended against resistance. The *erector spinae* and *semispinalis* muscles have already been described, and the *levator scapulae* is illustrated in Figure 16.4. It will be further described in Part VI. The *suboccipitals,* like the deep posterior muscles will not be described in further detail. All of these muscles are located on the posterior side of the spine.

The *splenius capitis* is attached at one end to some of the thoracic and cervical vertebrae and at the other end to the skull (Figure 16.2). The *splenius cervicis* is also attached at one end to some of the thoracic vertebrae and at the other end to some of the cervical vertebrae (Figure 16.2). You can feel both these muscles in action by placing your fingers on the back of your neck, just behind the *sternocleidomastoid* muscle, while you extend the neck against resistance.

Lateral Flexion of the Neck

The primary muscles that produce lateral flexion have all been described. They are the *splenius capitis* and *cervicis*, the upper portions of the *erector spinae* and *semispinalis*, the three *scalenes*, and the *sterno- cleidomastoid*. Lateral flexion is produced when the muscles on one side of the neck contract.

Rotation of the Neck

The *sternocleidomastoid, splenius, erector spinae* and *suboccipital* muscles have all been discussed. They are all active in producing neck rotation.

17

Questions and Answers

Note: The questions and answers that follow concern improvement in technique and prevention of injuries to the trunk and neck.

1. What is the correct alignment of the spine and pelvis?

When viewed from the front or back, the properly aligned spine and pelvis will appear symmetrical. A plumb line should pass through the center of the head, chest, abdomen, and buttocks. The shoulders, shoulder blades, and hips will be horizontally level unless a structural deviation precludes this. Structural deviations include conditions such as a difference in leg length or a curvature in the spine.

When viewed from the side, a plumb line will fall through the ear lobe, through the center of the shoulder joint, and hip joint (Figure 17.1). The anterior superior iliac spines, or "hip bones," will be in the same vertical plane as the *symphysis pubis,* or juncture of the pubic bones. The spinal curves will also be apparent.

There are four natural curves in the spine (Figures 16.1 and 17.1). The forward curve in the neck is called the *cervical curve;* the backward curve in the middle back is called the *thoracic curve;* the forward curve in the lower back is called the *lumbar curve;* and the backward curve in the *sacrum* is called the *sacral curve.* These curves are formed by the architecture of the vertebrae and intervertebral disks. They strengthen the spine so it can support the body's weight.

Correct alignment of the spine involves maintaining the integrity of this curved architecture. As we go about daily living, the spinal curves are constantly being increased and decreased in order to allow movement to occur. When we look down at our feet we decrease the natural forward curve of the neck. If we look up at the ceiling we increase this curve. If we round over to pick something up, we increase the thoracic curve and decrease the lumbar curve. This kind of activity is in harmony with spinal structure.

Problems and injuries arise when permanent changes are made in the structure of the spinal curves. These changes are usually the result of postural deviations that become habitual, or are the result of repeated movements that weaken the spinal structure. Because the

Figure 17.1 Correct alignment of the spine.

body is a closed system, a permanent increase or decrease in one spinal curve will alter other curves in the spine as well as affecting other joints in the body.

2. *What happens if the spine is not properly aligned?*

When a spinal curve is permanently increased or decreased, the weight of the body is no longer transmitted through the centers of vertebrae and the intervertebral disks. Depending on the alignment problem, the weight of the body falls toward the front, back, or sides of the vertebrae.

This stresses the vertebrae and spinal ligaments. Improper alignment can also pinch the intervertebral disks, making them vulnerable to rupture and other injury. It can also irritate or injure the spinal nerves. The problem is compounded each time you jump and land with increased force on a structure that is improperly placed.

Incorrect alignment can also affect the spinal muscles. When curves are permanently changed, spinal muscles are stretched or contracted as they adjust to the improper alignment. This makes them less efficient and more vulnerable to injury.

One area of the spine, the lumbar curve, is particularly susceptible to injury. This is due to several factors. First, the accumulated weight of the head, cervical spine, shoulder girdle, arms, rib cage, and thoracic spine pass through the lumbar spine. When the dancer is partnering, the added weight of another body is transmitted to the lumbar spine. The lumbar spine is also vulnerable because it does not have the rib cage to help support its alignment, as does the thoracic spine. Finally, the joint between the fifth lumbar vertebrae and the *sacrum* is the site of a great deal of movement. Whenever you flex, extend, or hyperextend the spine, the lumbar-sacral joint is involved.

Injuries to the lumbar spine include a wide range of problems. This is the common site for disk herniations, stress fractures, and *vertebral subluxation* (partial sliding out of alignment). This area is also susceptible to muscle cramps, spasms, chronic aches, and ligament tears.

3. What are some of the most common spinal and pelvic alignment problems?

Some of the more common alignment problems seen in dance result from an increase or decrease in the natural lumbar curve. Figure 17.2a illustrates an increase in the lumbar curve. This postural deviation is often referred to as a hyperextended or "overarched" back. The medical term is *lordosis*. By looking carefully at the example you can see other alignment problems have occurred as a result. These include hyperextended knees, an anterior tilt of the pelvis, and a slightly forward chest and head.

Figure 17.2b illustrates another example of an increased lumbar curve. In this case the upper torso is leaning back, accentuating the lumbar curve. In an effort to compensate, the head is thrust forward, thus compounding the problem.

Figure 17.2c illustrates a postural problem related to "tucking under." In this case the posterior pelvic tilt is accompanied by a decrease in the lumbar curve. Note the resulting compensations in the knees and chest.

Other common alignment problems relate to the thoracic area of the

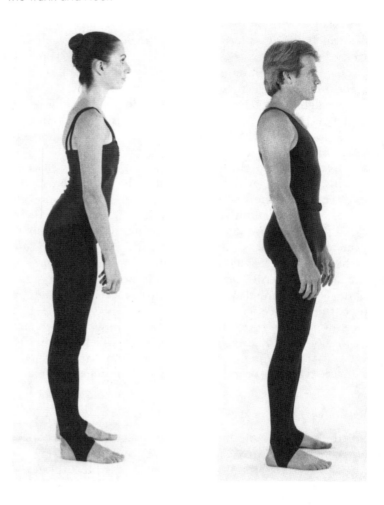

Dancer (a) is overarching her back.   **Dancer (b)** is leaning back.
Figure 17.2 Incorrect alignment of the spine.

spine. For example, increasing the thoracic curve rounds the back, brings the shoulders forward, and depresses the chest. This misalignment is commonly referred to as "round shoulders."

Another alignment problem in this area occurs when dancers incorrectly "pull-up" and push the ribs and chest forward. In Figure 17.2d the ribs and chest have caused the weight of the whole body to shift forward and the knees to hyperextend.

Dancer (c) is tucking the pelvis under.

Dancer (d) is pressing her ribs and chest forward.

It is important to identify and correct alignment problems as soon as possible. The longer the problem continues, the more difficult it will be to correct later on. In some cases, alignment problems that begin as muscular imbalances or incorrect postural habits cause structural changes that become permanent.

Related information may be found in the answers to questions 5–8, 22 and 23.

Figure 17.2 continued.

Dancer (e) is tilting the pelvis forward.

4. *If a student has several alignment problems, one affecting another, how do I know which one to correct first?*

When alignment problems involve several parts of the body, we suggest you work in one of two ways. Some people prefer to correct spinal alignment first. They believe that once the center of the body is correctly placed, it is easier to correct problems in the legs, arms, or head. Others recommend beginning with the feet and working up. They find that establishing a firm base of support at the feet facilitates changes in trunk, arm, and head alignment.

No matter which way you choose to work, it is critical that you remember to evaluate the entire body. Some problems are more easily recognized, others require more time and thought. Changes in torso alignment will never be completely successful if placement errors in the feet, ankles, arms, or head are left unrecognized. By the same token, problems in the feet and knees will not be satisfactorily resolved until errors in torso, arms, and head alignment are corrected.

It is also very important to remember that some alignment problems are structural in nature, and cannot be changed. Students with problems such as limited *demi-plié* due to bone structure, structural knock knees, differences in leg length, and so on, should not be expected to change these problems by "working harder." Instead, we suggest you help them make whatever technical adjustments are necessary to work safely within their anatomical parameters, and teach them to maintain a balance of strength and stretch in the surrounding musculature.

Related information can be found in the answers to questions 5–8, 22 and 23.

5. What is a hyperextended back, and can it be changed?

A hyperextended back is an increase in the lumbar curve of the spine usually accompanied by an anterior tilt of the pelvis (Figures 17.2a and e). It may be an acquired posture or may be due to a growth spurt. In this postural deviation, the trunk extensors and hip flexors are tight and the trunk flexors and hip extensors are weak. In some cases, the gluteals may be weak while the hamstrings are tight.

The hyperextended back places particular stress on the lumbar spine. This stress can precipitate serious problems in the lower back. These injuries were discussed in the answer to question 2, above.

A hyperextended back also hinders the successful performance of many dance movements. For example, it can limit leg extension to both the front and back, as well as making it impossible to correctly lift the turned-out leg to the side. Other accompanying alignment problems may make balancing, turning, and jumping more difficult.

Sometimes dancers intentionally assume an anterior pelvic tilt and hyperextended back posture in order to increase their turnout. Tilting the pelvis does relax the iliofemoral ligament at the front of the hip, and this results in a slight increase in turnout. Because of the many problems associated with this posture, however, it is not wise to try to improve turnout in this way. Chapter 14 contains a detailed discussion of turnout and alternative ways to improve it.

To help correct a hyperextended back and anterior pelvic tilt, it will be advantageous to strengthen the trunk flexors and stretch the trunk extensors. At the same time, the hip extensors should be strengthened and stretched, while the hip flexors should be stretched. Exercises to do this are listed below. Teachers may want to specifically recommend the flexibility exercises to students who are going through a growth spurt.

Related information can be found in questions 2 and 3, above, as well as question 6, and in question 24, Chapter 14.

Recommended exercises may be found in Chapter 15 to strengthen and stretch the hip extensors (15.A, 15.G). Chapter 15 also presents an exercise to stretch the hip flexors (15.I). Exercises may be found in Chapter 18 to strengthen and stretch the trunk flexors (18.A, 18.E). Chapter 18 also presents a flexibility exercise for the trunk extensors (18.F).

6. *As a teacher I want to be certain that I accurately identify an anterior pelvic tilt. Do I do this by looking for an exaggerated curve in the lower back?*

In evaluating an anterior pelvic tilt, it is important to remember that the natural curve in the lower back varies widely among individuals, as does the shape of the gluteal muscles. If the appearance of the lumbar curve is the only factor considered, it is possible to make mistakes in evaluating pelvic placement. The pelvis of someone whose natural curve is slightly greater than the "norm" may appear to be tilted, even though the spine and pelvis are correctly aligned for that body structure. The same is true of someone with large gluteal muscles. Large gluteal muscles can cause the lower back to appear hyperextended and the pelvis to appear incorrectly aligned.

Dancers with either of these anatomical structures should not be told to tuck in the pelvis and decrease the lumbar curve. While the visual result may be a more normal curve, they are changing their natural curve and stressing the integrity of their structure. This can lead to the series of injuries discussed in question 2, above.

There is another way of evaluating pelvic placement that can help safeguard against this error. This requires an assessment of the relationship between the "hip bones" and the symphysis pubis. Recall from the anatomy section that when the pelvis is correctly aligned, the anterior-superior spines, or "hip bones," are in the same vertical plane as the symphysis pubis. In an anterior pelvic tilt, the *ilium* is moved forward and the symphysis pubis is moved backward. As a result, the vertical plane through the anterior-superior spines is forward of the vertical plane through the symphysis pubis. Figure 17.2e illustrates this point.

Related information can be found in questions 2, 3, and 5.

7. *When my teacher says to "lift up" and stand up straight, my ribs stick out. I can't seem to lift up without sticking out my rib cage. Is there an exercise I could do to correct this?*

Recall from Chapter 16 the location and function of the trunk flexors and extensors. The trunk flexors are attached to the ribs and pelvis. When the pelvis is stationary, the trunk flexors act to pull down on the ribs. The thoracic attachment of the trunk extensors is such that a contraction of these muscles causes the ribs to lift and stick out. When a dancer pulls up correctly, the trunk flexors and extensors work in a balanced partnership. This gives the dancer a lifted or elongated appearance without projecting the ribs forward.

Some dancers find it difficult to lift up correctly. The problem begins when they attempt to lift up by contracting the trunk extensors alone. This causes the ribs to stick out. Their error is compounded if they try to correct the rib position by contracting the trunk flexors with a force greater than that of the trunk extensors. While this action pulls the ribs into better alignment, it leaves the dancer trapped in a tight corset of muscle contraction. Movement of the torso is inhibited and breathing is restricted.

A better solution is to lift up by using both the trunk flexors and extensors. Should the ribs still protrude, a partial relaxation of the trunk extensors will help. What is important is to restore a balance between the two muscle groups without excessive muscular tension. This balance permits a lift of the torso in addition to freedom of movement and ease in breathing.

If a dancer habitually stands with the ribs protruded, the trunk extensors can become shortened and tight while the trunk flexors become weak. When this happens, additional conditioning work is needed to restore a balance between the two muscle groups.

Recommended exercises may be found in Chapter 18 to strengthen and stretch the trunk flexors (18.A, 18.E). Chapter 18 also presents a flexibility exercise for the trunk extensors (18.F.).

8. *I have heard that it isn't good to "grip with the gluteals" or "tuck under the pelvis" in order to control turnout. Why is that?*

Numerous muscles work to control turnout. Some, like the six deep outward rotators or the adductors, are active in a variety of situations. Other muscles help with turnout on a more limited basis. The *gluteus maximus* acts as an outward rotator when the hip is extended. It does not contribute to turnout when the hip is flexed.

To strongly contract the gluteals to the point of tucking the pelvis under changes the lumbar curve, stresses the spine, and can lead to alignment problems in other parts of the body. Furthermore, it places too much importance on this one muscle group for turnout control. A better way to improve turnout is to work with all of the muscle groups that are active in outward rotation (see Chapter 14).

If a dancer has worked with the pelvis tucked under for a period of time, a muscle imbalance may have developed. In an exaggerated posterior pelvic tilt, the tight muscles are usually the hip extensors and trunk flexors. The weak muscles are the hip flexors and trunk extensors. Exercises to stretch and strengthen these muscles are listed below.

Related information may be found in Chapter 14, question 24.

Recommended exercises may be found in Chapter 15 to strengthen and stretch the hip flexors (15.C, 15.I). Chapter 15 also presents a flexibility exercise for the hip extensors (15.G). Exercises may be found in Chapter 18 to strengthen and stretch the trunk extensors (18.B, 18.F). Chapter 18 also presents a flexibility exercise for the trunk flexors (18.E).

Exercises that stretch the trunk flexors must necessarily hyperextend the back. There is some concern about the advisability of hyperextending the back and some discussion as to the safest way to do it. This matter is explained in question 10, below, which should be read before performing the exercise to stretch the trunk flexors.

9. *I have heard that bending back or a back* port de bras *can be dangerous. Why is that, and what is the correct way to bend back?*

When the back is arched, the curve primarily takes place in the cervical and lumbar regions of the spine. Recall from Chapter 16 that the cervical, thoracic, and lumbar vertebrae are shaped differently. The shape of the cervical and lumbar vertebrae permit hyperextension, while the anatomical structure of the thoracic vertebrae allow very little hyperextension to occur in the middle back. This limited hyperextension in the thoracic spine does not seem apparent when one first looks at a back *port de bras*. This is because the forward curve of the rib cage completes the visual line. In reality, however, an arched back primarily occurs in the cervical and lumbar regions of the spine.

When you bend back, it is important that the arch be properly controlled in order to protect the cervical and lumbar structures. Question 2, above, explains the vulnerability of the lumbar spine and some of the injuries that occur in that area. Bending back can stress the lumbar area if performed incorrectly. Incorrect technique can also stress the cervical vertebrae, disks, nerves, and ligaments.

Injuries to these areas can occur if the weight of the head or body is allowed to fall into the cervical and lumbar curves. To avoid injury to the cervical region, the head position should be controlled by the neck flexors in an eccentric muscle action. The head should appear to be an extension of the spine. It should not look as if it has fallen back. To avoid injury to the lumbar region, the position of the torso should be controlled by the trunk flexors in an eccentric muscle action. The torso should be "lifted" before starting to bend, and the "lift" should continue throughout the movement. This will keep the weight of the body from sinking into the lower back.

Some dancers cheat when they perform a back *port de bras.* Instead of using the trunk muscles, they achieve the arched appearance by tilting the pelvis forward. This cheating does not produce the proper line. Furthermore, it creates stress on the lower back, particularly the lumbar-sacral joint.

Recommended exercises may be found in Chapter 18 to strengthen and stretch the trunk flexors (18.A, 18.E), and the neck muscles (18.D: Parts 1 and 2; 18.H: Part 4).

10. I would like to be able to bend back further in back port de bras *and similar movements. How can I safely improve the arch in my back?*

First of all, it is important to realize that there are anatomical factors that ultimately determine hyperextension of the spine. These factors differ from one dancer to another and help to explain the wide range of back flexibility seen among dancers. Some of the structural factors that affect hyperextension include the shape of the vertebrae and disks as well as the laxity or looseness of the ligaments. Exercise cannot change an individual's spinal architecture.

Another factor that affects hyperextension is the strength and flexibility of the anterior trunk muscles. When you bend back, the trunk flexors function in an eccentric muscle action to produce the movement. This means they must be strong enough to control the movement and flexible enough to accommodate the hyperextended position. Conditioning these muscles will help improve the position of your back when you arch backwards.

Exercises that stretch the trunk flexors must necessarily hyperextend the spine. While hyperextension is a natural spinal movement, care must be taken to protect the vertebrae, disks, nerves, and ligaments from improper stress. As explained in question 9, above, the shape of the thoracic vertebrae limits hyperextension, while the shape of the lumbar vertebrae favors hyperextension. Because the lumbar spine is particularly susceptible to injury, it is important that hyperextension in that area be wisely controlled.

The flexibility exercise recommended below is designed to stretch the trunk flexor muscles safely and thereby increase hyperextension of the spine in most dancers. The exercise is presented in a series of graduated positions that offer dancers an opportunity to find the stretch most appropriate for them. The exercise should *not* be performed by any one with low back problems, nor should it be continued if there is any pain.

Recommended exercises may be found in Chapter 18 to strengthen and stretch the trunk flexors (18.A, 18.E).

11. What can I do to improve the line of my arabesque *and back* attitude?

When the leg is lifted to *arabesque* or back *attitude,* the spine is hyperextended. Question 10 discuses the structural limitations that determine hyperextension of the spine. These factors must be considered when evaluating the line of your *arabesque* or back *attitude.* Different dancers with different spinal anatomies will have different lines in *arabesque;* this does not mean you cannot improve the line of your *arabesque.* There are things you can do to improve within your anatomical parameters.

The first thing you must do to improve your line is to be certain you are working correctly. Incorrect technique in *arabesque* and back *attitude* not only distorts the line, but also accounts for many of the back injuries that occur in dancers. To protect the spine, it is important to avoid faulty placement of the upper torso and hip. The upper torso should be allowed to move or lean slightly forward. If it is held too straight and upright, the spine can be harmfully hyperextended and the disks may be pinched. The hip should not be lifted or allowed to twist. If the hip is allowed to twist, rotary forces can pinch the nerves and disks. To avoid this, the hip should be kept down, parallel with the shoulder.

Conditioning work can also help to improve your *arabesque* and back *attitude.* Exercises to strengthen the trunk extensors will help the position of the back. The trunk flexors should also be conditioned. They must be strong enough to maintain a lift in the front of the body and flexible enough to accommodate the hyperextended position. Properly conditioned muscles at the hip will also improve the position of the leg. Exercises for the muscle groups acting on the hip are discussed in Chapter 14.

Related information may be found in Chapter 14, question 19.

Recommended exercises may be found in Chapter 18 to strengthen and stretch the trunk flexors (18.A, 18.E) and extensors (18.B, 18.F).

12. When I try to sit with my legs apart in second position, I can't sit up straight. What can I do to improve the line of my back?

Sometimes the problem is due to bone structure and cannot be helped by exercise. Many times, however, the problem is due to tightness in the hip extensors and weakness in the trunk extensors. Chapter 14 discusses the role of the hip extensors in contributing to this problem. An exercise for the trunk extensors is recommended below.

Related information may be found in Chapter 14, question 20.

Recommended exercises may be found in Chapter 18 to strengthen and stretch the trunk extensors (18.B, 18.F).

13. What can I do to improve my knee hinge and back hinge fall?

In performing both the knee hinge and back hinge fall, you must be careful to protect the lower back. If the trunk muscles are weak, the back can hyperextend and cause stress to the lumbar spine. You should also review Chapter 14, where we discussed the importance of protecting the knee during these movements.

Related information may be found in Chapter 14, questions 4 and 9.

Recommended exercises may be found in Chapter 18 to strengthen and stretch the trunk flexors (18.A, 18.E).

14. In my modern dance and jazz classes we are learning front layouts (Figure 17.3) and back layouts (Figure 17.4). How can I improve my layout positions?

The front layout requires strong muscles in both the hip and torso. Chapter 14 discusses the hip conditioning exercises needed to improve the position of the lifted leg. The position of the torso is controlled by the trunk and hip extensors. The trunk muscles function in an isometric muscle action to maintain the position of the torso. They must be strong enough to hold the flat back position as the trunk leans forward. The hip extensors function in an eccentric muscle action as the hip flexes. These muscles must be strong enough to control the movement and flexible enough to accommodate the final stretched position. The exercises listed below should help improve your performance of the front layout.

In the back-layout position, the trunk flexors function in an eccentric muscle action to control the position of the torso. Strengthening these

Figure 17.3 Performing a front layout.

muscles will help you avoid overarching. It is also important to strengthen the neck flexors. These muscles function in an eccentric muscle action to control the head position. If they are weak, the head will fling back too far and the neck might be injured. Exercises to condition the trunk and neck muscles are listed below. Strategies to improve the forward leg position are discussed in Chapter 14.

Related information may be found in Chapter 14, question 18.

Recommended exercises may be found in Chapter 15 to strengthen and stretch the hip extensors (15.A, 15.G). Exercises may be found in Chapter 18 to strengthen and stretch the trunk flexors (18.A, 18.E), trunk extensors (18.B, 18.F), and neck flexors (18.D: Parts 1 and 2; 18.H: Part 4).

15. *When I stand on one leg, my weight sinks into the standing hip. What will improve the position of my pelvis?*

When you stand on one leg, the hip abductors control the position of the pelvis on the supporting leg. Other muscles control the position of the pelvis on the nonsupported side. These muscles are the lateral trunk flexors. Recall from Chapter 16 that some of the lateral trunk

Figure 17.4 Performing a back layout.

flexors connect the pelvis with the ribs and/or lower vertebrae. When the ribs and vertebrae are held steady, these lateral trunk flexors can pull up on the pelvis and help to position it correctly.

If you sink in the standing hip, strengthening the hip abductors and lateral trunk flexors may help. Chapter 14 recommends exercises for the hip abductors. Exercises to condition the lateral trunk flexors are listed below.

Related information may be found in Chapter 14, question 26.

Recommended exercises may be found in Chapter 18 to strengthen and stretch the lateral trunk flexors (18.C, 18.G).

16. *In my modern and jazz classes, we often perform side tilts, laterals, and other movements in which the torso leans away from the midline of the body. How can I improve my line in these positions?*

Leaning the torso away from the midline requires the lateral flexors of the trunk to work in an eccentric muscle action. This means they must be flexible enough to lengthen and strong enough to exert controlling force.

Recommended exercises may be found in Chapter 18 to strengthen and stretch the lateral trunk flexors (18.C, 18.G).

17. What is the best exercise to strengthen the abdominal muscles? I have heard that both sit-ups and double leg raises are best. Which is correct?

Partial sit-ups are the best exercise for the abdominal muscles. In the initial stages of the sit-up, the abdominal muscles are active in flexing the spine. In the last part of a full sit-up, the hip flexors act as the primary movers and the abdominals act as stabilizers. Performing only the first part of the sit-up gives you maximum abdominal activity. If you twist the body while doing this partial sit-up then you will also strengthen the oblique abdominal muscles.

Sit-ups should be performed with the legs bent, because the hip flexors show greater activity in the straight leg sit-up position. In addition, there is evidence to show that straight leg sit-ups can increase the lumbar curve of the spine, thereby placing too much stress on the lower back.

Double leg raises should not be performed by most people, because of possible harm to the lower spine. Double leg raises usually cause the lower back to hyperextend, unless the person performing them already has very strong abdominal muscles. This stresses the lower back and can lead to injury.

Recommended exercises may be found in Chapter 18 to strengthen and stretch the trunk flexors (18.A, 18.E).

18. Can a stress fracture occur in the spine?

Yes. This condition, called *spondylolysis,* occurs most often in the forth and fifth lumbar vertebrae. Spondylolysis is more common in dancers and gymnasts than in the general public. Some experts believe it may be caused by repetitive flexion and extension of the spine. Others believe the problem may be precipitated by weak abdominals and hyperextended posture. In either case, dancers are cautioned against hyperextending the back in order to increase turnout.

Spondylolysis is often identified by chronic low back pain especially on one side of the spine. This pain becomes acute when executing a back *arabesque* or *attitude* on the injured side. The treatment for this condition usually includes rest and possible immobilization. After the stress fracture is healed, a conditioning program to strengthen the abdominals is usually recommended along with exercises to correct any other muscular imbalances.

If a stress fracture is bilateral and goes untreated, other complications can result. One problem is vertebral subluxation, or partial sliding out of place of a vertebra, a condition called *spondylolisthesis*. Sometimes the fifth lumbar vertebra slides forward on the *sacrum*. At other times the fourth lumbar vertebra slides forward over the fifth lumbar vertebrae. If you suspect that you have a stress fracture of the spine, you should see a physician as soon as possible.

19. What is scoliosis?

Scoliosis is a serious postural deviation that requires medical attention. In the majority of cases the cause is unknown; however, dancers with a parent or sibling with scoliosis are at increased risk. If the spine is affected by scoliosis, the vertebrae do not fall in a straight line. When viewed from the back, they form either a simple curve that resembles the letter C, or a more complex curve that resembles the letter S. If the condition is noticed soon enough, it may be stopped or slowed from progressing further.

Generally speaking, scoliosis produces bilateral asymmetry. The result can often be seen in a series of postural deviations such as an uneven horizontal line in the shoulders, shoulder blades, and uneven arm hang. Deviations in leg length are also associated with scoliosis. It should be noted, however, that almost everyone has a slight degree of asymmetry, sometimes owing to the dominance of one hand and overuse of the muscles on the dominant side. These deviations should not be confused with scoliosis. The asymmetry caused by scoliosis is far more pronounced.

Dance teachers are in an excellent position to check for the possible beginning of scoliosis. One way to check for this problem is to have the dancer bend over so the head is in line with the knees and the arms hang freely. The teacher can then look to see if the vertebrae fall in a straight line. In addition, the teacher should look at the back to see if both sides of the spine appear equal. If one shoulder blade is more pronounced, if the rib cage looks higher on one side, or if the muscles of the lumbar spine are more developed on one side, the dancer should consult a medical professional for further evaluation.

20. How can male dancers prevent back injuries that result from lifting their partners?

Correct alignment of the spine is critical in partnering. The most common error is to have the back in a hyperextended position while lifting. When this happens, the full weight of the partner is transmitted to the already stressed lower back.

Lifting with the back in hyperextension can cause one of the more serious back injuries, the *herniated disk*. When the spine is out of alignment, the disks can become pinched between the adjacent vertebrae. The added weight of the partner can create enough force to rupture the outside ring of one of the disks. If the jelly-like center protrudes through the break, it can press on spinal nerves and cause further complications. The conditioning exercises recommended in the answer to question 5, above, will help correct hyperextension and help to protect the back from hyperextending in partnering situations.

In addition to correct alignment, another protection for the back is to develop strength and flexibility in the upper torso, shoulders, and arms. Dance technique classes usually concentrate on building strength in the legs but do not generally develop sufficient upper body strength for partnering. In Chapters 20–23, we discuss conditioning exercises to prepare the shoulder girdle and arms for partnering work.

Partnering is a complex skill that depends on proper timing. In many instances, the timing can be off and the lift can "go wrong." When this happens, the man is usually responsible for saving the situation. This not only calls for additional strength, but can demand additional flexibility of many muscle groups. To cope safely with these situations, the total body must be both strong and flexible. We recommend that dancers involved in partnering follow a conditioning program designed to develop strength and flexibility throughout the entire body. In Part VII, programs to achieve this goal are discussed.

Related information can be found in question 5, above, and in question 10, in Chapter 20. See also Part VII.

21. My back always aches after dance class. Should I be concerned about this?

While some degree of muscle fatigue is common after a strenuous class, it is not wise to accept repeated pain in the same area of the body. If your lower back aches, you should speak with your teacher or see a physician. Ask your teacher to help you assess your posture. It is not always possible for dancers to see alignment problems that occur as they are moving. Sometimes a dancer will be correctly placed during the warm-up or *barre*, but slip into an incorrect alignment when dancing more complicated movement sequences. Your teacher can help you identify this problem.

In addition to working with your teacher to identify possible problems in technique, you should also consider seeking medical advice. Many serious injuries start with chronic back ache as the first warning sign. Pain is something to be evaluated and alleviated, not ignored.

22. When I try to stand in correct alignment, my shoulders round forward. What can I do?

In some cases round shoulders may be caused by structural increase in the throacic curve known as *kyphosis*. As a result, the upper back and shoulders appear unusually rounded. Conditioning exercises will not correct this problem.

Round shoulders may also be caused by a muscular imbalance. When this is the case, conditioning exercises for the trunk and shoulder girdle muscles can help solve the problem. Exercises to strengthen and stretch the trunk extensor muscles are recommended below. Chapter 20 discusses the shoulder girdle and the muscles that need to be strengthened and stretched along with conditioning the trunk extensors.

Related information can be found in Chapter 20, question 4.

Recommended exercises may be found in Chapter 18 to strengthen and stretch the trunk extensors (18.B, 18.F).

23. I have noticed that some of the students in my dance class have a forward head. Can I recommend exercises to correct this?

The position of the head is controlled by a complex coordination of neck flexor and extensor muscles. A forward head is usually associated with tightness in the neck flexors and weakness in the neck extensors. Correcting this problem calls for restoring a balance of strength and flexibility in both muscle groups. Exercises to condition these muscles are listed below.

A forward head is often associated with other alignment problems. These include carrying the arms too far back in second position and hyperextending the back. Correcting these problems will also help to improve head alignment.

Recommended exercises can be found in Chapter 18 to strengthen and stretch the neck muscles (18.D: Part 4, 18.H).

24. My neck muscles hurt after performing several head rolls. What can I do about this problem?

The head, which weighs about fifteen-to-twenty pounds, is heavier than many people realize. It is possible to pinch disks and nerves as well as stress ligaments and muscles if you fling your head or let it drop too far in any direction. Particular care should be taken when the head rolls toward the back. If you tip your head back and find it difficult to talk, or if you feel tingles or a sensation of pins and needles, you have allowed the head to go too far.

Strong and flexible neck muscles are needed to control head movements like spotting when you turn, as well as head circles or head rolls.

Recommend exercises can be found in Chapter 18 to strengthen and stretch the neck muscles (18.D, 18.H).

18

Strength and Flexibility Exercises

Note: Be sure to read Part II before performing any of the following exercises.

18.A Strength Conditioning Exercise for the Trunk Flexors

Optional equipment

Towel or small pillow to place under your pelvis if your sacral bones press uncomfortably against the floor during this exercise.

Part 1.

Starting position

1. Begin double-V horizontal.
2. Pull your abdominal muscles in and up so that your lower back is pressed flat against the floor. This position is called the *posterior pelvic tilt.* Do not perform the posterior pelvic tilt by pinching your buttocks together and lifting the pelvis off the floor. Do not push your feet against the floor in order to tilt the pelvis and flatten your back. If you correctly use your abdominal muscles, the abdominal area will feel scooped out. Your lower back will be pressed into the floor, and your buttocks will be in contact with the floor (Figure 18.1a)

Action

1. Curl your head forward so your chin is close to your chest. Do not force it to touch your chest.
2. Reach forward with your hands and curl your torso forward and up (Figure 18.1b). Continue to curl up until your shoulder blades and rib cage no longer touch the floor. Stop curling up before your waistline comes off the floor. (If you curl up further, your hip flexors will be doing most of the work). Your feet should remain in contact with the floor.
3. Uncurl until your upper back comes in contact with the floor. Maintain your head and arm positions. Try to touch each vertebra individually as you roll back down.
4. Complete all repetitions for Part 1 before going further.

Part 2.

Starting positions

1. Begin double-V horizontal with a posterior pelvic tilt and head lift as in Part 1.
2. Turn your upper torso to face the right diagonal. Let your hands reach to the right front diagonal.

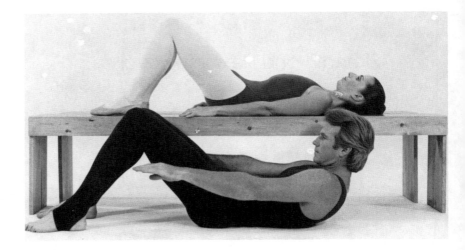

Dancer (a) is on the bench. **Dancer (b)** is on the floor.

Dancer (c).

Figure 18.1 Performing part of the exercise to strengthen the trunk flexors.

Action

1. Curl your torso forward and up toward the right diagonal. Continue to curl up until your right shoulder blade and the right side of your rib cage no longer touch the floor. Stop curling up before the right side of your waistline comes off the floor. Your feet should stay in contact with the floor.

2. Uncurl until the right side of your upper back comes in contact with the floor. Maintain your head and arm positions.

3. Complete all repetitions on the first side before changing sides.

Part 3.

Starting position

1. Begin double-V horizontal with pelvic tilt and hips flexed approximately 90 degrees.

2. Extend the right leg until the knee is straight. The right foot should be slightly off the floor (Figure 18.1c).

Action

1. Exchange leg positions so the left leg is extended and the right hip is flexed approximately 90 degrees. Maintain the pelvic tilt so your lower back is in contact with the floor during the movement.

2. Continue to exchange leg positions until you complete all repetitions for this part of the exercise. One repetition consists of extending the right leg then extending the left leg.

3. If you cannot maintain the pelvic tilt position and your lower back arches during the leg exchanges, increase the distance between the extended leg and the floor. As you gain strength, you will be able to lower the extended leg closer to the floor and keep your back in contact with the floor.

Repetitions
4 of Parts 1 and 2; 8 of Part 3.

Timing patterns
A, B, C.

Increasing the difficulty for Parts 1 and 2

Change the positions of your arms. The following list progresses from the easiest position to the most difficult:

1. Arms at your sides and reaching forward or toward a front diagonal while you are curling up.

2. Arms across your chest.

3. Hands clasped back of your head, elbows pointing forward. Do not let your elbows go out to the side and then swing forward to help you come up.

Increasing the difficulty for Part 3

Lower the extended leg so it is closer to the floor. Be certain to maintain the pelvic tilt. It is also possible to add ankle weights. If you feel any stress on the knee, place the ankle weights above the knee.

Comment

Parts 1 and 2 primarily strengthen the upper abdominal muscles, while Part 3 strengthens the lower abdominal muscles. In Part 3 the lower abdominal muscles perform an isometric muscle action to hold the trunk in place while the legs move. This is the way these muscles are used whenever you are standing and do a *développé, grand battement,* or even a *tendu.*

Exercise 18.A adapted from: Arnheim (1980), p. 109; Arnheim (1985) p. 643; Como, Ed. (1966), pp. 38, 40, 44; Daniels and Worthingham (1977), p. 54–5; Fitt (1988), p. 333; Hobby and Hoffmaster (1986), p. 39; Howse and Hancock (1988), pp. 146–47; Kendall and McCreary (1983), p. 220; Kisner and Colby (1985), pp. 443–46; Roy and Irvin (1983), p. 282; Ryan and Stephens (1988), p. 171.

18.B   Strength Conditioning Exercise for the Trunk Extensors

Equipment
Small pillow or bath towel folded to make a small pillow.

Starting position
Front horizontal, forehead on the floor, and a small pillow placed under the abdominals between your pelvis and your ribs.

Action
1. Lift your upper torso at the same time you maintain the relationship of your chin to your chest. Do not let your head tip back in an effort to help you come up. If you do this movement correctly, your head will be an extension of the spine, and you will be looking at the floor, not the wall.
2. Rotate your torso to the right (Figure 18.2a). Keep the right hip bone on the floor.
3. Return to the starting position by rotating the torso back to the center position, then lowering the torso.
4. Rotate the torso to the left on the next repetition.

Timing pattern
D.

Increasing the difficulty
Change the positions of your arms. The following list progresses from the easiest position to the most difficult:

1. Arms at your sides.
2. Arms in the right-angle position.
3. Hands clasped back of your head.
4. Arms in diagonal fifth position.

Exercise 18.B adapted from: Arnheim (1980), p. 112; Barnes and Crutchfield (1971), pp. 41–42; Fitt (1988), p. 332; Hobby and Hoffmaster (1986); p. 37; Howse and Hancock (1988), pp. 148–51; Kisner and Colby (1985), p. 441; Ryan and Stephens (1988), p. 172.

8.C   Strength Conditioning Exercise for the Lateral Trunk Flexors

Starting position
Stand in good dance alignment, legs in parallel first or second position, arms at your sides.

Action
1. Lift up through your torso and maintain that lift as you lean as far as possible to one side (Figure 18.2b). Reach out with your arms and be sure your shoulder stays directly in line with your hip. Do not let your torso twist, ribs stick out, or back hyperextend. Do not let your hips shift to one side.
2. Return to the starting position.
3. Complete all repetitions on the first side before changing sides.

Figure 18.2 **Dancer (a),** on the floor, is strengthening the trunk extensors. **Dancer (b),** standing, is strengthening the lateral flexors of the trunk.

Timing Pattern
   B.

Increasing the difficulty
   Add wrist weights.

Exercise 18.C adapted from an interview with S. Anthony, physical therapist, November 1987. At the time of this interview, Ms. Anthony was affiliated with the National Center for Sports Medicine; Howse and Hancock (1988), pp 152–53.

18.D   Strength Conditioning Exercise for the Neck Flexors, Lateral Flexors, Extensors, and Rotators

Equipment
   Small pillow or bath towel folded to make a small pillow.

Part 1.
Starting position
   Double-V horizontal.

Action
   1. Raise your head by pulling your chin toward your *sternum*. Do not force the chin to touch the chest (Figure 18.3a).
   2. Return to the starting position by trying to touch the back of your neck to the floor before the back of your head.
   3. Complete all repetitions of Part 1 before going further.

Part 2.
Starting position
   Double-V horizontal with your head turned so you can see your right underarm.

Action
   1. Bring your face toward your right underarm. Do not force your chin to touch your chest (Figure 18.3b).
   2. Return to the starting position. Try to touch the back of your neck to the floor before the back of your head.
   3. Complete all repetitions on the first side before changing sides.

Part 3.
Starting position
   Side horizontal on your right side. Your right arm should be straight.

Action
   1. Raise your head by pulling your left ear toward your left shoulder. Do not hunch your left shoulder or let your head turn (Figure 18.3c).
   2. Return to the starting position.
   3. Complete all repetitions on the first side before changing sides.

Dancer (a) is on the bench. **Dancer (b)** is on the floor.

Dancer (c) is on the bench. **Dancer (d)** is on the floor.

Figure 18.3 Strengthening the neck muscles.

Part 4.

Starting position

Front horizontal, forehead on the floor, and a small pillow placed under your abdominals, between your pelvis and your ribs.

Action

1. Raise your forehead slightly off the floor, keeping your chin tucked in. You should be looking at the floor (Figure 18.3d). If you raise your forehead incorrectly by tilting your head back, your chin will lift and you will be able to see the wall.

2. Turn your head to the right. Keep your chin tucked in.

3. Return to the starting position by turning the head back to the center, then lowering it to the floor.

4. Turn your head to the left on the next repetition.

Repetitions
4 of Parts 1 and 2; 8 of Part 3; 16 of Part 4.

Timing patterns
A, B, C for Parts 1–3; D for Part 4.

Exercise 18.D adapted from: Alter (1986b), pp. 34–37; Daniels and Worthingham (1977), p. 64; Kisner and Colby (1985), p. 441.

18.E   Flexibility Exercise for the Trunk Flexors and Hyperextension of the Spine

Starting position:
1. Begin front horizontal with your forehead on the floor.

2. Place your hands up by your ears and let your forearms rest on the floor close by your shoulders.

3. Lift your chest off the floor. Move your forearms toward the midline until they are under your shoulders and can comfortably support your weight. Look up, but do not let your head tip back so far that you are looking directly up at the ceiling.

Figure 18.4 Stretching the trunk flexors. **Dancer (a)** is on the bench. **Dancer (b)** is on the floor.

4. Use the abdominal muscles so your weight does not sink into the lower back.

Action

Hold the stretch (Figure 18.4a). Feel the stretch along the front of the body between the *sternum* and *pubic* bone. Many people feel compression, but not pain, in the back.

Increasing the difficulty

Straighten your elbows, but do not let your thighs lose contact with the floor. You can walk your hands slightly forward if you need to (Figure 18.4b.) The difficulty can be further increased by walking your hands in, toward your chest, until they are under your shoulders. Your upper thighs should not lose contact with the floor.

Comment

Read the discussion following question 10 in Chapter 17 before you perform this exercise. It explains this stretch and who should do it. Do not do this exercise if you have any low back problems, and stop the exercise if you feel any pain in your back.

Exercise 18.E adapted from: Gelabert (1986), pp. 185–86; Hobby and Hoffmaster (1986), p. 37; Kisner and Colby (1985), p. 438; Ryan and Stephens (1988), p. 172.

18.F   Flexibility Exercise for the Trunk Extensors

Starting position

1. Begin L-sitting and grasp your right ankle with your left hand.
2. Cross your right arm over your left and reach toward your left foot.
3. Let your back round over.
4. Pull your right hip back, increasing the distance between your left foot and your right buttock. Your upper torso may twist slightly to the right.

Action

1. Hold the stretch (Figure 18.5a). Feel the stretch across the right side of your back from your shoulder to your hip.
2. Stretch the other side.

Comment

If you cannot keep your knees straight, it is all right to let them bend slightly. If your lower back is particularly tight, you may need to first stretch that area with a less strenuous exercise. One way to do this is to begin in the double-V horizontal position. Bring your thighs toward your chest. Your knees will remain flexed. Clasp your hands around the backs of your thighs and pull your legs toward your chest. Hold that stretch position.

Exercise 18.F adapted from an interview with S. Anthony, physical therapist, in November 1987. At the time of this interview, Ms. Anthony was affiliated with the National Center for Sports Medicine.

Figure 18.5 **Dancer (a),** on the left, is stretching the trunk extensors. **Dancer (b),** on the right, is stretching the lateral flexors of the trunk.

18.G Flexibility Exercise for the Lateral Flexors of the Trunk

Starting position
1. Begin back horizontal with your arms in fifth position.
2. Keep your left buttock in contact with the floor as you move your feet and hands as far to the right as possible. Your body position will resemble the letter *C*.
3. Grasp your left wrist with your right hand and gently pull toward the right side.
4. Flex your right hip and knee until they reach the turned-out *passé* position. Let the right leg relax on the floor.

Action
1. Hold the stretch (Figure 18.5b). Feel the stretch along the left side of your body, from your ribs to your upper thigh.
2. Stretch the other side.

Exercise 18.G adapted from: Fitt (1988), p. 335.

18.H Flexibility Exercise for the Neck Flexors, Lateral Flexors, Extensors, and Rotators

Equipment
Chair or bench, thick bath or hand towel.

Part 1.

Starting position
   1. Sit with your left hand at your side or relaxed in your lap.
   2. Grasp the crown of your head with your right hand. Your right elbow will be pointing forward.
   3. Carefully and slowly pull your head forward and down. Do not force your chin to touch your chest.

Action
   Hold the stretch (Figure 18.6a). Feel the stretch along the back of your neck and upper back. Some people feel the stretch from the base of their skull to their shoulder blades; others feel the stretch continue further down the back.

Part 2.

Starting position
   1. Sit and hold the left edge of the seat with your left hand.
   2. Turn your head to face the right diagonal.
   3. Grasp the crown of your head with your right hand. Your right elbow will point to the right diagonal.
   4. Carefully and slowly pull your head forward and down. Your chin will move toward your right underarm. Do not force your chin to touch your chest. Do not let the left shoulder pull up.

Action
   1. Hold the stretch (Figure 18.6b). Feel the stretch along the back of your neck and upper back, just to the left of your spine. Some people feel the stretch extend from their ears to their shoulder blades; others feel the stretch continue further down their back.
   2. Stretch the other side.

Part 3.

Starting position
   1. Sit and hold the left edge of the seat with your left hand.
   2. Lift your right arm over the top of your head and grasp the top of your left ear with your right hand. Your right elbow will be pointing to the right side.
   3. Carefully and slowly pull your head to the right. Do not let your left shoulder pull up.

Action
   1. Hold the stretch (Figure 18.6c). Feel the stretch along the left side of your neck from your ear to your shoulder.
   2. Stretch the other side.

Part 4.

Starting position
   1. Sit and loop a thick bath or hand towel around your neck. Let the fabric bunch together to form a wide band. Hold the ends of the towel in your hands and keep the fabric pulled taut.

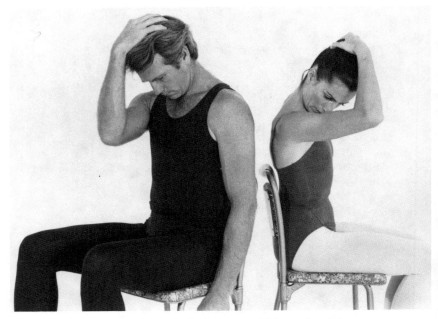

Dancer (a) is on the left. **Dancer (b)** is on the right.

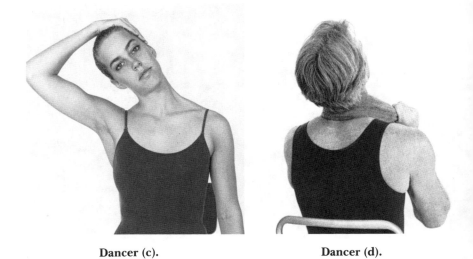

Dancer (c).   **Dancer (d).**

Figure 18.6 Stretching the neck muscles.

2. Reach forward with your chin and look up. Stop when you feel a stretch in the front of the neck. Do not let your head tip back so far that you can see the ceiling.

3. Keep your mouth closed and your lower teeth in contact with the upper teeth.

Action

Hold the stretch (Figure 18.6d). Feel the stretch along the front of your neck.

Increasing the difficulty for Part 4

Turn your head to face the right diagonal, then perform the stretch. Repeat on the other side.

Comment

Flexibility exercises for the neck flexors necessarily hyperextend the cervical spine, and there is a difference of opinion among experts as to whether these exercises should be performed. While hyperextension is a natural movement in the neck, there is concern that the head may tip too far back and injure the cervical structure (Alter, 1983, p. 20.) On the other hand, tightness in the neck flexors is associated with a forward head, and stretching this muscle group may help in correcting the alignment problem (Fitt, 1988, p. 370.) Part 4 of this exercise is designed to stretch the neck flexors without excessive hyperextension; a thick rolled towel is wrapped around the neck to add support for the head. If Part 4 of this exercise causes you any pain, however, you should not do it.

Exercise 18.H adapted from: Alter (1986b) pp. 32–34; Arnheim (1985), p. 662; Fitt (1988), p. 350.

PART

VI

The Shoulder and Arm

The arms are very important in dance movement. They contribute to the success of many turns, falls, leaps, and lifts. The arms communicate feeling as well as adding to the quality and style of movement. Even if the rest of the body is moving correctly, the movement can appear stiff and awkward if the arms are not well positioned and moving gracefully.

The positions of the elbow and wrist are particularly crucial in producing a fluid, aesthetically pleasing line. While audiences, choreographers, or teachers may forgive a structurally unaesthetic foot, they do not overlook elbows and wrists that are incorrectly placed.

In most technique classes, much time is spent exercising the lower limbs and, to a lesser extent, the torso; comparatively little time is spent training the upper limbs. For some dancers, the arm exercises performed in class are sufficient to develop strength and control, but others find that class work is not sufficient to correct errors in arm placement. These dancers constantly struggle with problems such as droopy wrists, sagging elbows, and tense shoulders. Specific conditioning exercises for the shoulders and arms can help these dancers.

Partnering requires a great deal of strength and flexibility in the arms, shoulders, and upper torso of both men and women. The average dance technique class, with its emphasis on the legs and torso, does not adequately prepare a dancer for partnering. In Chapters 20 and 21, specific exercises are recommended to help dancers prepare for partnering work.

19

The Major Muscles of the Shoulder and Arm

The Structure of the Shoulder

The shoulder can be divided into two parts, the shoulder joint and the shoulder girdle. The one bone that both parts have in common is the *scapula*, or the shoulder blade (Figure 19.1).

The right *scapula* articulates with the shoulder joint and shoulder girdle on the right side of the body. The left *scapula* articulates with the shoulder joint and the shoulder girdle on the left side of the body.

The plural form of the word *scapula* is *scapulae*. This term is used whenever reference is made to both the right and left *scapula*. For example, if a dancer pinches her shoulder blades together, it can be said she is pinching her *scapulae*.

The *scapula* is a triangular bone lying on top of the ribs at the back of the torso. It has two forward projections found near the shoulder, called the *acromion* and the *coracoid process*. The *scapula* also has a shallow cup or dish formation at the shoulder, called the *glenoid fossa*. These features allow the shoulder blade to articulate with other bones in the shoulder.

The shoulder joint is comprised of the *scapula* and the *humerus*, the upper arm bone (Figure 19.1). The head of the *humerus* fits into the glenoid fossa of the *scapula*. The articulation is called the *glenohumeral joint*.

The shoulder girdle is comprised of the *scapula,* the *clavicle*, or collar bone, and the *sternum*, the breast bone (Figure 19.1). The acromion, one of the forward projections of the *scapula,* articulates with the *clavicle*. This articulation is called the *acromioclavicular joint*, and can be palpated at the shoulder. The *clavicle* also articulates with the *sternum;* this is called the *sternoclavicular joint*. It is located right at the base of the throat.

The sternoclavicluar joint is the only joint that connects the three bones in the shoulder girdle with the rest of the body. The *scapulqe* do not articulate with any other bones at the back of the body. They are held in place by muscle attachments alone.

Both the shoulder joint and the shoulder girdle are stabilized by

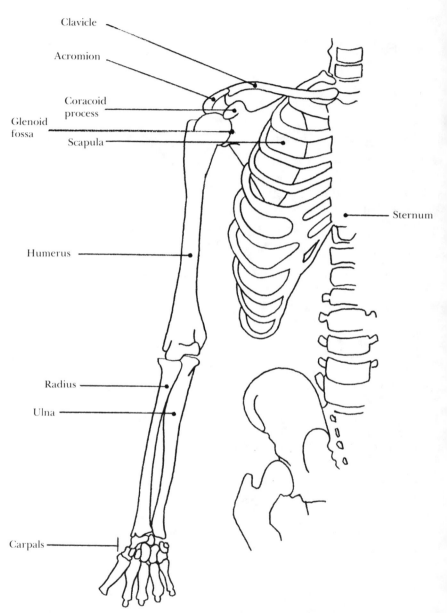

Figure 19.1 Anterior view of right shoulder girdle and arm bones.

ligaments and muscles. A description of the most important muscle groups is included in the material that follows.

Movements of the Shoulder Joint

Movements at the glenohumeral joint include: *flexion* (from resting at the side, the arms move in a forward, upward direction until they reach fifth position); *hyperflexion* (the arms move from fifth position in a backward direction behind the head); *extension* (return from flexion); *hyperextension* (from resting at the side, the arms move in a backward, upward direction); *abduction* (from resting at the side, the arms move through second position and up to fifth position); *adduction* (return from abduction); *outward rotation* and *inward rotation* of the upper arm; *horizontal adduction* (the arms move from second position toward the front of the body); *horizontal abduction* (return from horizontal adduction); and *circumduction* (full circle of the arms).

Movements of the Shoulder Girdle

Movements of the shoulder girdle change the position of the *scapulae*. Some of these movements include *elevation* of the *scapulae* (shrugging the shoulders); *depression* (return from elevation); *abduction* (pulling the *scapulae* away from the midline of the back, as when stretching the arms forward); and *adduction* (pulling the *scapulae* toward the midline of the back, as when "pinching" the shoulder blades together). Other movements of the *scapulae* are not included in this discussion.

Interaction of the Shoulder Joint and the Shoulder Girdle
The movements of the shoulder joint and the shoulder girdle are closely interwoven. Recall, from the discussion of anatomy, that the head of the *humerus* articulates with the glenoid fossa of the *scapula*. Whenever the arm moves, the *scapula* on that side of the body also moves. This movement of the *scapula* positions the glenoid fossa in such a way that the *humerus* can have full range of movement. If the *scapula* was unable to move, the *humerus* would be greatly limited in its range of motion.

Movements of the shoulder joint involve the interaction of eighteen different muscles. Some of these muscles position the *scapula* while others move the *humerus*. Studying these muscles need not be overwhelming if you first identify the muscles that control the position of the *scapula*. These muscles are called *shoulder girdle muscles*.

Once you understand the shoulder girdle muscles, you will be ready to study the movements of the shoulder joint. For each movement of

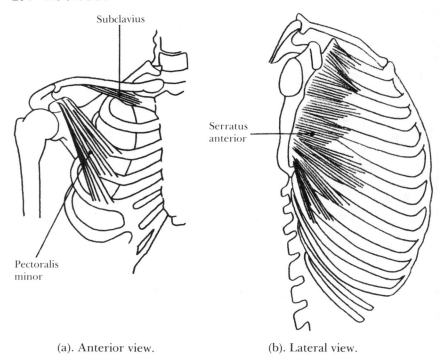

(a). Anterior view.   (b). Lateral view.

Figure 19.2 Anterior and lateral views of shoulder girdle muscles.

the shoulder joint, the muscles that move the *humerus* will first be presented. Then the muscles that position the *scapula* will be identified.

Shoulder Girdle Muscles

There are seven muscles that change the position of the *scapula* (Figures 19.2 and 19.3). These include the *subclavius* and *pectoralis minor* on the anterior side of the shoulder girdle, the *serratus anterior* on the lateral side of the shoulder girdle, the *levator scapulae, rhomboids major* and *minor*, and the *trapezius* on the posterior side of the shoulder girdle.

The *subclavius* is a small muscle band. It is attached on one end to the first rib cartilage, and the other end is attached to the *clavicle* (Figure 19.2). It is active in depressing the *scapula*.

The *pectoralis minor* is attached to the anterior surface of some of the ribs and to the coracoid process of the *scapula* (Figure 19.2). It assists in depressing the *scapula*.

The *serratus anterior* is attached at one end to the lateral surface of some of the ribs. At the other end it is attached to the anterior surface of the *scapula* (Figure 19.2). This muscle abducts the *scapula*.

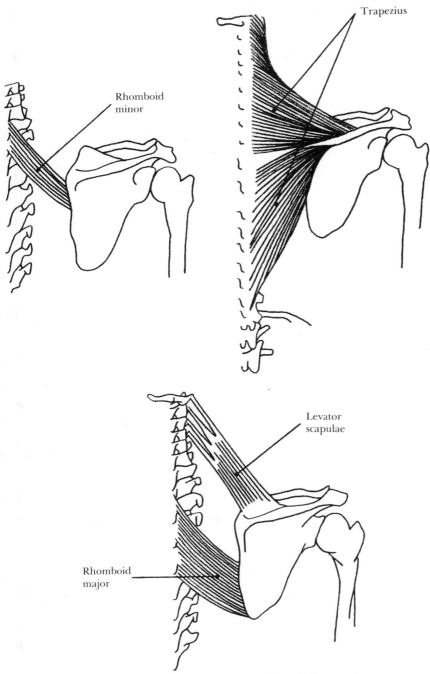

Figure 19.3 Posterior view of shoulder girdle muscles.

The *levator scapulae* is attached on one end to the upper four cervical vertebrae. At the other end it is attached to the *scapula* (Figure 19.3). It is responsible for elevating the *scapula* and assists in adduction.

The *rhomboid major* and *rhomboid minor* muscles form a wide band that is attached to the last cervical and the first five thoracic vertebra. The other end of this muscle band is attached to the *scapula* (Figure 19.3). These muscles adduct the *scapula* as well as elevate them.

The *trapezius* is attached on the base of the skull, the posterior ligaments of the cervical neck, as well as on the seventh cervical vertebra and all the thoracic vertebrae (Figure 19.3). The other end of this large muscle is attached on the back of the *scapula,* the acromion, and the *clavicle.* It is convenient to separate the *trapezius* into three sections, with the first being the upper-most and the third being the lower-most section. The first section is active during elevation and adduction of the *scapula;* the second is active in adduction; and the third is active in adduction and depression of the *scapula.*

Flexion and Hyperflexion of the Arms
At the shoulder joint the anterior portion of the *deltoid,* the *pectoralis major,* and the *biceps* muscle work together to flex the *humerus.* The *coracobrachialis* may also help to produce the movement. All of these muscles are found on the anterior side of the arm. At the shoulder girdle the *serratus anterior* as well as the *trapezius* are active in positioning the *scapula.* The shoulder girdle muscles have been described previously.

The *deltoid* is a muscle that covers the shoulder joint like a cap sleeve. It is attached to the *clavicle,* the acromion, and the back of the *scapula* on one end (Figure 19.4). On the other end it is attached to the lateral side of the *humerus.* This muscle can be palpated at the shoulder and upper arm. The anterior muscle fibers are active in all forward movements of the arm as well as the inward rotation of the arm. The posterior fibers can produce extension with outward rotation. The entire muscle functions to produce abduction. This muscle is commonly used in any lifting movement. Indeed, any movement of the *humerus* will generally involve some part of the *deltoid* muscle.

The *pectoralis major* is attached at one end to the *clavicle,* the *sternum,* and the anterior cartilage of the upper ribs. Its attachment on the other end is to the *humerus* (Figure 19.4). The *pectoralis major* can easily be palpated as the large muscle of the chest region. When different portions of the *pectoralis major* contract, a variety of movements are produced. These include flexion, adduction, horizontal adduction, inward rotation of the *humerus,* and extension against resistance. This muscle is important in partnering, especially during lifts.

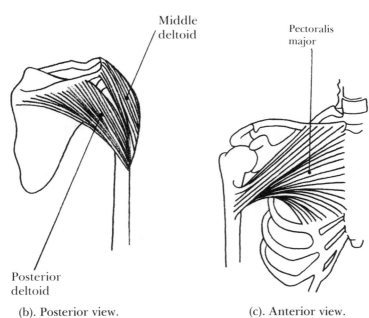

Anterior
deltoid

Middle
deltoid

(a). Anterior view.

Middle
deltoid

Pectoralis
major

Posterior
deltoid

(b). Posterior view.   (c). Anterior view.

Figure 19.4 Anterior and posterior views of shoulder muscles.

The *biceps brachii* is a two-joint muscle crossing both the shoulder joint and the elbow joint (Figure 19.5). The *biceps brachii* has two heads: one is attached to the coracoid process of the *scapula,* and the other to the glenoid fossa of the *scapula.* At the other end, the muscle is attached to the lower arm. Although its main action is at the elbow, it also flexes and abducts the *humerus* against resistance when the elbow is straight. It may also be active in horizontal adduction. This muscle can easily be palpated on the anterior side of the upper arm. It is the muscle people often contract when they "show off" the size of their arm muscles.

The *coracobrachialis* is a small muscle that is found on the anterior side of the arm. It is attached to the coracoid process of the *scapula* at one end and to the medial side of the *humerus* at the other end (Figure 19.5). The *coracobrachialis* flexes and adducts the *humerus* as well as moving the arm through horizontal adduction.

Extension of the Arms
Muscles responsible for arm extension include portions of the *pectoralis major* (described previously), the *latissimus dorsi,* the *teres major,* and probably the posterior *deltoid* (described previously). The long head of the *triceps* may also be involved. At the shoulder girdle the *pectoralis*

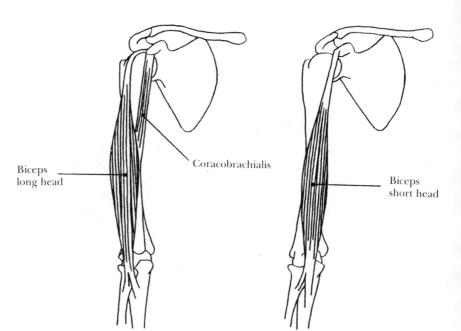

Biceps
long head

Coracobrachialis

Biceps
short head

Figure 19.5 Anterior view of shoulder and elbow muscles.

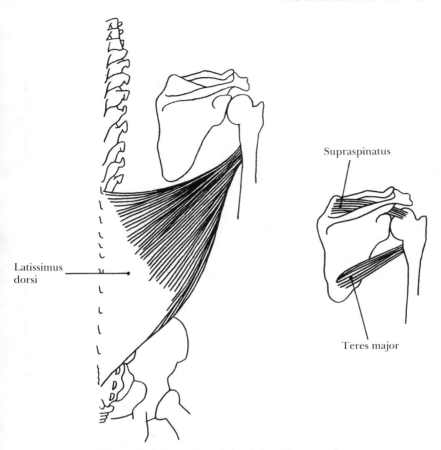

Supraspinatus

Latissimus dorsi

Teres major

Figure 19.6 Posterior view of shoulder muscles.

minor, the *subclavius,* the *rhomboids,* and the *trapezius* are active in positioning the *scapula.* These shoulder girdle muscles have been previously described.

The *latissimus dorsi* is located on the posterior of the body. It is attached at one end to the *sacrum,* the *ilium,* the lumbar vertebrae, the lower thoracic vertebrae, and the lower ribs (Figure 19.6). At the other end, it is attached to the anterior side of the *humerus.* This muscle covers the lower and middle portions of the back. It can be palpated on the lateral side of the torso below the armpit. Contraction of the *latissimus dorsi* results in extension and adduction of the arm against resistance. It also produces inward rotation of the arm.

The *teres major* is a muscle also located on the posterior of the body. It is attached to one end of the *scapula* and at the other end to the anterior side of the *humerus* (Figure 19.6). It functions to extend and adduct the arm. It can also rotate the *humerus* inward. Because this muscle has similar functions as the *latissimus dorsi*, it is sometimes referred to as the *latissimus dorsi's* "little helper."

The *triceps brachii* muscle (Figure 19.7), found on the posterior side of the arm, has three heads. The long head is a two-joint muscle that crosses both the shoulder joint and the elbow joint. The long head is attached to the *scapula* at one end and to the fascia (connective tissue) of the forearm at the other end. This fascia connects it to the *ulna*, one of the bones in the lower arm. The lateral and medial heads originate on the *humerus* and insert on the fascia and *ulna*. The *triceps brachii* can easily be palpated on the posterior side of the upper arm. Although its primary function is to extend the elbow, the long head assists in adduction, extension, and hyperextension of the *humerus*.

Hyperextension of the Arms

At the shoulder joint the *posterior deltoid*, the *latissimus dorsi*, and the *teres major* produce hyperextension of the arms. At the shoulder girdle, the *pectoralis minor* causes an adjustment in the position of the *scapula*. All these muscles were previously described.

Abduction of the Arms

At the shoulder joint the *deltoid* and the *supraspinatus* abduct the *humerus*. At the shoulder girdle, the *serratus anterior* and the second and fourth portion of the *trapezius* cause a change in the position of the *scapula*. With the exception of the *supraspinatus*, all these muscles have been described.

The *supraspinatus* is a small muscle attached to the top of the *scapula* and at the other end to the top of the *humerus* (Figure 19.6). Although its main action is to stabilize the head of the *humerus* in the glenoid fossa so that the *deltoid* can abduct, it also assists in flexion and horizontal abduction.

Adduction of the Arms

When arm adduction is performed against resistance, the *latissimus dorsi*, *teres major*, *pectoralis major* and possibly the *posterior deltoid* function to produce the movement. At the shoulder girdle the *rhomboids*, *pectoralis minor*, and *levator scapulae* are active in positioning the *scapula*. All these muscles have been described.

Inward Rotation of the Arms

At the shoulder joint, the muscles responsible for inward rotation of the *humerus* are the *subscapularis*, the *latissimus dorsi*, the *anterior deltoid*, and

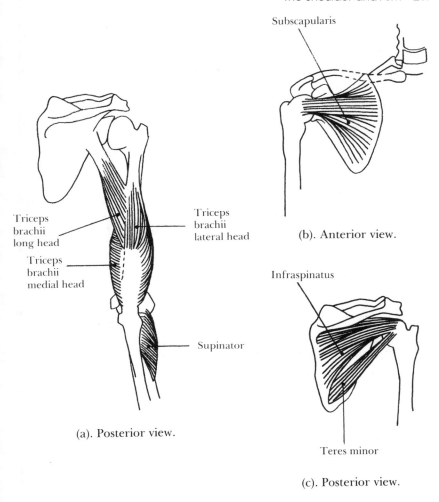

Subscapularis

Triceps
brachii
long head

Triceps
brachii
lateral head

Triceps
brachii
medial head

(b). Anterior view.

Infraspinatus

Supinator

(a). Posterior view.

Teres minor

(c). Posterior view.

Figure 19.7 Anterior and posterior views of shoulder and elbow muscles.

the *pectoralis major*. At the shoulder girdle the *serratus anterior* and the *pectoralis minor* are the primary muscles acting to position the *scapula*. With the exception of the *subscapularis*, these muscles were all described above.

The *subscapularis* is attached at one end to a large area of the anterior surface of the *scapula*. At the other end it is attached to the anterior side of the *humerus* (Figure 19.7). The *subscapularis* stabilizes the glenohumeral joint. Its primary action is to produce inward rotation of the upper arm.

Outward Rotation of the Arms

At the shoulder joint, the *infraspinatus* and the *teres minor* produce outward rotation of the *humerus*. At the shoulder girdle, the *rhomboids* and the trapezius are active in positioning the *scapula*. These shoulder girdle muscles have been described previously.

The *infraspinatus* and *teres minor* are muscles located on the posterior side of the body, attached to the *scapula*. At the other end they are attached to the *humerus* (Figure 19.7). They are active during outward rotation of the *humerus* and are also important in stabilizing the joint.

Horizontal Abduction of the Arms

At the shoulder joint, the *posterior deltoid*, the *infraspinatus*, the *teres minor*, and the long head of the *triceps* are active in horizontal abduction of the arms. At the shoulder girdle, the *rhomboids* and the *trapezius* muscles position the *scapula*. All of these muscles were described previously.

Horizontal Adduction of the Arms

At the shoulder joint, the *pectoralis major*, the *anterior deltoid*, and *coracobrachialis* are the chief muscles producing horizontal adduction of the arms. At the shoulder girdle, the *serratus anterior* and *pectoralis minor* are active in positioning the *scapula*. All of these muscles have previously been described.

Structure of the Elbow Joint

The elbow actually contains two joints. The first consists of the articulation of the *humerus* with the two forearm bones, the *ulna* and *radius*. The second consists of the articulation of the *ulna* with the *radius*. For our purposes we will use the term "elbow joint" to refer to both of these (Figure 19.1).

Movements of the Elbow Joint

Movements of the elbow are usually described from a starting position in which the palm of the hand is facing forward. These movements include *flexion* (moving the hand toward the shoulder), *extension* (return from flexion), *outward rotation of the forearm* (palms facing forward), and *inward rotation of the forearm* (palms facing backward).

Elbow Flexion

The chief muscles that produce elbow flexion are the *biceps brachii* (described previously), the *brachioradialis*, and the *brachialis*.

The *brachioradialis* is attached at one end to the lateral side of the *humerus* and at the other end to the lateral side of the *radius* (Figure 19.8). It can be felt by placing your hand on the anterior and lateral surfaces of the forearm near the elbow.

The *brachialis* is attached to the anterior side of the *humerus* on one side, and on the other end to the anterior side of the *ulna* (Figure 19.8). Since this muscle is located beneath the *biceps brachii*, it is difficult to palpate.

Elbow Extension

The chief muscles that produce elbow extension are the *triceps brachii* (described previously) and the *anconeus*. They are located on the posterior side of the elbow.

The *anconeus* is a small muscle attached at one end to the lateral side of the *humerus* (Figure 19.9). At the other end it is attached to the posterior side of the *ulna*. Because it is so small, this muscle is difficult to palpate.

Inward Rotation of the Forearm

The muscles that produce inward rotation are the *pronator teres* and the *pronator quadratus*. They are found on the anterior side of the arm and were shown in Figure 19.8.

The *pronator teres* is attached at one end to both the *humerus* and *ulna* and on the other end to the lateral side of the *radius*. It cannot be palpated.

The *pronator quadratus* is a small muscle attached to the *ulna* on one end, and to the *radius* at the other end. It cannot be palpated.

Outward Rotation of the Forearm

The muscles that produce outward rotation are the *biceps brachii* (already described) and the *supinator* (Figure 19.7).

The *supinator* is a short muscle attached to the lateral side of the *humerus* and to the *ulna* on one end. On the other end, it is attached to the lateral side of the *radius*. The *supinator* cannot be palpated.

Structure and Movements of the Wrist Joint

The wrist joint consists of the *radius, ulna,* and two rows of *carpal* bones (Figure 19.1). Movements of the wrist are usually described from a starting position in which the palm of the hand is facing forward. These movements include *flexion* (moving the palm of the hand toward the

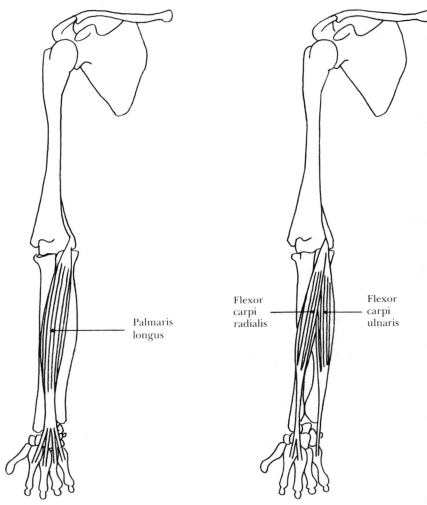

Figure 19.8 Anterior view of elbow and wrist muscles.

lower arm), *extension* (return from flexion), *hyperextension* (moving the back of the hand toward the lower arm), *abduction* (moving the hand away from the body), *adduction* (moving the hand toward the body), and *circumduction* (moving in a circle).

There are many muscles that contribute to the performance of these movements. Some of these are considered wrist muscles and others are muscles of the hand and fingers. Only the muscles that are considered wrist muscles will be described.

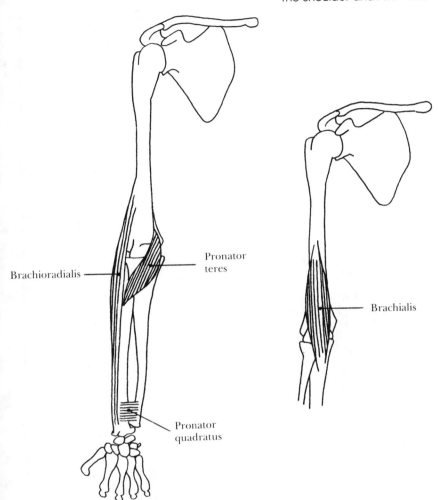

Brachioradialis —

Pronator teres

Pronator quadratus

Brachialis

Flexion of the Wrist

Some of the muscles that produce flexion of the wrist are the *flexor carpi radialis*, the *flexor carpi ulnaris*, and the *palmaris longus*. These muscles are located on the anterior side of the arm and are shown in Figure 19.8.

The *flexor carpi radialis* is attached to the medial side of the *humerus* at one end, and at the other end on the palm side of two of the hand bones.

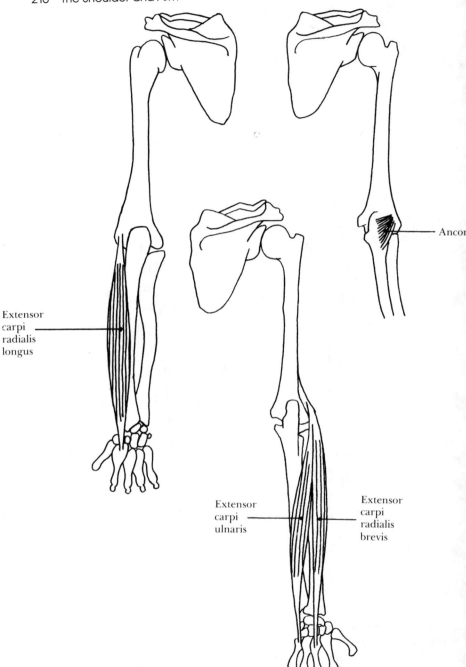

Figure 19.9 Posterior view of elbow and wrist muscles.

The *flexor carpi ulnaris* is also attached to the medial side of the *humerus*. At the other end it is attached to some of the wrist bones as well as to a hand bone.

The *palmaris longus*, like the *flexor carpi radialis* and *ulnaris*, is attached at one end to the medial side of the *humerus*. At the other end the attachment is to the middle hand bones. The *palmaris longus* is located between the *flexor carpi ulnaris* and the *flexor carpi radialis*. As you flex your wrist against resistance, you can see the prominent tendon of this muscle on the inside of your wrist.

Extension and Hyperextension of the Wrist

Some of the muscles that produce extension and hyperextension of the wrist are the *extensor carpi radialis longus*, the *extensor carpi radialis brevis*, and the *extensor carpi ulnaris*. These muscles are located on the posterior side of the arm and are shown in Figure 19.9.

The *extensor carpi radialis longus* is attached on one end to the lateral side of the *humerus*. At the other end it is attached to the back of one of the hand bones.

The *extensor carpi radialis brevis* is also attached to the lateral side of the *humerus*. At the other end it is attached to the back of one of the hand bones.

The *extensor carpi ulnaris* like the other two extensor muscles, is attached to the lateral side of the *humerus*. At the other end, it is attached to the back of one of the hand bones.

Abduction of the Wrist

Abduction is produced by the *extensor carpi radialis longus* and *brevis* and the *flexor carpi radialis*. Each of these muscles has already been described.

Adduction of the Wrist

Adduction is produced by the *extensor carpi ulnaris* and the *flexor carpi ulnaris*. Both of these muscles have been described.

20

Questions and Answers

Note: The questions and answers that follow concern improvement of dance technique and prevention of injuries in the shoulders and arms.

1. What is the correct alignment of the shoulder and arm?

There are four points to evaluate when observing arm and shoulder alignment. If the body is viewed from the front, the shoulders should be in horizontal alignment and the shoulder girdle should hang freely. If viewed from the back, the *scapulae* should be horizontally aligned. The *scapulae* should not wing, nor should they be pinched together. If the body is viewed from the side, a plumb line should pass through the ear lobe, through the center of the shoulder, and through the center of the hip (Figure 20.1). The arms should hang freely, and the hands should align with the center of the hip.

There may be structural problems such as scoliosis or unequal length of the arm bones that alter this ideal posture. Many times, however, incorrect shoulder and arm alignment is caused by muscular imbalance. Round shoulders, tense shoulders, and winged *scapulae* are some of the more common alignment deviations caused by muscular imbalance. These and other problems are discussed in the answers to the questions that follow.

Related information may be found in the answers to questions 4 through 7, below.

2. Some of my students have problems with "drooping" wrists whenever they lift their arms. Are there exercises I can recommend to them to help correct this problem?

In many styles of dance the hand should appear as an extended line from the arm. If the wrist droops, the line is broken. Drooping wrists often result from a weakness in the wrist extensors.

Recommended exercises can be found in Chapter 21 to strengthen and stretch the wrist extensors (21.N, 21.U).

3. My teacher is always telling me to correct my arms when they are in second position. What can I do to improve my arm placement in second?

Figure 20.1 Correct alignment of the shoulder and arm.

When the arms are correctly held in second position, the upper arm is rotated inward and the forearm is rotated outward. The arm should slope gradually downward from the shoulder to the hand. The elbow should flex slightly, giving the arm a curved appearance.

If the inward rotators of the upper arm are weak, the elbows will "sag" or "droop." If the outward rotators of the forearm are weak, the forearm will rotate inward and the palms will face the floor. If the abductors of the shoulder are weak, the arms will not be held at the correct height.

Recommended exercises can be found in Chapter 21 to strengthen and stretch the arm abductors (21.C, 21.R), and the arm inward rotators

(21.E, 21.Q). Chapter 21 also presents a strength conditioning exercise for the outward rotators of the forearm (21.L). The outward rotators of the forearm are difficult to stretch. Gentle massage can help them relax.

4. *My shoulders seem to round forward and my teacher is always telling me to pull them back. Are there exercises that can help me correct this problem?*

In many cases, round shoulders are caused by muscular imbalance. Chapter 17 presents information concerning possible muscle imbalances in the trunk that can contribute to round shoulders. Other imbalances involve the muscles at the front and back of the chest. Strengthening the shoulder girdle adductors at the back and stretching the chest muscles at the front will help solve this problem. If you also have a problem with the *scapulae* "winging" or sticking out, you may need to condition additional muscle groups. This is discussed further in the answer to question 5, below.

Related information can be found in question 5, below, and in the answer to question 22, Chapter 17.

Recommended exercises can be found in Chapter 21 to strengthen and stretch the shoulder girdle adductors (21.H, 21.R). Chapter 21 also presents a flexibility exercise for the muscles at the front of the chest (21.O).

5. *Some of my students have shoulder blades that protrude or "wing." What can be done about this?*

Winged or protruding *scapulae* may be caused by an imbalance in the muscles that control the position of the *scapulae*. This might include a tightness in the *pectoralis minor,* a weakness in the shoulder girdle adductors, and/or a weakness in the shoulder girdle abductors that also hold the medial border of the *scapulae* against the ribs. Restoring a balance of strength and stretch to all of these muscle groups can help improve scapular alignment. If winged *scapulae* are accompanied by round shoulders or accentuated curve in the thoracic spine, you may need to condition other muscle groups. Exercises for round shoulders are discussed in the answer to question 4, above. Exercises to condition the muscle groups related to winged *scapulae* are listed below.

Related information can be found in question 4, above.

Recommended exercises can be found in Chapter 21 to strengthen and stretch the shoulder girdle abductors (21.G, 21.O) and the shoulder girdle adductors (21.H, 21.R).

6. When I try to "lift up," my ribs stick out and my shoulder blades pinch together in the back. What can I do?

The answer to question 7, in Chapter 17 addresses the issue of lifting up without sticking out the ribs. If you are also pinching your shoulder blades together when you try to lift up, you will probably need to do some conditioning exercises for the shoulder girdle. If the shoulder blades are constantly pinched together, the shoulder girdle adductors may become tight, and the shoulder girdle abductors may become weak.

Related information can be found in the answer to question 7, Chapter 17.

Recommended exercises can be found in Chapter 21 to strengthen and stretch the shoulder girdle abductors (21.G, 21.O). Chapter 21 also presents a flexibility exercise for the shoulder girdle adductors (21.R).

7. My shoulders are tense and elevated. Are there exercises that can solve this problem?

Tense, elevated shoulders may be an indication of alignment problems elsewhere in the body. For example, one cause of elevated shoulders is incorrect placement of the arms when they are in second position. If the arms are held too far back, the shoulders may tense up. Other causes may involve incorrect placement in the head, torso, legs, or feet. If incorrect alignment is causing your shoulder elevation and tension, you will need to correct these problems at the same time you work on correcting your shoulder placement.

If you have determined that your alignment is correct, then the tension in your shoulders may have other causes. Some people, when they concentrate very hard, unconsciously tense some part of their body, often the shoulders. Learning to relax and release the added tension will help to correct shoulder placement.

If you have been continually tensing your shoulders, the muscles that elevate the shoulders are probably tight and need to be stretched. This can be done by performing part of the flexibility exercise for the neck muscles. In addition, you may find biofeedback techniques helpful in releasing unnecessary tension.

A *recommended exercise* can be found in Chapter 18 to stretch the neck muscles (18.H: Parts 1 and 2).

8. My teacher says that I have very awkward arms. Is there something I can do about this?

Graceful arm movement is the result of refined motor control by the nervous system. Some dancers are well endowed with a finely tuned nervous system. Other dancers must "train" their nervous system. This training involves the repetition of the movement until is is refined. These repetitions are performed in the dance class. Strength and flexibility conditioning will not help.

Sometimes, however, the arms reflect muscular tension elsewhere in the body. This tension can occur from concentrating very hard on other parts of the body as you try to improve technique. If the tension is continually generated, the arm muscles may become tight.

Related information is found in question 7, above.

Recommended exercises can be found in Chapter 21 to stretch all the arm muscles (21.O through 21.T.)

9. As a teacher, I notice certain students have trouble controlling the front fall (Figure 20.2) in modern class. How can I help them improve this movement?

A successful front fall requires strong arm and shoulder girdle muscles. In addition, the trunk flexors must be strong enough to prevent the spine from hyperextending.

Recommended exercises can be found in Chapter 18 to strengthen and stretch the trunk flexors (18.A, 18.E). Exercises can be found in Chapter 21 to strengthen and stretch the elbow extensors (21.K, 21.T).

10. I will soon be starting a partnering class. What should I do to prepare for this?

Before starting a partnering class it is important to condition the muscles of the upper torso, shoulder, and arm for both strength and flexibility. While both men *and* women need to condition these muscle groups, men generally need to work with heavier weights and build greater strength than women.

The recommended exercises will help you prepare for partnering. They are designed to be performed with wrist weights at first, then progress to the heavier weights made possible with a barbell. (See Chapter 6 for a description of how to prepare this equipment from items found around the house.) These exercises should build sufficient arm and shoulder strength for women, and provide a good start for men. Male dancers who need to develop further arm and shoulder strength should work with the weight machines found in most gyms. Chapter 23 provides an introduction to using this equipment.

Sometimes dancers mistakenly believe that conditioning work for partnering means immediately working with very heavy weights. This

Figure 20.2 Performing a front fall.

is not true. Follow the guidelines presented in Part II, and increase strength gradually. Do not lift weights that are so heavy that you can perform an exercise only once or twice.

When some dancers think about partnering, they assume that conditioning the upper body is all they need to be concerned about. In reality, successful partnering depends on strength and flexibility throughout the entire body. In Chapter 22 we present conditioning programs based on the exercises in this book. We strongly recommend that all dancers, especially those involved in partnering, adopt a regular conditioning program.

Recommended exercises include all of the exercises in Chapter 21. These exercises strengthen and stretch all muscle groups of the shoulders, arms, and wrists.

21

Strength and Flexibility Exercises

Note: Be sure to read Part II before doing any of the following exercises.

21. A Strength Conditioning Exercise for the Arm Flexors

Equipment
Wrist weights or barbell; chair (optional).

Starting position
1. Stand in a comfortable second position with your torso in good dance alignment, or sit with your torso in good dance alignment. Your arms should be at your sides.
2. If you are wearing wrist weights, rotate your forearms until your palms face the back. If you are using a barbell, grasp the bar with your arms shoulder-width apart and your palms facing the back.
3. Flex your elbows until the backs of your hands reach shoulder height. Your upper arms should touch the sides of your torso. Your palms will now be facing forward (Figure 21.1a).

Action
1. Extend your hands toward the ceiling. Straighten your elbows, but do not lock or hyperextend them. Your hands should be directly over your shoulders and your back should be in good dance alignment (Figure 21.1b).
2. Return to the starting position.

Timing patterns
A, B, C.

Increasing the difficulty
Add more weight.

Comment
This exercise will also help to strengthen the elbow extensors.

Exercise 21.A adapted from: Arnheim (1985), p. 134.

21.B Strength Conditioning Exercise for the Arm Extensors

Equipment
Wrist weights.

Starting position
Stand in a comfortable second position with your torso in good dance alignment. Your arms should be at your sides with wrist weights attached. Your palms should face your body.

Figure 21.1 Strengthening the arm flexors. **Dancer (a)** is on the left. **Dancer (b)** is on the right.

Action
1. Bring your arms behind you and up toward your shoulder. Your palms should continue to face your midline. Keep your elbows straight. Contract your abdominal muscles to keep your lower back from overarching (Figure 21.2a).
2. Return to the starting position.

Figure 21.2 **Dancer (a),** on the left, is strengthening the arm extensors. **Dancer (b),** on the right, is strengthening the arm abductors.

Timing pattern
   A, B, C.

Increasing the difficulty
   Add additional weight.

Exercise 21.B adapted from: Arnheim (1985), p. 721.

21.C Strength Conditioning Exercise for the Arm Abductors

Equipment
   Wrist weights; chair (optional).

Starting position
   Stand in a comfortable second position with your torso in good dance alignment or sit with your torso in good dance alignment. Your arms should be at your sides with wrist weights attached. Your palms should face your body.

Action
   1. Lift your arms to second position. Your elbows should be slightly flexed. The backs of your elbows should point to the back of the room, not the floor. (Figure 21.2b).
   2. Return to the starting position.

Timing patterns
   A, B, C.

Increasing the difficulty
   Add additional weight.

Exercise 21.C adapted from: Arnheim (1985), p. 721; Barnes and Crutchfield (1971), p. 14.

21.D Strength Conditioning Exercise for the Arm Adductors

Equipment
   Chair (optional), elastic resistance attached to a doorknob or *barre*. If you use a *barre*, tie the elastic close to the wall support bracket. If you are using rubber bands for elastic resistance, you will need to construct a "chain of elastic resistance." Directions for making this piece of equipment are found in Chapter 6.

Starting position
   1. Sit on the floor or in a chair with your right shoulder directly across from the elastic. Your legs should be parallel, and your back in good dance alignment. Grasp the tube sock or Thera-band with your right hand and raise your right arm to shoulder height or above shoulder height.
   2. Adjust the distance between you and the doorknob or *barre* so that there is tension in the elastic.

Action
1. Pull your right hand down to your right side. Keep your elbow straight and maintain your torso in good dance alignment (Figure 21.3).
2. Return to the starting position.
3. If you do not feel enough resistance throughout the exercise, sit further from the door or *barre.*
4. Complete all repetitions on the first side before changing sides.

Timing patterns
A, B, C.

Increasing the difficulty
Sit further from the doorknob or *barre;* add additional elastic resistance.

Exercise 21.D adapted from: Roy and Irvin (1983), p. 195.

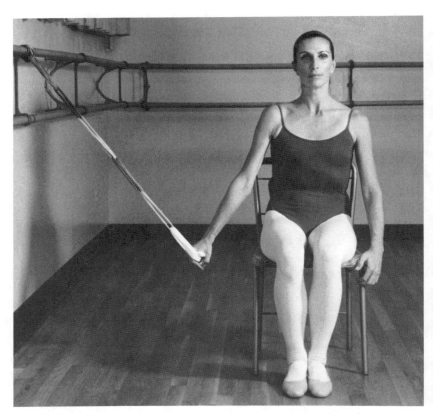

Figure 21.3 Strengthening the arm adductors.

21.E Strength Conditioning Exercise for the Inward Rotators of the Arm

Equipment
   Elastic resistance attached to the leg of a heavy piece of furniture.

Starting position
   1. L-sit with your right side to the heavy piece of furniture. Hold the loop in your right hand.
   2. Flex your right elbow 90 degrees. Your upper arm should be held against your right side. Your wrist should be straight and your palm should be facing the left wall.
   3. Adjust the distance between you and the piece of furniture so that there is some tension in the elastic.

Action
   1. Keep your upper arm held against your side, your wrist straight and pull your hand across your body. Your forearm will touch your torso (Figure 21.4a).
   2. Return to the starting position.
   3. If you do not feel a strong resistance from the elastic, sit further from the piece of furniture.
   4. Complete all repetitions on the first side before changing sides.

Figure 21.4 **Dancer (a),** on the left, is strengthening the inward rotators of the arm. **Dancer (b),** on the right, is strengthening the outward rotators of the arm.

Timing patterns
A, B, C.

Increasing the difficulty
Sit further from the piece of furniture; add more elastic resistance.

Comment
It is possible to combine this exercise with 21.F, below, the strength conditioning exercise for the outward rotators of the arm. See the comment in exercise 21.F for an explanation of how to do this.

Exercise 21.E adapted from: Kisner and Colby (1985), p. 257; Roy and Irvin (1983), p. 195.

21.F   Strength Conditioning Exercise for the Outward Rotators of the Arm

Equipment
Elastic resistance attached to the leg of a heavy piece of furniture.

Starting position
1. L-sit with your left side to the heavy piece of furniture. Hold the loop in your right hand.
2. Flex your right elbow 90 degrees and bring your right forearm across your torso. Your right upper arm should touch your right side,

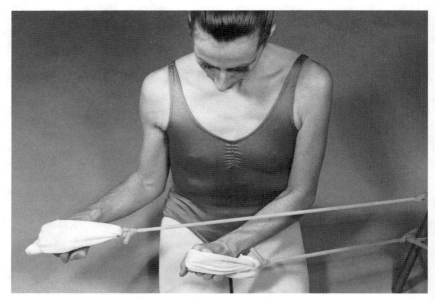

Figure 21.5 Combining exercises 21.E and 21.F.

your right wrist should be straight, and your right hand should be close to the midline of your body.

3. Adjust your distance from the piece of furniture so there is some tension in the elastic.

Action

1. Keep your right upper arm held against your side, your right wrist straight, and move your right hand away from the midline of your body. Your right palm will face the left diagonal at the completion of the movement (Figure 21.4b).

2. Return to the starting position.

3. If you do not feel a strong resistance from the elastic, sit further from the furniture.

4. Complete all repetitions on the first side before changing sides.

Timing patterns
A, B, C.

Increasing the difficulty
Sit further from the piece of furniture; add more elastic resistance.

Comment
It is possible to perform this exercise with the right arm at the same time you perform exercise 21.E with the left arm. Figure 21.5 illustrates how to combine these exercises.

Exercise 21.F adapted from: Kisner and Colby (1985), pp. 256–57.

21.G Strength Conditioning Exercise for the Shoulder Girdle Abductors

Starting position
1. Begin on your hands and knees and move your hands forward several inches.

2. Allow your chest to sink toward the floor. Your shoulder blades will move closer together. Contract your abdominal muscles so your lower back does not hyperextend (Figure 21.6a).

Action
1. Push your shoulder blades apart by pressing your upper back toward the ceiling and increasing the curve in your upper back (Figure 21.6b).

2. Return to the starting position.

Timing patterns
A, B, C.

Increasing the difficulty
Support your weight on your hands and feet in the full push-up position (Figure 21.9b).

Exercise 21.G adapted from: Barnes and Crutchfield (1971), p. 17; Fitt (1988), p. 348.

Figure 21.6 Strengthening the shoulder girdle abductors. **Dancer (a)** is on the floor. **Dancer (b)** is on the bench.

21.H Strength Conditioning Exercise for the Shoulder Girdle Adductors

Equipment
   Small pillow or bath towel folded to make a small pillow.

Starting position
   1. Begin front horizontal, forehead on the floor, arms in second position, and a small pillow placed under your abdominals between your pelvis and your ribs.
   2. Rotate your arms until your thumbs point to the ceiling. Be sure to rotate the entire arm, not just the forearm.

Action
   1. Lift your thumbs toward the ceiling. Keep your chest and forehead on the floor (Figure 21.7).
   2. Return to the starting position.

Timing patterns
   A, B, C.

Figure 21.7 Strengthening the shoulder girdle adductors.

Increasing the difficulty
Add wrist weights.

Exercise 21.H adapted from an interview with S. Anthony and M. Calitri, physical therapists, in June 1985. At the time of the interview, Ms. Anthony and Ms. Calitri were affiliated with the Center for Health and Sports Medicine of the National Hospital for Orthopaedics and Rehabilitation; Kisner and Colby (1985), p. 441.

21.I   Strength Conditioning Exercise for the Shoulder Girdle Depressors

Equipment
Two or four telephone books. Each pair of telephone books should be of equal size.

Starting position
1. L-sit with one telephone book placed beside each hip joint.
2. Put your hands on the telephone books and straighten your elbows. Your shoulders should elevate. If your shoulders do not elevate, you will need more than one telephone book under each hand.

Action
1. Press down on the phone books and pull your shoulders down into alignment. Your hips will rise (Figure 21.8a). *Note:* the model is sitting on a table for photographic clarity. You can do this exercise sitting on the floor.
2. Return to the starting position.

Timing patterns
A, B, C.

Increasing the difficulty
Use two sturdy chairs of equal size. Kneel between them and place one hand on each chair seat. Straighten your elbows and allow your shoulders to elevate. If your shoulders do not elevate, you will need to put a telephone book under each hand. As you press your shoulders down, your body will rise. If you keep your knees flexed 90 degrees, you will finish suspended between the two chairs. This makes the exercise even

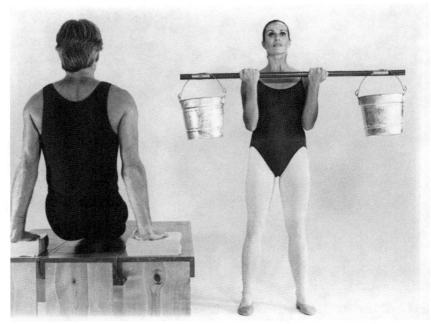

Figure 21.8 **Dancer (a),** on the left, is strengthening the shoulder girdle depressors. **Dancer (b),** on the right, is performing part of the exercise to strengthen the elbow flexors.

more difficult. Be careful when you return to the starting position. Do not let your body weight suddenly drop to your knees.

Exercise 21.I adapted from an interview with S. Anthony and M. Calitri, physical therapists, in June 1985. At the time of the interview Ms. Anthony and Ms. Calitri were affiliated with the Center for Health and Sports Medicine of the National Hospital for Orthopaedics and Rehabilitation; Alter (1986b), p. 56; Barnes and Crutchfield (1971), p. 15; Fitt (1988), p. 348; Kisner and Colby (1985), p. 83.

21.J   Strength Conditioning Exercise for the Elbow Flexors

Equipment
Wrist weights or barbell.

Part 1

Starting position
1. Stand in a comfortable second position, your torso in good dance alignment, and your arms at your sides.
2. If you are using wrist weights, rotate your forearms until your palms face forward.

3. If you are using a barbell, grasp the bar with your hands shoulder-width apart and your palms facing forward.

Action
1. Flex your elbows until your hands reach shoulder height. Your palms will now be facing the back (Figure 21.8b).
2. Return to the starting position.

Part 2

Starting position
1. Stand in a comfortable second position, as in Part 1.
2. If you are using wrist weights, rotate your forearms until your palms face the back.
3. If you are using a barbell, grasp the bar with your arms shoulder-width apart and your palms facing the back.

Action
1. Flex your elbow until your hands reach shoulder height. Your palms will now be facing the front.
2. Return to the starting position.

Repetitions
8 of Parts 1 and 2.

Timing patterns
A, B, C.

Increasing the difficulty
Add additional weight.

Exercise 21.J adapted from: Arnheim (1985), p. 134; Barnes and Crutchfield (1971), p. 7; Kisner and Colby (1985), p. 84.

21.K   Strength Conditioning Exercise for the Elbow Extensors and Other Related Action Muscles

Starting position
1. Begin front horizontal.
2. Place your hands on the floor by your shoulders. Your elbows will be facing the sides.

Action
1. Straighten your elbows and push your torso away from the floor. This is called the *modified push-up position* (Figure 21.9a). Do not lock or hyperextend your elbows. Contract your abdominal muscles so your torso remains straight and your lower back does not overarch. If you need to flex your hips slightly to protect your lower back, that is all right.
2. Return to the starting position, but stop just before your chest rests on the floor.

Timing patterns
A, B, C.

Figure 21.9 Strengthening the elbow extensors. **Dancer (a),** on the bench, is in the modified push-up position. **Dancer (b),** on the floor is in the full push-up position.

Increasing the difficulty

Change to a *full push-up position* so that your weight is supported on your hands and feet (Figure 21.9b). Be sure to contract the abdominal muscles so the lower back does not overarch. If you need to flex your hips slightly to protect the lower back, that is all right.

You can further increase the difficulty by tying weights around your waist. If you do this, it is particularly important to keep the lower back from overarching.

Exercise 21.K adapted from: Alter (1986b), pp. 65–67; Arnheim (1985), pp. 722–23; Fitt (1988), p. 346.

21.L   Strength Conditioning Exercise for the Inward and Outward Rotators of the Forearm

Equipment

Chair or bench, hand weights.

Starting position

1. Begin sitting and hold a hand weight in each hand.
2. Rest your elbows on your thighs with your palms facing up. Your forearms should extend beyond your knees (Figure 21.10a).

Action
   1. Rotate your forearms so your palms face down (Figure 21.10b).
Keep your wrist straight.
   2. Return to the starting position.

Timing pattern
   B.

Increasing the difficulty
   Add additional weight.

Comment
   Holding the weights will help to strengthen your hand muscles. Some
dancers find small barbells easier to hold. These may be purchased in
sporting goods stores.

Exercise 21.L adapted from: Arnheim (1985), p. 136; Barnes and Crutchfield (1971), p.
8; Kisner and Colby (1985), pp. 289–90.

Figure 21.10 The male dancer is strengthening the inward and outward
rotators of the forearm. **Arm (a)** has the palm facing up. **Arm (b)** has the palm
facing down. The female dancer is strengthening the wrist flexors and
extensors. **Arm (c)** has the palm facing toward the dancer. **Arm (d)** has the palm
facing away from the dancer.

21.M Strength Conditioning for the Wrist Flexors

Equipment
  Hand weights.

Starting position
  1. Double-V sit with a hand weight in each hand.
  2. Place your forearms on your knees with your hands extending beyond your knees, your palms facing up.
  3. Relax your wrists so your palms face forward.

Action
  1. Flex your wrists (Figure 21.10c).
  2. Return to the starting position.

Timing pattern
  B.

Increasing the difficulty
  Add additional weight.

Comment
  Holding the weights will help to strengthen your hand muscles. Some dancers find small barbells easier to hold. These may be purchased in sporting goods stores.

Exercise 21.M adapted from: Barnes and Crutchfield (1971), p. 8; Kisner and Colby (1985), pp. 289–90; Roy and Irvin (1983), p. 225.

21.N Strength Conditioning Exercise for the Wrist Extensors

Equipment
  Hand weights.

Starting position
  1. Double-V sit and hold a hand weight in each hand.
  2. Rest your forearms on your knees with your hands extending beyond your knees and your palms facing down.
  3. Relax your wrists until your palms face your shins.

Action
  1. Extend your wrists (Figure 21.10d).
  2. Return to the starting position.

Timing pattern
  B.

Increasing the difficulty
  Add additional weight.

Comment
  Holding the weights will help to strengthen your hand muscles. Some dancers find small barbells easier to hold. These may be purchased in sporting goods stores.

Exercise 21.N adapted from: Barnes and Crutchfield (1971), p. 8; Kisner and Colby (1985), pp. 289–90; Roy and Irvin (1983), p. 225.

21.O Flexibility Exercise for the Arm Flexors, Shoulder Girdle Abductors, and Other Related Action Muscles

Equipment
Bath towel and chair.

Part 1

Starting position
1. Sit with your torso in good dance alignment and hold the ends of a bath towel.
2. Bring the towel back until it is slightly behind your head. Your elbows may be straight or bent, whichever provides the best stretch. If they are straight, be certain they are not locked or hyperextended.

Action
Hold the stretch (Figure 21.11a). Feel the stretch across the front of your chest.

Part 2

Starting position
1. Sit holding the bath towel as in Part 1.
2. Bring the towel back until your hands are even with your shoulders. Your elbows may either be straight or bent, whichever provides the best stretch. If they are straight, be certain they are not locked or hyperextended.

Action
Hold the stretch (Figure 21.11b). Feel the stretch across the front of your chest. Some people feel an additional stretch along the inner arm.

Part 3

Starting position
1. Sit with the bath towel as in Part 1.
2. Bring the towel back over your head until your hands are lower than your shoulders. Your elbows may be bent or straight, whichever provides the best stretch.

Action
Hold the stretch. Feel the stretch across the front of your chest. Some people feel an additional stretch along the inner arm.

Increasing the difficulty
Place your hands closer to the center of the towel.

Exercise 21.O adapted from: Alter (1986b), pp. 46–7; Como (1966), p. 16; Daniels and Worthingham (1977), p. 72; Kisner and Colby (1985), pp. 429–31; Roy and Irvin (1983), pp. 192–93.

Figure 21.11 Performing part of the exercise to stretch the arm flexors, shoulder girdle abductors and related action muscles. **Dancer (a)** is on the left. **Dancer (b)** is on the right.

21.P   Flexibility Exercise for the Arm Extensors and Adductors

Starting position
  1. Sit with the soles of your feet together. Your feet should be a comfortable distance from your body.
  2. Rest your right hand on the floor and reach up with your left hand.
  3. Lean to the right as you reach out with the left hand.
  4. Twist slightly to the right and increase the curve in your upper back. Maintain a feeling of reaching out with the left hand.

Action
  1. Hold the stretch (Figure 21.12). Feel the stretch in your back and left side.
  2. Stretch the other side.

Exercise 21.P adapted from: Fitt (1988), p. 336.

Figure 21.12 Stretching the arm extensors and adductors.

21.Q Flexibility Exercise for the Inward Rotators of the Arm

Starting position
1. Stand facing the wall with your right arm held against the side of your body.
2. Flex your right elbow 90 degrees and put the palm of your hand against the wall.
3. Move your feet so your body turns to the left. Keep your upper arm in contact with the side of your torso and your palm in contact with the wall. Use your abdominals to maintain alignment of your torso.

Action
1. Hold the stretch (Figure 21.13a). Feel the stretch along the inner portion of your upper arm.
2. Stretch the other side.

Exercise 21.Q adapted from: Kisner and Colby (1985), p. 26.

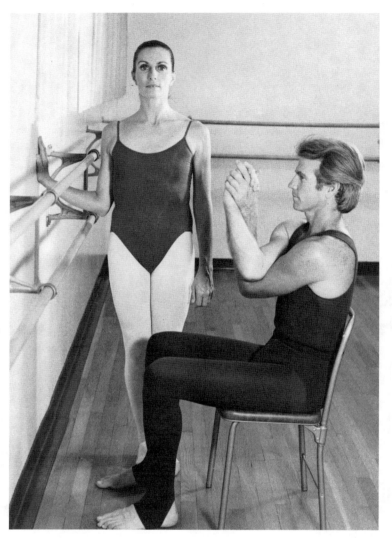

Figure 21.13 **Dancer (a),** on the left, is stretching the inward rotators of the arm. **Dancer (b),** on the right, is stretching the arm abductors, outward rotators, and shoulder girdle adductors.

21.R   Flexibility Exercise for the Arm Abductors, the Outward Rotators of the Arm, and the Shoulder Girdle Adductors

Starting position
1. Sit.
2. Flex your left elbow and bring it toward the center of your torso. Your fingers should point to the ceiling.

3. Flex your right elbow and place it in the bend of your left elbow. Your fingers should point to the ceiling.

4. Rotate your left hand to the left (away from you). At the same time, bring your left hand in front of your right until you can grasp your right wrist and palm. Clasp hands. The palm of your right hand will be facing the floor. The palm of your left hand will be facing away from you.

Action
1. Hold the stretch (Figure 21.13b). Feel the stretch across your upper back, shoulders, and upper arms.
2. Stretch the other side.

Increasing the difficulty
Pull your elbows into your chest and bend forward, increasing the curve in your upper back.

Exercise 21.R adapted from: Roy and Irvin (1983), p. 198.

21.S Flexibility Exercise for the Elbow Flexors

Note: This exercise should be performed within the frame of a door.

Starting position
1. Stand approximately one foot in front of the door frame with your arms at your sides.
2. Rotate your arms inward until the backs of your hands are next to your thighs and your palms face out.
3. Reach back with your hands until your thumbs catch hold of the door frame. Contract your abdominal muscles to prevent your lower back from overarching.

Action
Hold the stretch (Figure 21.14a). Feel the stretch along the upper arm.

Exercise 21.S adapted from: Kisner and Colby (1985), pp. 19, 28.

21.T Flexibility Exercise for the Elbow Extensors and Shoulder Girdle

Starting position
1. Sit.
2. Reach back with your left arm and place the back of your left hand against your spine.
3. Raise your right arm beside your right ear, bend your elbow, and place your right palm on your spine.
4. Bring your right and left hands together and curl your fingers around each other. Do not let your back hyperextend.

Figure 21.14 **Dancer (a),** standing, is stretching the elbow flexors. **Dancer (b),** seated, is stretching the elbow extensors and shoulder girdle muscles.

Action
1. Hold the stretch (Figure 21.14b). Feel the stretch along the back of your right arm. Some dancers feel an additional stretch in the left chest and upper arm.
2. Stretch the other side.

Comment
If your fingers are unable to grasp each other, you can hold a towel between your hands. Alternately pull up and down on the hand towel. Hold each stretch position.

Exercise 21.T adapted from: Arnheim (1980), p. 98; Arnheim (1985), p. 719.

21.U Flexibility Exercise for the Wrist Flexors and Extensors

Equipment
Chair or bench.

Figure 21.15 Stretching the wrist flexors.

Starting position

1. Sit in good alignment. Flex your right shoulder to 90 degrees. If you are stretching your wrist flexors, extend your wrist until your fingers point to the ceiling. Your palm will face away from you. If you are stretching your wrist extensors, flex your wrist until your fingers point to the floor. Your palm will face toward you.

2. Use your left hand to press your right hand back toward your forearm. The fingers of your right hand can bend slightly.

Action

1. Hold the stretch (Figure 21.15). If you are stretching the wrist flexors, you will feel the stretch along the right palm and the under side of the right forearm. If you are stretching the wrist extensors, you will feel the stretch along the top of your right forearm.

2. Stretch the other side.

Exercise 21.U adapted from an interview with S. Anthony and M. Calitri, physical therapists, in June 1985. At the time of the interview Ms. Anthony and Ms. Calitri were affiliated with the Center for Health and Sports Medicine of the National Hospital for Orthopaedics and Rehabilitation.

PART

VII

Putting it All Together

There are many different ways to structure a personal conditioning program. The information in this part will help you plan a program based on the exercises recommended in this book. This part also presents general information about programs that use exercise machines. No matter which way you plan your conditioning program, it is important that you develop a balance of strength and stretch throughout your body. Then you will be better prepared to meet the challenges of technique class and performance. You will be able to dance longer and stronger.

22

Conditioning Programs

There are many different ways to organize a conditioning program based on the exercises in this book. This chapter presents three sample conditioning programs that can be used as designed, or used as guidelines in creating other strategies. Program I includes all of the exercises used throughout the book. Program II includes all of the exercises for the trunk and legs and allows each dancer to choose the neck, arm, and shoulder exercises that are most important to them.

Program III presents a more individualized approach in structuring a conditioning program. Under this system, a dancer is responsible for analyzing the important muscle groups not specifically strengthened and stretched in technique class. The dancer then plans a basic program to condition these neglected muscles.

Dancers who want assistance in planning their individualized program can check with their teacher, or they can start with the sample plan presented in Program III below. This sample plan is designed to condition muscle groups commonly neglected in many ballet, modern, and jazz technique classes. For example, all dance styles depend on a strong "center," yet many technique classes do not specifically condition the trunk muscles. For this reason, the sample plan in Program III includes strength conditioning for the trunk. It also includes stength conditioning for some of the arm and shoulder girdle muscles often neglected in technique class. Finally, the sample plan in Program III includes flexibility exercises for some of the muscle groups usually conditioned for strength during a technique class, but not generally given an opportunity to stretch out.

Once the individualized exercise program has been established, the dancer is responsible for an ongoing evaluation of his or her technique. As technical deficiencies are recognized, the appropriate conditioning exercises are added to the basic exercise program. These exercises will change from time to time as changes occur in the dancer's technique and choreographic assignments.

Program I: The Complete Program

Monday/Wednesday/Friday Exercises
These exercises are to be performed on Monday, Wednesday, and Friday by dancers who want to increase strength and flexibility.

Dancers who want to maintain their present level of conditioning will probably need to perform these exercises twice a week, on Monday and Wednesday, for example.

The timing patterns for the strength conditioning exercises are to be used in rotation. Dancers performing the exercises three times per week should use pattern A on Monday, pattern B on Wednesday, and pattern C on Friday. Dancers performing the exercises twice a week should use pattern A on Monday, pattern B on Wesnesday, pattern C on the following Monday, and so on. The specific exercises for this group are listed in Table 22.1

Tuesday/Thursday/Saturday Exercises
These exercises are to be performed on Tuesday, Thursday, and Saturday by dancers who want to increase strength and flexibility. Dancers who want to maintain their present level of conditioning will probably need to perform these exercises twice a week, on Tuesday and Thursday, for example.

The timing patterns for the strength conditioning exercises are to be used in rotation. Dancers performing the exercises three times a week should use pattern A on Tuesday, pattern B on Thursday, and pattern C on Saturday. Dancers performing the exercises twice a week should use pattern A on Tuesday, pattern B on Thursday, pattern C on the following Tuesday, and so on. The specific exercises for this group are listed in Table 22.1

Program II: Emphasizing Legs and Trunk

Monday/Wednesday/Friday Exercises
Perform all of the Monday, Wednesday, Friday exercises outlined for the trunk and legs in Table 22.1. Evaluate the conditioning work you need to do for your neck, arms, and shoulders. Select the appropriate exercises from those listed in the Monday/Wednesday/Friday group. All of these exercises should be performed according to the instructions given for Program I.

Tuesday/Thursday/Saturday Exercises
Perform all of the Tuesday/Thursday/Saturday exercises outlined for the trunk and legs in Table 22.1. Select appropriate arm and shoulder exercises from those listed in the Tuesday/Thursday/Saturday group. All of these exercises should be performed according to the instructions given for Program I.

Table 22.1

The Complete Program and the Program Emphasizing Legs and Trunk

Monday/Wednesday/Friday Exercises

Legs and Trunk
1. Hip abductors/inward rotators, 15.A, 15.J
2. Hip outward rotators, 15.F, 15.L, 15.M
3. Hip adductors, 15.E, 15.K
4. Knee flexors/hip extensors, 15.A, 15.G
5. Knee extensors, 15.B, 15.H
6. Muscles that support the arch, 12.A (These muscles are difficult to stretch. Massage can help them relax.)

Neck, Arm, and Shoulder
1. Shoulder girdle abductors, 21.G
2. Arm flexors, 21.A
3. Shoulder girdle depressors, 21.I
4. Stretch for the muscles strengthened in numbers 1–3, 21.O
5. Neck, 18.D, 18.H
6. Inward and outward rotators of the forearm, 21.L (These muscles are difficult to stretch. Massage can help them relax.)
7. Wrist flexors, 21.M, 21.U
8. Wrist extensors, 21.N, 21.U

Tuesday/Thursday/Saturday Exercises

Legs and Trunk
1. Trunk flexors, 18.A, 18.E
2. Trunk extensors, 18.B, 18.F
3. Lateral trunk flexors, 18.C, 18.G
4. Hip flexors, 15.C, 15.I
5. Ankle plantar flexors, 12.F, 12.H
6. Foot inverters and everters, 12.C, 12.D (These muscles are difficult to stretch. Performing ankle circles, massage, and gentle hand manipulation in the directions of inversion and eversion can help them relax.)
7. Ankle dorsiflexors, 12.E, 12.G
8. Toe flexors, 12.B. (These muscles are difficult to stretch. Massage and gentle hand manipulation in the direction of toe extension can help them relax.)

Arms and Shoulder
1. Elbow extensors, etc., 21.K, 21.T
2. Elbow flexors, 21.J., 21.S
3. Arm extensors, 21.B
4. Arm adductors, 21.D
5. Stretch for muscles strengthened in numbers 3–4, 21.P
6. Arm abductors, 21.C
7. Shoulder girdle adductors, 21.H
8. Arm inward and outward rotators, 21.E, 21.F
9. Stretch for some of the muscles strengthened in numbers 6–8, 21.R
10. Stretch for the inward rotators, 21.Q

Table 22.2

The Individualized Approach/Sample Plan

Monday/Wednesday/Friday
Exercises
 1. Trunk flexors, 18.A, 18.E
 2. Elbow extensors, etc., 21.J, 21.T
 3. Other exercises as needed.
*Additional flexibility exercises to be used
following class, rehearsal, or performance*
 1. Ankle plantar flexors, 12.H
 2. Knee extensors, 15.H
 3. Hip flexors, 15.I
 4. Hip outward rotators, 15.L, 15.M
 5. Trunk extensors, 18.F

Tuesday/Thursday/Saturday
Exercises
 1. Trunk extensors, 18.B, 18.F
 2. Shoulder girdle adductors, 21.H,
     21.R
 3. Other exercises as needed.
*Additional flexibility exercises to be used
after class, rehearsal, or performance*
 1. Ankle plantar flexors, 12.H
 2. Knee extensors, 15.H
 3. Hip flexors, 15.I
 4. Hip outward rotators, 15.L, 15.M

Program III: The Individual Approach/Sample Plan

Monday/Wednesday/Friday Exercises
These exercises are listed in Table 22.2. They should be performed according to the instructions given in Program I.

Tuesday/Thursday/Saturday Exercises
These exercises are also listed in Table 22.2. They should be performed according to the instructions given in Program I.

23

Conditioning with Exercise Machines

Weight machines are designed to strengthen the large muscle groups used in various athletic movements. They can be used to enhance some, but not all, dance movements. Nevertheless, dancers can benefit from strength training on weight machines.

The same concepts governing strength conditioning exercises presented in Chapter 2 apply to exercises performed on weight machines. These machines can offer moderate resistance exercises that are similar to the exercises presented in this book. When the equipment is used in this way, gains in strength will be moderate, and there will be little muscle hypertrophy. The machines can also be used to provide considerable resistance. When used in a high resistance program, large gains in strength and muscle mass are made possible, particularly for men.

Some dancers in college or university settings have free access to weight rooms and exercise equipment. Most dancers, however, must join a gymnasium or health club to use weight machines. Before making any financial commitment to join one of these programs, dancers should consider the pros and cons.

Dancers who do not need to make large gains in strength can choose an exercise program on the basis of personal preference and financial resources. Many dancers find it easier to do conditioning work in a gym where others are also working out. Some enjoy having access to the stationary bicycles and treadmills that can be used for warming up. This equipment can also be used to improve the body's aerobic capacity and can aid dancers in losing weight. On the other hand, some dancers find it difficult to get to a gym when it is open and do not always have the time to travel to the gym for regular sessions.

It is not necessary to use exercise machines to strengthen the body for most of the movements performed in dance. Although weight machines enable one to perform moderate exercise, it may be easier and less expensive for dancers to workout without using this equipment. On the other hand, weight machines will be needed by men who require greater strength to lift a partner or who wish to increase their musculature.

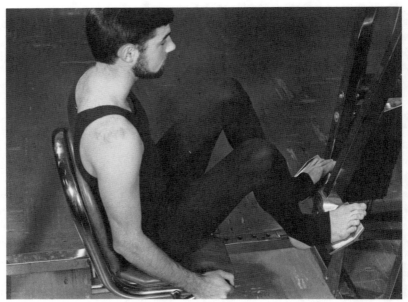

(a) Starting position.

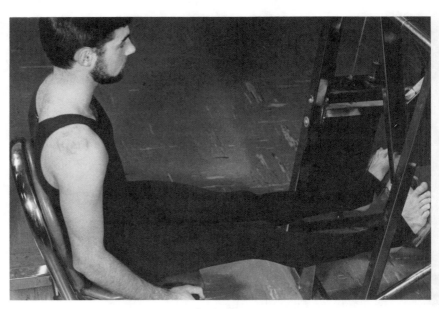

(b) Action.

Figure 23.1 Strengthening the hip and knee extensors. Photographs courtesy of the School of Physical Education, University of Massachusetts, Amherst.

Different Types of Machines

Many companies make exercise machines, and each brand is different. One way that equipment can differ is in the way resistance is added to the movement. Some machines have variable resistance and some do not. Machines with variable resistance control the resistance throughout the range of movement. In this way, the angle where your muscle is the weakest encounters the least resistance, and the angle where your muscle is the strongest encounters the greatest resistance.

Weight equipment also differs in the way the muscles are exercised. Some machines are designed to work the same muscle group in both a concentric muscle action and an eccentric muscle action. Figures 23.1a and 23.1b illustrate such equipment. As the dancer moves from the position shown in Figure 23.1a to the one in Figure 23.1b, the hip and knee extensors function in a concentric muscle action. If the dancer moves from the position shown in Figure 23.1b to the one in Figure 23.1a with control, the muscles function in an eccentric muscle action. This particular machine is part of the *Universal Gym* brand of exercise equipment.

Other machines are designed so both muscles in a pair of muscles perform a concentric muscle action. Figure 23.2 illustrates this kind of machine. As the dancer flexes the elbow, the resistance makes the elbow flexors function in a concentric muscle action. As the dancer straightens the elbow, the resistance causes the elbow extensors to function in a concentric muscle action. This equipment is manufactured by *Hydra-Fitness, Inc.*

General Guidelines for Using Weight Machines

This section gives general guidelines about the use of exercise equipment, but does not provide you with specific descriptions of all the exercises possible on all machines. Dancers who use weight equipment for the first time should be properly trained by the weight-room personnel. These people can demonstrate how to use the specific equipment, check to be sure that the dancer is working correctly, and answer any questions that may arise. Dancers who would like to read more about weight machines will find there are many excellent books. We have included a few in our reference list (Berger, 1984; Fleck & Kraemer, 1987; Pearl & Moran, 1986; and Westcott, 1982).

How to Select the Proper Resistance
Strength training programs that utilize weight machines are often based upon the concept of the ten RM (repetition maximum) weight load. This is the heaviest amount of weight you can lift in ten

Figure 23.2 Strengthening the elbow flexors and extensors. Photograph courtesy of The Body Shop, Department of Exercise Science, University of Massachusetts, Amherst.

repetitions. Different types of training programs have been designed using this concept, and we refer you to the many books written on weight training for a full description. The example we will use is the DeLorme-Watkins Program (Westcott, 1982, pp. 71–72). Under this system you determine your 10RM, or repetition maxium. Then you perform 10 repetitions using 50 percent of the 10RM weight, followed by 10 repetitions using 75 percent of the 10RM weight, followed by 10 repetitions using 100 percent of the 10RM weight. A new 10RM is determined as strength develops.

As an illustration, let's say that Mike's 10RM is 100 lbs. For his first set of exercises he would perform 10 repetitions using 50 lbs (50 percent 10RM). For the second set of exercises he would perform 10 repetitions using 75 lbs (75 percent 10RM). For the third set of exercises he would perform 10 repetitions using 100 lbs (100 percent 10 RM).

How to Set the Machine for the Resistance You Want to Use
Most weight machines have either a dial or pin that controls the resistance. Figure 23.3 shows a dial control on which the position of the black dot indicates whether the resistance is at level 1, 2, 3, or 4. (Level 1 offers the least resistance.) Figure 23.4 shows a pin control. On this type of equipment, each weight in the stack is marked with its poundage. To select the desired resistance, you simply count down the number of weights you wish to use. The pin is placed in the slot at the bottom of the stack you want to lift.

Figure 23.3 Dial Control. Photograph courtesy of The Body Shop, Department of Exercise Science, University of Massachusetts, Amherst.

Figure 23.4 Pin Control. Photograph courtesy of the School of Physical Education, University of Massachusetts, Amherst.

How to Select Exercise Equipment

When you first go into a weight room, you will see several pieces of exercise equipment. Most weight rooms are orgnaized in different "areas" or "stations." Each station is designed to strengthen a particular muscle group. For example, the first station may be set up with equipment to strengthen the legs. The next station may have equipment to exercise the upper arms. This may be followed by a third

(a) Starting position.

(b) Action.

Figure 23.5 Strengthening the hips, legs, and feet. Photographs courtesy of The Body Shop, Department of Exercise Science, University of Massachusetts, Amherst.

(a) Starting position.

(b) Action.

Figure 23.6 Strengthening the elbow extensors. Photographs courtesy of the School of Physical Education, University of Massachusetts, Amherst.

station with equipment to exercise the abdominal muscles, and so forth. Thus, by making a circuit around the weight equipment and exercising at each station, a person would be able to strengthen each of the major muscle groups in the body. Figures 23.5a and 23.5b show a station manufactured by *Hydra-Fitness, Inc.* This station strengthens the hips, legs, and feet. Figures 23.6a and 23.6b illustrate a station made by *Universal Gym*, designed to strengthen the arms and shoulder girdle.

Most weight rooms have a monitor or instructor whose job it is to teach people to use the equipment. You can either ask the assistant to show you a basic program for overall conditioning, or say which muscle groups you particularly want to strengthen. The assistant can then show you which pieces of equipment to use, and how to exercise on each one.

Words of Caution

Weight equipment is not dangerous, but it needs to be used wisely. Proper instruction for the use of each piece of equipment is crucial. Specific attention should be given to the alignment of the body as you work. For example, during a bench press you should be careful not to arch your lower back.

As you use the weight equipment, remember to check your breathing. Review Chapter 7 for the principles of strength conditioning as they relate to breath control. Men who work with heavier weights need to be absolutely certain that they breathe correctly as they build strength.

Finally, be careful not to work with weights that are too heavy. Too much resistance, particularly at an extreme range of motion, can lead to injury. If you can only lift the weight once or twice before fatique sets in, the weight is too heavy. If you experience painful muscle soreness the next day, you used too much weight. Increase the weight and the number of repetitions gradually. Remember to work with your body, not against it.

If you have any questions about the equipment or the exercise, be certain to ask the professional personnel who are hired to monitor the gym. They are trained to supervise the equipment and explain its many possible uses. Do not try to adapt the exercises or make changes in the indicated body positions without asking. The equipment is designed for specific purposes, and can be of benefit to dancers if it is used correctly.

References

Alter, J. (1983). *Surviving exercise: Judy Alter's safe and sane exercise program.* Boston: Houghton Mifflin.

Alter, J. (1986a). A few more thoughts on the snapping hip. *Kinesiology for Dance, 8*(3), 6–7.

Alter, J. (1986b). *Stretch and strengthen.* Boston: Houghton Mifflin.

Arnheim, D. D. (1980). *Dance injuries: Their prevention and care.* (2nd Edition.) St. Louis: C. V. Mosby (republished 1988, Princeton, NJ: Dance Horizons/ Princeton Book Co., Publishers).

Arnheim, D. D. (1985). *Modern principles of athletic training.* 6th Edition. St. Louis: C. V. Mosby.

Ashley, M. (1984). *Dancing for Balanchine.* New York: E. P. Dutton.

Bachrach, R. M. (1984, July). *Supplemental materials.* Distributed at the International Symposium on the Scientific Aspects of Dance, an associative program of the 1984 Olympic Scientific Congress, University of Oregon, Eugene, OR.

Bachrach, R. M. (1986a). Diagnosis and management of dance injuries to the lower back: An osteopathic approach. In C. G. Shell (Ed.), *The dancer as athlete* (pp. 83–94). Champaign, IL: Human Kinetics.

Bachrach, R. M. (1986b). A physician's primer of dance injuries. *Kinesiology for Dance, 9*(1), 5–10.

Bachrach, R. M. (1986c). The relationship of low back/pelvic somatic dysfunctions to dance injuries. *Kinesiology for Dance, 8*(3), 11–14.

Bachrach, R. M. (1987). Injuries to the dancer's spine. In A. J. Ryan and R. E. Stephens (Eds.), *Dance medicine: A comprehensive guide* (pp. 243–266). Chicago: Pluribus Press.

Bachrach, R. M., Skinner, H. B., Brunet, M. E., & Cook, S. D. (1983). Joint laxity and proprioception in the knee. *Physician and Sportsmedicine, 11*(6), 130–135.

Bakst, F. (1985). The ups and downs of heels. *Dance Magazine, 59*(11), 80–81.

Barnes, M. R., & Crutchfield, C. (1971). *The patient at home: A manual of exercise programs, self help devices and home care procedures.* Thorofare, NJ: Slack.

Basmajian, J. V., & De Luca, C. J. (1985). *Muscles alive: Their functions revealed by electromyography* (5th ed.). Baltimore, MD: Williams & Wilkins.

Benjamin, B. (1980a). Creating your own warm-up. *Dance Magazine, 54*(11), 86–88.

Benjamin, B. (1980b). The do's and don'ts of stretching. *Dance Magazine, 54*(12), 86–89.

Benjamin, B. (1981). Alignment: The best prevention. *Dance Magazine, 55*(1), 84–87.

Berger, R. A. (1984). *Introduction to weight training.* Englewood Cliffs, NJ: Prentice-Hall.

Bergfeld, J. A. (1982). Medical problems in ballet. *Physician and Sportsmedicine*, 10(3), 98–112.

Bonnor-Moris, J (1986). Assessment and management of common dance injuries and conditions: A physiotherapist's approach. In D. Peterson, G. Lapenskie, & A. W. Taylor (Eds.), *The medical aspects of dance* (pp. 65–70). Ontario: Sports Dynamics.

Clanin, D. R., Davison, D. M., & Plastino, J. G. (1986). Injury patterns in university dance students. In C. G. Shell (Ed.), *The dancer as athlete* (pp. 195–199). Champaign, IL: Human Kinetics.

Clarkson, P. M., James, R. J., Watkins, A., & Foley, P. (1986). The effect of augmented feedback on foot pronation during barre exercise in dance. *Research Quarterly for Exercise and Sport*, 57(1), 33–40.

Clarkson, P. M., & Skrinar, M. (Eds.). (1988). *The science of dance training*. Champaign, IL: Human Kinetics.

Clippenger-Robertson, K. S. (1985). The snapping hip phenomenon. *Kinesiology for Dance*, 7(4), 12–13.

Clippenger-Robertson, K. S. (1986). Increasing functional range of motion in dance. *Kinesiology for Dance*, 8(3), 8–10.

Clippenger-Robertson, K. S., Hutton, R. S., Miller, D. I., & Nichols, T. R. (1986). Mechanical and anatomical factors relating to the incidence and etiology of patellofemoral pain in dancers. In C. G. Shell (Ed.), *The dancer as athlete* (pp. 53–72). Champaign, IL: Human Kinetics.

Como, W. (Ed.). (1964). *Raoul Gelabert's anatomy for the dancer with exercises to improve technique and prevent injuries: As told to William Como*. New York: Dance Magazine.

Como, W. (Ed.) (1966). *Raoul Gelabert's anatomy for the dancer with exercises to improve technique and prevent injuries* (Vol. 2). New York: Dance Magazine.

Daniels, L., & Worthingham, C. (1977). *Therapeutic exercise: For body alignment and function* (2nd Ed.). Philadelphia: W. B. Saunders.

DeLorme, T. L., & Watkins, A. L. (1951). *Progressive resistance exercise*. New York: Appleton-Century-Crofts.

Dowd, I. (1984a). How to arch your back. *Dance Magazine*, 58(4), 118–119.

Dowd, I. (1984b). How to find the turnout. *Dance Magazine*, 58(6), 100.

Dowd, I. (1984c). What it means to "pull up." *Dance Magazine*, 58(5), 142.

Ende, L. S., & Wickstrom, J. (1982). Ballet injuries. *Physician and Sportsmedicine*, 10(7), 101–118.

Featherstone, D. F. (1970). *Dancing without danger: A guide to the prevention of injury for the amateur and professioanl dancer*. New York: A. S. Barnes.

Fitt, S. (1985). A few thoughts on the snapping hip. *Kinesiology for Dance*, 7(4), 9–12.

Fitt, S. (1988). *Dance kinesiology*. New York: Schirmer Books.

Fleck, J., & Kraemer, W. J. (1987). *Designing resistance training programs*. Champaign, IL: Human Kinetics.

Fox, E. L. (1984). *Sports physiology*. Philadelphia: W. B. Saunders.

Friedman, P., & Eisen, G. (1981). *The pilates method of physical and mental conditioning*. New York: Warner Books.

Galea, V. (1985). Foot and ankle forces in pointe shoes. *Kinesiology for Dance*, 7(3), 10.

Gans, A. (1985). The relationship of heel contact in ascent and descent from jumps to the incidence of shin splints in ballet dancers. *Physical Therapy*, 65(8), 1192–1196.

Gantz, J. (1985). Comments on the snapping hip. *Kinesiology for Dance, 7*(4), 13–14.

Gelabert, R. (1977a). The myth of dance-induced pain. *Dance Magazine,* 51(5), 96–97.

Gelabert, R. (1977b). Posture. *Dance Magazine,* 51(10), 85–87.

Gelabert, R. (1977c). Turning out. *Dance Magazine, 51*(2), 86–87.

Gelabert, R. (1980). Preventing dancer's injuries. *Physician and Sportsmedicine,* 8(4), 69–76.

Gelabert, R. (1986). Dancers' spinal syndromes. *Journal of Orthopaedic and Sports Physical Therapy,* 7(4), 180–191.

Getchell, B. (1979). *Physical fitness: A way of life.* New York: John Wiley.

Grace, T. G. (1985). Muscle imbalance and extremity injury a perplexing relationship. *Sports Medicine,* 2, 77–82.

Gyn, G. H. Van. (1986). Contemporary stretching techniques: Theory and application. In C. G. Shell (Ed.), *The dancer as athlete* (pp. 109–116). Champaign, IL: Human Kinetics.

Hamilton, W. G. (1978a). Ballet and your body: An orthopedist's view. *Dance Magazine,* 52(2), 79.

Hamilton, W. G. (1978b). Ballet and your body: An orthopedist's view. *Dance Magazine,* 52(3), 84–85.

Hamilton, W. G. (1978c). Ballet and your body: An orthopedist's view. *Dance Magazine,* 52(4): 126–127.

Hamilton, W. G. (1978d). Ballet and your body: An orthopedist's view. *Dance Magazine,* 52(5), 98–99.

Hamilton, W. G. (1978e). Ballet and your body: An orthopedist's view. *Dance Magazine,* 52(6), 84–85.

Hamilton, W. G. (1978f). Ballet and your body: An orthopedist's view. *Dance Magazine,* 52(7), 86–87.

Hamilton, W. G. (1978g). Ballet and your body: An orthopedist's view. *Dance Magazine,* 52(8), 84–85.

Hamilton, W. G. (1978h). Ballet and your body: An orthopedist's view. *Dance Magazine,* 52(9), 90–91.

Hamilton, W. G. (1978i). Ballet and your body: An orthopedist's view. *Dance Magazine,* 52(10), 86–87.

Hamilton, W. G. (1978j). Ballet and your body: An orthopedist's view. *Dance Magazine,* 52(12), 91–92.

Hamilton, W. G. (1982a). The best body for ballet. *Dance Magazine,* 56(10), 82–83.

Hamilton, W. G. (1982b, May 30). The dancer's ankle. *Emergency Medicine,* 42–49.

Hamilton, W. G. (1982c). Sprained ankles in ballet dancers. *Foot and Ankle,* 3(2), 99–102.

Hamilton, W. G. (1982d). Stenosing tenosynovitis of the flexor hallucis longus tendon and posterior impingement upon the os trigonum in ballet dancers. *Foot and Ankle,* 3(2), 74–80.

Hamilton, W. G. (1984). The use and misuse of muscle, tendons, and ligaments. *Dance Magazine,* 58(5), 144.

Hamilton, W. G., & Molnar, M. (1983). Back to dancing after injury. *Dance Magazine,* 57(4), 88–90.

Hardaker, W. T., Erickson, L., & Myers, M. (1986). The pathogenesis of dance injury. In C. G. Shell (Ed.), *The dancer as athlete* (pp. 11–29). Champaign, IL: Human Kinetics.

Hardaker, W. T., & Moorman, III, C. T. (1986). Foot and ankle injuries in dance and athletics: Similarities and differences. In C. G. Shell (Ed.), *The dancer as athlete* (pp. 31–41). Champaign, IL: Human Kinetics.

Hardaker, W. T., Margello, S., & Goldner, J. (1985). Foot and ankle injuries in theatrical dancers. *Foot and Ankle, 6*(2), 59–69.

Hardy, L., & Jones, D. (1986). Dynamic flexibility and proprioceptive neuromuscular facilitation. *Research Quarterly for Exercise and Sport, 57*(2), 150–153.

Hartley-O'Brien, S. J. (1980). Six mobilization exercises for active range of hip flexion. *Research Quarterly for Exercise and Sport, 51*(4), 625–635.

Henricson, A. S., Fredriksson, K., Persson, I., Pereira, R., Rostedt, Y., & Westlin, N. E. (1984). The effect of heat and stretching on the range of hip motion. *Journal of Orthopaedic and Sports Physical Therapy, 6*(2), 110–115.

Hobby, K., & Hoffmaster, L. (1986). Supplementing traditional training for dancers. In D. Peterson, G. Lapenskie, & A. W. Taylor (Eds.), *The medical aspects of dance* (pp. 31–42). Ontario: Sports Dynamics.

Horosko, M. (1980). Happy hands and feet. *Dance Magazine, 54*(9), 84.

Horosko, M. (1981). Making friends with yourself. *Dance Magazine, 55*(12), 76–77.

Horosko, M. (1982). Feet: Avoiding painful pitfalls. *Dance Magazine, 56*(5), sc–24.

Horosko, M. (1984a). Avoiding arthritis. *Dance Magazine, 58*(3), 100–101.

Horosko, M. (1984b). Cures and myths about arthritis. *Dance Magazine, 58*(4), 108.

Horosko, M. (1986a). If the shoe fits . . . Part I. *Dance Magazine, 60*(4), 81–82.

Horosko, M. (1986b). If the shoe fits . . . Part II. *Dance Magazine, 60*(5), 98–99.

Howse, A. J. G. (1972). Orthopedists aid ballet. *Clinical Orthopaedics and Related Research, 89*, 52–63.

Howse, A. J. G. (1982). Posterior block of the ankle joint in dancers. *Foot and Ankle, 3*(2), 81–84.

Howse, A. J. G. (1983). Disorders of the great toe in dancers. *Clinics in Sports Medicine, 2*(3), 499–505.

Howse, A. J. G., & Silver, D. (1985). L.A. dance clinic: Hip problems. *Dance Magazine, 59*(5), 99.

Howse, A. J. G., & Hancock, S. (1988). *Dance technique and injury prevention*. New York: Theater Arts Books/Routledge.

Hughes, L. (1985). Biomechanical analysis of the foot and ankle for predisposition to developing stress fractures. *Journal of Orthopaedic and Sports Physical Therapy, 7*(3), 96–101.

Jacob, E. (1981). *Dancing: A guide for the dancer you can be*. New York: Danceways.

Kapurian, W. (Ed.), (1981). *Physical therapy for sport*. Philadelphia: W. B. Saunders.

Katch, F. I., & McArdle, W. D. (1983). *Nutrition, weight control, and exercise* (2nd Ed.). Philadelphia: Lea & Febiger.

Kendall, H. O., Kendall, F. P., & Boynton, D. A. (1952). *Posture and pain*. Baltimore, MD: Williams & Wilkins.

Kendall, F. P., & McCreary, E. K. (1983). *Muscles: Testing and function*, (3rd Ed.). Baltimore: Williams & Wilkins.

Kisner, C., & Colby, L. A. (1985). *Therapeutic exercise: Foundations and techniques*. Philadelphia: F. A. Davis.

Kleiger, B. (1982). Anterior tibiotalar impingement syndromes in dancers. *Foot and Ankle, 3*(2), 69–73.

Kleiger, B. (1987). Foot and ankle injuries in dancers. In A. J. Ryan and R. E. Stephens (Eds.), *Dance medicine: A comprehensive guide.* (pp. 115–134). Chicago, IL: Pluribus Press.

Klemp, P., & Learmonth, I. D. (1984). Hypermobility and injuries in a professional ballet company. *British Journal of Sports Medicine, 18*(3), 143–148.

Kravitz, S. R., Huber, S., Murgia, C. J., Fink, K. L., Shaffer, M., & Varela, L. (1985). Biomechanical study of bunion deformity and stress produced in classical ballet. *Journal of the American Podiatric Medical Association, 75*(7), 338–345.

Kravitz, S. R., Murgia, C. J., Huber, S., Fink, K., Shaffer, M., & Varela, L. (1986). Bunion deformity and the forces generated around the great toe: A biomechanical approach to analysis of pointe dance, classical ballet. In C. G. Shell (Ed.), *The dancer as athlete* (pp. 213–225). Champaign, IL: Human Kinetics.

Kravitz, S. R., Murgia, C. J., Huber, S., & Saltrick, K. R. (1986). Biomechanical implication of dance injuries. In C. G. Shell (Ed.), *The dancer as athlete* (pp. 43–51). Champaign, IL: Human Kinetics.

Lemberg, D. (1985). Get rid of that pain in the neck. *Dance Magazine, 59*(7), 61.

Liederbach, M. B. (1985). Performance demands of ballet. *Kinesiology for Dance, 8*(2), 6–7.

Long, M. (1986). The biomechanical aspects of dance injuries. In D. Peterson, G. Lapenskie, & A. W. Taylor (Eds.), *The medical aspects of dance* (pp. 75–78). Ontario: Sports Dynamics.

Luttgens, K., & Wells, K. F. (1982). *Kinesiology: Scientific basis of human motion.* Philadelphia: W. B. Saunders.

Marr, S. J. (1983). The ballet foot. *Journal of the American Podiatry Association, 73*(3), 124–132.

McArdle, W. D., Katch, F. I., & Katch, V. O. (1981). *Exercise physiology: Energy, nutrition, and human performance.* Philadelphia: Lea & Febiger.

McQueen, C. (1986). Conditioning for dancers. In D. Peterson, G. Lapenskie, and A. W. Taylor (Eds.), *The medical aspects of dance* (pp. 43–47). Ontario: Sports Dynamics.

Micheli, L. J. (1983). Back injuries in dancers. *Clinics in Sports Medicine, 2*(3), 473–484.

Micheli, L. J., (1988). Dance injuries: The back, hip, and pelvis. In P. M. Clarkson & M. Skrinar (Eds.), *Science of dance training* (pp. 193–207). Champaign, IL: Human Kinetics.

Micheli, L. J., & Micheli, E. R. (1986). Back injuries in dancers. In C. G. Shell (Ed.), *The dancer as athlete* (pp. 91–94). Champaign, IL: Human Kinetics.

Micheli, L. J., & Solomon, R. (1987). Training the young dancer. In A. J. Ryan & R. E. Stephens (Eds.), *Dance medicine: A comprehensive guide.* (pp. 51–72). Chicago: Pluribus Press.

Millar, A. P. (1987). Injuries to the neck and upper extremity. In A. J. Ryan & R. E. Stephens (Eds.), *Dance Medicine: A Comprehensive Guide* (pp. 267–273). Chicago: Pluribus Press.

Miller, E. H., Schneider, H. J., Bronson, J. L., & McLain, D. (1975). A new consideration in athletic injuries: The classical ballet dancer. *Clinical Orthopaedics and Related Research, 11,* 181–191.

Molnar, M. E. (1987). Rehabilitation of the injured dancer. In A. J. Ryan & R. E. Stephens (Eds.), *Dance medicine: A comprehensive guide* (pp. 302–320). Chicago: Pluribus Press.

Morris, A. F. (1983). The problem: Adding weights to a walker's ankle. *Physician and Sportsmedicine,* 11(4), 34.

Myers, M. (1982). Is the grand plié obsolete? *Dance Magazine,* 56(6), 78–80.

Myers, M. (1983a). Facts and fantasies: Stretching. *Dance Magazine,* 57(6), 66–70.

Myers, M. (1983b). What to do before you dance: Warming up. *Dance Magazine,* 57(5), 136–138.

Myers, M. (1986). Perceptual awareness in integrative movement behavior: The role of integrative movement systems (body therapies) in motor performance and expressivity. In C. G. Shell (Ed.), *The dancer as athlete* (pp. 163–172). Champaign, IL: Human Kinetics.

Nash, H. L. (1986). Sports activity and arthritis: Individually determined or preplanned? *Physician and Sportsmedicine,* 14(4), 148–156.

Nawoczenski, D. A., Owen, M. G., Ecker, M. L., Altman, B., & Epler, M. (1985). Objective evaluation of peroneal response to sudden inversion stress. *Journal of Orthopaedic and Sports Physical Therapy,* 7(3), 107–109.

Nelson, A. G., Chambers, R. S., McGown, C. M., & Penrose, K. W. (1986). Proprioceptive neuromuscular facilitation verses weight training for enhancement of muscular strength and athletic performance. *Journal of Orthopaedic and Sports Physical Therapy,* 7(5), 250–253.

Nixon, J. E. (1983). Injuries to the neck and upper extremities of dancers. *Clinics in Sports Medicine,* 2(3), 459–472.

Novella, T. M. (1987). Dancer's shoes and foot care. In A. J. Ryan & R. E. Stephens (Eds.), *Dance medicine: A comprehensive guide* (pp. 139–176). Chicago: Pluribus Press.

Paskevska, A. (1981). *Both sides of the mirror: The science and art of ballet.* Princeton, NJ: Dance Horizons/Princeton Book Co., Publishers.

Pearl, B., & Moran, G. T. (1986). *Getting stronger.* Bolinas, CA: Shelter Publications.

Peterson, C. (1986). Learning through observation: The dancer's technique. In D. Peterson, G. Lapenskie, & A. W. Taylor (Eds.), *The medical aspects of dance* (pp. 49–62). Ontario: Sports Dynamics.

Quirk, R. (1982). Talar compression syndrome in dancers. *Foot and Ankle,* 3(2), 65–68.

Quirk, R. (1983). Ballet injuries: The Australian experience. *Clinics in Sports Medicine,* 2(3), 507–513.

Quirk, R. (1987). The dancer's knee. In A. J. Ryan & R. E. Stephens (Eds.), *Dance medicine: A comprehensive guide* (pp. 177–219). Chicago: Pluribus Press.

Rovere, G. D., Webb, L. X., Gristina, A. G., & Vogel, J. M. (1983). Musculoskeletal injuries in theatrical dance students. *American Journal of Sports Medicine,* 11(4), 195–198.

Roy, S., & Irvin, R. (1983). *Sports medicine: Prevention, evaluation, management, and rehabilitation.* Englewood Cliffs, NJ: Prentice-Hall.

Ryan, A. J., & Stephens, R. E. (1987). The epidemology of dance injuries. In A. J. Ryan & R. E. Stephens (Eds.), *Dance medicine: A comprehensive guide* (pp. 3–15). Chicago: Pluribus Press.

Ryan, A. J., & Stephens, R. E. (1988). *The dancer's complete guide to healthcare and a long career.* Princeton, NJ: Dance Horizons/Princeton Book Company, Publishers.

Sammarco, G. J. (1982, May 30). The dancer's forefoot. *Emergency Medicine,* 49–57.

Sammarco, G. J. (1983). The dancer's hip. *Clinics in Sports Medicine, 2*(3), 485–498.

Sammarco, G. J. (1984). Diagnosis and treatment in dancers. *Clinical Orthopaedics and Related Research, 187,* 176–187.

Sammarco, G. J. (1987). The dancer's hip. In A. J. Ryan & R. E. Stephens (Eds.), *Dance medicine: A comprehensive guide* (pp. 220–242). Chicago: Pluribus Press.

Schaberg, J. E., Harper, M. C., & Allen, W. C. (1984). The snapping hip syndrome. *American Journal of Sports Medicine, 12*(5), 361–365.

Scranton, P. E., Jr., Whitesel, J. P., & Farewell, V. (1985). Cybex evaluation of the relationship between anterior and posterior compartment lower leg muscles. *Foot and Ankle, 6*(2), 85–89.

Shellock, F. G. (1983). Physiological benefits of warm-up. *Physician and Sportsmedicine, 11*(10), 134–139.

Siegel, R. H. (1986). Unjam your hamstrings. *Dance Magazine, 60*(6), 66–67.

Silver, D. M. (1985). Knee problems and solutions in dancers. *Kinesiology for Dance, 8*(2), 9–10.

Silver, D. M., & Campbell, P. (1985). Arthroscopic assessment and treatment of dancers' knee injuries. *Physician and Sportsmedicine, 13*(11), 75–82.

Smith, W., Winn, F., & Parette, R. (1986). Comparative study using four modalities in shinsplint treatments. *Journal of Orthopaedic and Sports Physical Therapy, 8*(2), 77–80.

Solomon, R., & Micheli, L. (1986a). Concepts in the prevention of dance injuries: A survey and analysis. In C. G. Shell (Ed.), *The dancer as athlete* (pp. 201–212). Champaign, IL: Human Kinetics.

Solomon, R. L., & Micheli, L. (1986b). Techniques as a consideration in modern dance injuries. *Physician and Sportsmedicine, 14*(8), 83–92.

Sparger, C. (1971). *Anatomy and ballet.* New York: Theater Arts Books.

Stephens, R. E. (1987). The etiology of injuries in ballet. In A. J. Ryan & R. E. Stephens (Eds.), *Dance medicine: A comprehensive guide* (pp. 16–50). Chicago: Pluribus Press.

Teitz, C. C. (1982). Sports medicine concerns in dance and gymnastics. *Pediatric Clinics of North America, 29*(6), 1399–1421.

Teitz, C. C. (1986). First aid immediate care, and rehabilitation of knee and ankle injuries in dancers and athletes. In C. G. Shell (Ed.), *The dancer as athlete* (pp. 73–81). Champaign, IL: Human Kinetics.

Thompson, C. W. (1977). *Manual of structural kinesiology.* St. Louis: C. V. Mosby.

Todd, M. E. (1972). *The thinking body.* Princeton, NJ: Dance Horizons/Princeton Book Company, Publishers.

Torbjorn, A., & Nilsson, B. E. (1978). Degenerative changes in the first metatarso-phalangeal joint of ballet dancers. *Acta Orthapaedica Scandinavica, 49,*317–319.

Tropp, H., Askling, C., & Gillquist, J. (1985). Prevention of ankle sprains. *American Journal of Sports Medicine, 13*(4), 259–262.

Vincent, L. M. (1978). *The Dancer's Book of Health.* Kansas City: Andrews & McMeel (Reprinted 1988, Princeton, NJ: Dance Horizons/Princeton Book Company, Publishers).

Vincent, L. M. (1989). *Competing with the sylph: The quest for the perfect dance body* (2nd ed.). Princeton, NJ: Dance Horizons/Princeton Book Company, Publishers.

Wallin, D., Ekblom, B., Grahn, R., & Nordenborg, T. (1985). Improvement of muscle flexibility: A comparison between two techniques. *American Journal of Sports Medicine, 13*(4), 263–268.

Washington, E. L. (1978). Musculoskeletal injuries in theatrical dancers: Site, frequency, and severity. *American Journal of Sports Medicine*, 6(2), 75–98.

Washington, E. L. (1982). The dancer's hip. *Dance Medicine-Health Newsletter*, 1(1), 1–2.

Weiker, G. G. (1982, May 30). The dancer's spine. *Emergency Medicine*, 28–41.

Wescott, W. L. (1982). *Strength fitness.* Boston: Allyn & Bacon.

Woodruff, J. (1984). Plies—Some food for thought. *Kinesiology for Dance*, 7(1), 8–9.

Wright, S. (1985). *The dancer's guide to injuries of the lower extremity: Diagnosis, treatment and care.* Cranbury, NJ: Cornwall Books.

Index